The United States and Democracy in Chile

D0874909

The *United States*
and Democracy in Chile

Paul E. Sigmund

A Twentieth

Century

Fund Book

The

Johns Hopkins

University Press

Baltimore and

London

© 1993 The Twentieth Century Fund
All rights reserved
Printed in the United States of
America on acid-free paper

The Johns Hopkins University Press
2715 North Charles Street
Baltimore, Maryland 21218-4319
The Johns Hopkins Press Ltd., London

Library of Congress
Cataloging-in-Publication Data

Sigmund, Paul E.
    The United States and democracy in
    Chile / Paul E. Sigmund.
        p.   cm.
    "A Twentieth Century Fund Book."
    Includes bibliographical references and
index.
    ISBN 0-8018-4580-7 (alk. paper).
—ISBN 0-8018-4581-5 (pbk. : alk. paper)
    1. United States—Foreign relations—
Chile.   2. Chile—Foreign relations—
United States.   3. Chile—Politics and
government—1973–   I. Title.
E 183.8.C4S57   1993
327.73083—dc20   92-39230

A catalog record for this book is available
from the British Library.

To Barbara Boggs Sigmund, 1939–1990,
who shared my enthusiasm and love for Chile
and the Chilean people

Contents

Foreword

F OR MANY OBSERVERS, the recent history of Chile is one of the more positive developments of the past few years in Latin America. Considered among the continent's most dynamic economies and heralded for its successful transition from dictatorship to democracy, Chile is also at the forefront of Latin America's efforts to move toward closer hemispheric trade relations. Today, Chile's relations with the United States are warm, as are those of a growing number of Latin American countries. As in the rest of Latin America, however, a snapshot of the present yields only superficial understanding; political and economic change in Chile, as well as its evolving relationship with the United States, must be seen in historical context.

Paul Sigmund's study for the Twentieth Century Fund offers this context. Sigmund shows that Chile's progress toward democracy was at times impeded and at other times encouraged by U.S. policy. He demonstrates that U.S. policy toward democracy in Chile was an important element in U.S. foreign policy as early as the 1960s, but that it often lost out to other, mainly security, considerations. Along the way, U.S. policy—from support for the 1973 coup that overthrew a democratically elected government, to the sharply critical human rights policies of the Carter administration, and the at times contradictory policies of the two Reagan administrations— shaped the external environment within which Chile's transition to democratic rule took place.

Sigmund's analysis of the U.S.-Chilean relationship also helps illuminate the unique aspects of Chile's economic success. The move toward a market economy began under the Pinochet regime and was influenced strongly by economists trained in the United States. The nature of this transition raised difficult questions about whether the stringent austerity imposed by the Pinochet regime was facilitated by Chile's very lack of democracy; while the Chilean economy has continued to perform well even under the new democratic government, these questions remain to a large degree unanswered.

Chile's bid for closer trade and economic relations with the United States is the most recent development in the U.S.-Chilean relationship. Chile is receiving a warm reception because its efforts come at a time when world events and domestic economic pressures have forced the United States to take a closer look at its own hemisphere. But as observers of the region know, the spotlight of U.S. attention has moved on and off Latin America throughout this century (U.S. influence, of course, has been constant, whether visible or not). The Enterprise for the Americas Initiative and the North American Free Trade Agreement (NAFTA) negotiations suggest that we are in a relatively attentive phase.

Paul Sigmund's study of the relationship between the United States and a key Latin American country over three decades thus comes at a propitious time. The latest in a long tradition of Fund-sponsored studies of this region, it should provide an invaluable historical context for those seeking to understand or shape policy over the balance of the decade. Along with Jerome Levinson and Juan de Onis's *The Alliance That Lost Its Way* (1970); *Latin American Debt,* by Pedro-Pablo Kuczynski (1988); and Sigmund's earlier Fund-supported book, *Multinationals in Latin America* (1980); as well as a number of recently published and ongoing projects in this area, including a series of papers examining the international debt crisis that recently culminated in *In the Shadow of the Debt* (a collection of essays on Latin America's future) and Juan de Onis's *The Green Cathedral,* Sigmund's book is part of the Twentieth Century Fund's effort to ensure that public attention to this critical region of the world does not wane.

Richard C. Leone, President
The Twentieth Century Fund

Preface

I FELL IN LOVE with Chile from the time of my first visit nearly thirty years ago. It seemed a humane, literate, democratic society that took politics seriously as a way to deal with common problems. For a professor of political philosophy, the Chilean concern with the role of ideas in politics was especially appealing. A stint teaching on a Rockefeller Foundation grant at two universities in Santiago in 1967 reinforced my feelings. I was not prepared, however, for the destructive effect that some of those ideas subsequently had, nor for my role as observer, in over twenty visits, of the successive torments undergone by Chileans in the 1970s and 1980s, now fortunately only an unhappy memory.

Ask an educated American what he or she knows about Chile, and you are likely to get a response that alludes to the U.S. role in overthrowing a Marxist regime in 1973 and in "propping up" a brutal dictatorship that followed. If that person has seen the film *Missing,* you may even get a reference to the murder of Charles Horman "because he knew too much" about that role. This book is intended to set the record straight, "warts and all," about these and other aspects of U.S. policy toward a country that has been surprisingly important to the United States during the last three decades. It aims to measure the impact not only of the United States on Chile but also of Chile on domestic and international policy debates within the United States.

Chileans who read this study will think that it exaggerates the U.S. role—and to some degree they will be right. As my books and articles on Chile over the last three decades have repeatedly emphasized, the Chileans themselves, not the Americans, have been the most important actors in the dramatic events described in this book. They established constitutional democracy early in the nation's history, they produced the polarization and breakdown that led to the 1973 coup, and they are the ones most responsible for the reestablishment of the democratic society, concerned with liberty and social justice, which has now emerged again in Chile. The U.S. role, as I hope this book will demonstrate, was supportive but not determinative.

I am grateful to the Princeton University Committee on Research in the Humanities and the Social Sciences and to the Latin American Studies

Committee for supporting my research and repeated travel to Chile since 1963. Carol J. Bowers and the Center for International Studies provided essential logistical support. I owe a special debt of gratitude to the Twentieth Century Fund, which sponsored this study and supported its publication.

I also want to express my thanks to the hundreds of Chileans whom I have been privileged to know over the last thirty years for their generosity, hospitality, and friendship.

The United States
and Democracy in Chile

1

Introduction

ALTHOUGH SANTIAGO is farther from New York or Washington than is Moscow, Chile has had a strong fascination for Americans in recent decades. Ideological groups from the extreme left to the extreme right have interpreted its recent stormy history as a confirmation of their own views of political, economic, and international relations. Ever since the radicalization of the Cuban revolution in 1960 awakened Americans to the fact that Latin America existed, Chile has provided a series of case studies in the successes and failures of U.S. policy toward Latin America. U.S. interest and attention have had an impact on the course of recent Chilean history which has been better publicized and more thoroughly documented than U.S. relations with any other Latin American country. Memoirs, congressional hearings, and many declassified documents provide a rich set of resources for the scholar—and, on a more selective basis, the ideologue.

A central theme in the debates over U.S. policy toward Chile is the question of its impact on Chilean democratic institutions. As a country that, until 1973, had been under civilian constitutional rule since 1833—with only two exceptions, a brief civil war in 1891, and several years of military rule between 1924 and 1932—it appeared to be an exception to the pattern of authoritarian dictatorship which characterized most of the other countries of Latin America. Then when a bloody coup ended civilian rule and was followed by a military dictatorship that only ended in March 1990, one of many explanations put forward was to attribute much of the responsibility to U.S. intervention, covert and overt, as a contributing or even central cause of the collapse of Chilean democracy.

There is a very large literature on the issue of U.S. responsibility for the 1973 coup.[1] Most of that literature, however, focuses narrowly on the presidency of Salvador Allende (1970–73) and fails to take a broader view of both the causes and consequences of the coup. This study has been undertaken in the belief (1) that U.S. policy toward democracy in Chile must be seen as an important element in American foreign policy since the early 1960s, (2) that it has been a significant, although not decisive, variable influencing recent Chilean history, and (3) that the course of U.S.-Chilean relations over the last three decades has contributed to an important overall shift in the focus of U.S. foreign relations toward support for democracy around the world.

U.S. support for democracy in Chile has varied in its content and saliency over the last three decades. It has always had to compete with, or to complement, other more traditional goals of states in international relations, especially national security—defined in the period under consideration as opposition to the extension of Soviet influence—and the protection of the rights of U.S. citizens, including property rights. One of the questions to be examined in this study is the relation of support for democracy to security considerations; what happens if they conflict? And how does the protection of U.S. property rights relate to the promotion of democracy and human rights among the objectives of U.S. foreign policy making?[2] I identify at least a few instances in which support for democracy in Chile overrode more narrowly defined security or property-related considerations and argue that democracy and human rights more often complement and reinforce, rather than impede, the attainment of security, stability, and mutually beneficial economic relations.

The Structure of the Argument

This study begins with an examination of Chile's role in the Alliance for Progress—the U.S. effort during the 1960s to promote economic and social reform under democratic auspices in Latin America. Initiated by the Kennedy administration in 1961 as a response to the challenge of the Cuban revolution, the alliance was an effort to use U.S. economic aid and technical assistance to promote structural reforms that would broaden the support for and increase the appeal of democratic government by demonstrating its capacity to respond to social problems. Chile offered an especially attractive case study for the alliance because of its long history of constitutional government, its awareness of the need for social and economic change, and, more narrowly, because of the existence of a well-organized left, an alliance of the Communist Party of Chile with a Socialist Party that was strongly attracted to the Cuban model. Particularly after the election in 1964 of Eduardo Frei, the candidate of the center-left Christian Democratic Party, who was committed to a "Revolution in Liberty" to carry out far-reaching structural changes within a democratic framework, Chile seemed to offer an attractive "showcase" for the alliance. Yet the Chilean example also illustrated the tensions that can develop between support for a re-forming democratic government and the protection of U.S. investment as foreign policy goals, since included among Frei's reforms was the partial nationalization of the U.S.-owned copper mines. Similarly, U.S. security concerns seemed to be threatened by Chile as it challenged U.S. hegemony in the interamerican system on such issues as the expulsion of Cuba from the Organization of American States (OAS) in 1964, the creation of an Interamerican Peace Force to stabilize the Dominican Republic after the U.S. intervention in 1965, and a Chilean-sponsored effort to form a common Latin American front critical of U.S. policy which produced the Consensus of Viña del Mar in 1969. Further strains on U.S. support for Chilean democracy were created by the radicalization of Chilean politics in the late 1960s, which increased the strength of the left, both within and outside the Christian Democratic Party, just as a Republican administration under Richard Nixon was taking office in the United States. In the late 1960s as well, a series of military takeovers in Latin America suggested that democ-racy was not necessarily "the wave of the future" in Latin America, and led to modifications of U.S. policy toward democracy in Latin America—notably Nixon's adoption of a "low profile" in the visibility of U.S. diplo-macy and his sending of a mission to Latin America headed by Nelson Rockefeller, which recommended closer relations with military govern-ments.

The chapter on Chile, the United States, and the Alliance for Progress examines these developments with a particular emphasis on the question of the viability of a policy of support for democratic reform in Latin America. Was it an alliance "that lost its way" (the title of an article by President Frei in *Foreign Affairs* in 1969 and of a book by Jerome Levinson and Juan de Onis, published under the auspices of the Twentieth Century Fund in 1970)? Did it succeed in changing social and economic structures, and did those changes help or hinder democracy? Was the emphasis on agrarian reform in the alliance program justified in terms of its potential for responding to Latin American social and economic problems? To what extent were its democratic goals subordinated to the interests of U.S. investors in Latin America—in the Chilean case, to those of the large copper companies? What was the impact of U.S. covert Central Intelligence Agency (CIA) support for the democratic reformers, and what are the more general policy lessons that can be drawn from the Chilean example?

The tension between support for democracy and security concerns—that is, anti-Communism—was brought into dramatic focus with the election of Salvador Allende by a narrow margin in a three-way race in September

1970. In actions that became the subject of a major U.S. Senate investigation in 1975, the United States engaged in a massive covert effort that included encouraging a military coup to prevent Allende from taking office; when he did so, it gave covert funds to various opposition groups, including a few whose democratic credentials were dubious. While persuasive evidence indicates that the United States had no direct role in the 1973 coup that overthrew Allende, it engaged in economic pressures, propaganda efforts, and behind-the-scenes maneuvers aimed at making life as difficult as possible for the Allende government. The hearings, memoirs, investigations, and secondary literature—as well as a flawed Hollywood film, *Missing*—dealing with this period are reviewed in Chapter Three with a view to (1) assessing the role of economic interests in influencing U.S. foreign policy and its relation to U.S. commitments to democracy, (2) contributing to the continuing debate over the place of covert action in U.S. foreign policy, and (3) evaluating the place of anti-Communist power politics in U.S. policy toward Latin America during the 1960s and 1970s.

Chapter Four reviews the ways in which the Chilean example influenced the emergence and institutionalization of human rights as a permanent component of U.S. policy. Although Jimmy Carter made a commitment to human rights a major theme of his election campaign, and specifically criticized the U.S. role in Chile in one of his televised debates with President Ford, the U.S. Congress had already been upgrading the importance of human rights, including the right to self-government, as a goal of U.S. policy. In the case of Chile, it began to place restrictions on U.S. aid programs shortly after the 1973 coup, and in 1976 imposed an absolute ban on all military aid and sales to that country which with minor modifications remained in effect until the early 1990s. The chapter assesses the effectiveness of the ban on military aid and sales and reviews its impact on Chile—as part of a more general evaluation of economic pressures as an instrument to promote democracy and human rights. It also considers the stronger pressures that were proposed by congressional liberals—most notably a cutoff of all private bank lending—as well as the accusation by some liberals and radicals that the executive branch effectively undercut congressional intent by allowing private and multilateral support to blunt the effectiveness of the congressional sanctions.

After the coup the Pinochet government reacted against the statism and nationalizations of the Allende government by privatizing large sectors of the economy and social services. The changes were carried out under the direction of a group of free-market–oriented civilians, the so-called Chicago boys, many of whom had been trained at the University of Chicago on fellowships from the U.S. government and the Ford and Rockefeller foundations. After a deep recession in 1975, the Chilean economy bounced back and a few years later began to grow so rapidly that the *Wall Street Journal* described it as "the Chilean economic miracle." In 1982, however, the economy suffered another severe recession and massive unemployment, from which it later recovered. The checkered but successful economic policy it pursued was responsible for a certain ambivalence in the attitudes toward the Chilean dictatorship of U.S. investors, bankers, and economic conservatives. This study examines the impact of the imposition of a free-market economic policy in what had been an economy that had been heavily influenced by the state, and it assesses the U.S. role as an exporter of ideas and development policies to Latin America which stress market incentives and the reduction of government involvement. The analysis of U.S. policy toward the Pinochet government in the 1970s also serves as a useful case study for a critical evaluation of two hypotheses that were widely accepted in the postcoup period: first, that the U.S. government and business interests prefer authoritarian over democratic governments in Latin America, and second, that openings to a market economy can only take place under a dictatorial government that is willing to use force to impose the laissez-faire model.

Chile was cited again in American domestic debates during the 1980 presidential campaign when Ronald Reagan criticized President Carter's human rights policy for leading to the overthrow of rightist pro-American authoritarian regimes in Nicaragua and Iran and their replacement by anti-American totalitarians. Jeane Kirkpatrick, the author of the authoritarian-ism-totalitarianism distinction, visited Chile on behalf of President Reagan in August 1981, and a strongly anti-Communist conservative, James Theberge, was sent as U.S. ambassador. Yet when the Reagan administration sought to lift the 1976 congressional prohibition on military aid to Chile, the U.S. Congress prevented this from happening by voting as a precondition of any military aid a presidential certification of significant progress in the area of human rights and of Chilean cooperation in the prosecution of the murderers of Allende's former ambassador to the United States, Orlando Letelier, who had been killed in Washington in September 1976 by a car bomb planted by a Chilean agent.

The administration argued that it had not given up the U.S. commitment to democracy but had only shifted to "quiet diplomacy" as a way to achieve it. As early as 1982, in a speech to the British Parliament, President Reagan called for a program of support for democracy around the world. Chapter Six examines the turnaround of U.S. policy on democracy which by the mid-1980s produced a public policy of support for a transition to democracy in Chile.

Chapter Seven describes the active role of the U.S. government in promoting a return to democracy in Chile in the late 1980s, including a detailed examination of its assistance to the opponents of Pinochet in the 1988 plebiscite on his continuation as president. The chapter examines the impact of funding from the National Endowment for Democracy and the Agency for International Development and of other U.S. government diplomatic and economic pressures in promoting the return of Chile to democracy in the 1988–90 period. The Chilean case is evaluated to draw policy conclusions concerning the appropriateness and effectiveness of public support for democracy against repressive dictatorships.

The last stages of the transition to democracy in Chile coincided with the democratization of Eastern Europe and *perestroika* in the Soviet Union. The elected government of Patricio Aylwin, which took office in Chile in March 1990 with more U.S.-trained cabinet and subcabinet members than any other contemporary government, had reasons to expect substantial U.S. economic assistance, but at the outset U.S. economic problems and the competing demands of Panama, Nicaragua, and Eastern Europe reduced the possibilities of assistance. In fact, an argument can be made that now that the dictatorship, which the United States had at least some responsibility for producing, has left office, the reasons for a continued special interest in Chile have been seriously weakened. In addition, the security argument for U.S. interest in Chile has been sharply reduced as the Communist threat has disappeared, both domestically and internationally. The relative salience of the U.S. economic presence in Chile has also diminished, as other countries, notably Australia, Spain, and Japan, have expanded their economic involvement. Yet there are still reasons, I argue, to promote democracy in Chile and in the hemisphere. The book concludes with the June 1991 Santiago meeting of the OAS which formally adopted a hemisphere-wide commitment, strongly encouraged by the United States, to take active measures to support democratic governments against attempts to overthrow them by force.

Chile and U.S. Foreign Policy

In many ways, Chile typifies in microcosm the broader problems that have characterized U.S.–Latin American relations since the early 1960s. The issues that have been successively highlighted in the Chilean case—

economic aid, U.S. investment, the nature of U.S. links to the Latin American military, overt and covert intervention, policy toward authoritarian regimes, the relevance of market systems for developing countries, and the efficacy of U.S. support for human rights and democracy—have a broad applicability to the rest of Latin America—indeed, to the developing world in general. And those issues in turn are related in one way or another to the commitment that the United States made at the outset of the Kennedy administration to support and promote democracy in the Western Hemisphere. That commitment, however much it may have been honored in the breach during the last thirty years, has become formally institutionalized as one of the goals of U.S. foreign policy and has received bipartisan support in a way that makes it very unlikely to be reversed by any future administration. As later chapters argue, the course of U.S.-Chilean relations had a decisive influence on the development and strengthening of that commitment.

Support for democracy as a foreign policy goal has been questioned by those who see international relations in realist terms as primarily a struggle for power. The old realist-idealist debate in the study of international relations thus comes into play in a study such as this. I attempt in the concluding section to relate the experiences and policies of the last three decades of U.S.-Chilean relations to that controversy, since the sharp contrast between the Kissinger/Nixon and the Carter policies toward Chile, and the changes that took place during the two administrations of Ronald Reagan, provide instructive illustrations of the debate.

Ideological Shifts

Both the idealist and the realist positions can be described as ideological, since they provide their adherents with an overarching framework of ideas to explain and orient reality. But Chile has provided case studies for approaches that are more ideological in the specific sense of the term—that is, related to the broad sets of philosophical views of modern society which have emerged since the French Revolution to influence and structure government programs and policies. Until 1973, Chile had a multiparty system that encouraged ideological interpretations of its economics, politics, and international relations. On the left, ideas of imperialism, the international class struggle, and the inevitability and necessity of a revolutionary transformation of society from capitalism to socialism led to policies and attitudes by the Marxist parties which I examine and evaluate in the following pages—and to important modifications of those policies and attitudes which now make the likelihood of democratic stability much greater than at any time in Chile's recent history. In the center, a belief in development, modernization, democracy, and human rights dominated the outlook of the Christian Democrats, adherents of the Radical Party, and various social democratic groups and linked them to the United States ideologically, even when they differed on specific policies. This book examines how that center became eroded and undermined, and later rejuvenated and expanded, and it evaluates the U.S. role in that process. On the right, the traditional commitment to hierarchy, order, religion, and anti-Communism which characterized the Latin American right at the beginning of the period under study has gradually shifted in the direction of libertarianism, the promotion of market economics, and a belief in economic growth as the solution to societal ills which is more and more dominant among Latin American conservatives. Each group has had its set of prescriptions for the solution of Chile's problems, and each has had an opportunity to apply them, sometimes with the support of the United States, sometimes over its opposition, and often with its benevolent or not-so-benevolent neutrality. This study thus provides an opportunity to review and evaluate those formulations, especially as they affect the U.S. role.

Intervention

A further issue that recent Chilean history is uniquely adapted to illustrate is the nature, scope, limits, and successes and failures of U.S. intervention in Latin America. More than any other South American country, Chile has been the object of deep U.S. involvement in a variety of ways over the last three decades. This study enables us to define, evaluate, and perhaps prescribe the character of U.S. involvement in Latin America at a time when its longstanding raison d'être, defense of the West against Soviet expansionism, has ceased to have the compelling force it had in the past.

The last chapter also provides an opportunity to discuss the future of U.S. policy toward Latin America. The initial impetus to the establishment of the policy of support for democracy in Latin America was the need for a response to the Cuban revolution, and one of the arguments for that policy since that time has been that authoritarian governments are likely to lead to political polarization that can produce a Communist victory in the turbulence that follows. That policy could be established in the first place because of the belief that U.S. dominance in the hemisphere was so great that its political preferences were likely to be implemented if enough money, diplomacy, and pressure were exerted. Today, the "illusion of American omnipotence" has been dispelled, and the limits of U.S. influence in Latin America are more evident. This has occurred both because of the expansion of the presence of other powers in the area and because of the increased capacity and legitimacy of Latin American governments today.

With the multilateralization of Latin American relations, the virtual disappearance of the Communist threat, and the emergence of new issues such as debt, narcotics, the environment, and immigration, what analytic tools are available to help us in the formation of policy? The period discussed in this book has seen the rise and decline of a number of such formulations, including modernization, dependency, corporatism, and bureaucratic authoritarianism, as ways to understand the causes and consequences of change in Latin America. The examination of the Chilean case provides an opportunity to review and evaluate these approaches as they relate to Chile, and perhaps to develop new ways to explain what has happened in Latin America over the last three decades.

This study seeks more than explanation, however. If the period of what many academics have described as "mindless anti-Communism" has come to a close, what goal or goals can replace it as the orienting principle of policy, and what policies are most conducive to the pursuit of those goals? On the basis of the lessons that we have learned over thirty years, how can one define the U.S. national interest in Latin America, and does support for democracy form a central or important element in it? Or, as critics on the left argue, does support for democracy provide nothing more than a rhetorical fig leaf to clothe the interventionist impulse that has characterized U.S. policy toward Latin America throughout our history? Is there a difference on the part of both the United States and Latin America in the way support for democracy is now understood and implemented? Once again, recent Chilean history provides a useful case study to help to answer these questions.

Does the end of the Cold War mean the end of U.S. interest in democracy in Latin America—or at least in South America? If Chile is, in Henry Kissinger's words, "a dagger pointed at the heart of Antarctica," how should the U.S. national interest be defined in its relations with that country? How does the existence or nonexistence of a democratic government relate to the traditional diplomatic goals of avoidance of international conflict, promotion of mutually beneficial trade and investment, and friendly diplomatic and military relations? The Chilean case, which had so much to do with the establishment of the promotion of democracy as a continuing aim of U.S. foreign policy, may also serve as a test of its qualities of endurance in a situation in which the factors that produced that change in U.S. policy are no longer operative. To understand how that change in U.S. policy took place, and to judge its likelihood of survival, it is necessary to take a closer look at the turbulent history of the relations between the two countries over the last thirty years.

2

Chile, the United States, and the Alliance for Progress

CHILE WAS SETTLED principally by Spaniards, including a significant group of Basques, and in the nineteenth century important English and German colonies were established, but there was little U.S. presence in that country before the twentieth century except for occasional contact between Chile and California at the time of the gold rush. The United States recognized Chile in 1823, but during the nineteenth century Chile was more oriented toward Europe. American entrepreneurs, notably William Wheelwright in steamships and Henry Meigs in railroads, helped to develop the country, but U.S. investment was not substantial until the early twentieth century, when Guggenheim interests developed large copper mines at El Teniente and Chuquicamata and American investors took an interest in Chile's iron and nitrate deposits.

As American investments in copper, nitrate, and iron increased, U.S. influence in Chile rose dramatically, and the expansion of trade caused the United States to replace Britain as Chile's principal trading partner. By the 1920s, 90 percent of Chilean copper was American owned, and one-third of Chile's trade was with the United States. Diplomatically, the United States acted as a mediator in the settlement of the Tacna-Arica border controversy between Chile and Peru during the 1920s, although the final settlement in 1929 was the result of direct negotiations between the two countries. In the 1930s, the popularity of Franklin Roosevelt and the Good Neighbor policy led to an improvement of the relations between Chile and the United States, but in World War II, relations soured. For reasons related to its strong German minority and the vulnerability of its lengthy coastline, Chile resisted U.S. pressures to break relations with the Axis. The rupture of relations with Germany only took place in January 1943, after the United States had revealed instances of German subversive activity in Chile. And Chile only formally declared war on Japan in early 1945, upon learning that this was a precondition for participation in the San Francisco conference that created the United Nations.[1]

Following the break with the Axis, Chile began to receive Lend-Lease war materials from the United States and to participate in the joint defense of the west coast of South America and in the newly created Interamerican Defense Board. The American-owned copper companies cooperated with the U.S. government in a wartime price freeze that set the selling price of copper at 11.7 cents to 17.5 cents per pound—an action that Chileans still recall as costing the country hundreds of millions of dollars in lost revenues and taxes, particularly since when the accumulated wartime revenues were spent on imports after the war, price increases following the removal of wartime price controls meant still another loss to Chile.

In 1947, Chile joined the United States and the other Latin American countries at Rio de Janeiro in signing the Interamerican Treaty of Mutual Assistance, which provided for collective defense of the Americas against external attack. Along with the other Latin American republics, Chile also participated at Bogotá in 1948 in the establishment of the Organization of American States. The Charter of Bogotá committed the member nations to continental solidarity, social justice, and representative democracy ("The solidarity of the American States . . . require[s] the political organization of those States on the basis of the effective exercise of representative democracy"—Article 5d) and stipulated that "no State or group of States has the right to intervene directly or indirectly, for any reason whatsoever, in the internal or external affairs of any other State. The foregoing principle prohibits not only armed force but any other form of interference or attempted threat against the personality of the State or against its political, economic, or cultural elements" (Article 15). (Collective security measures called for under the Rio Treaty were not to constitute intervention.)

The Latin American countries did not participate in the Korean War, with the exception of Colombia, which sent a single battalion, but its significance for Chile was that the United States again attempted to impose a price ceiling on copper sales. In May 1951, a Chilean delegation secured an increase in the price from 24.5 cents to 27.5 cents a pound as well as the right to sell 20 percent of its production on the London metals market (where it received as much as 55 cents a pound, or double the fixed price). An attempt to establish a state monopoly on copper sales in 1952 failed when copper prices collapsed at the end of the Korean War. Continuing Chilean efforts to receive greater benefits from its principal natural resources resulted in the conclusion of a new set of agreements with the copper companies—the so-called Nuevo Trato ("New Deal") in 1955, which provided for a lower tax rate in exchange for increased production.[2]

During the Korean War, the U.S. government extended to Latin

America the Mutual Security Program of military assistance which had been initiated earlier with the NATO countries. Over the opposition of the leftist parties, Chile signed a Mutual Defense Assistance Pact with the United States in 1952, and the Chilean military began to participate in U.S. training programs and to receive grants and low-interest loans for military purchases. Chile was already receiving small technical assistance missions under the Point Four program, which had been established a few years earlier. However, the principal U.S. impact on Chile during the 1950s was a controversial anti-inflation program of economic stabilization designed by the Klein-Saks mission of U.S. economists, the failure of which produced a longstanding Chilean resistance to the imposition of strong anti-inflation programs.[3]

The Eisenhower administration (1953–61) resisted pressures from Latin America for public assistance for development purposes. However, the anti-American riots that accompanied Richard Nixon's visit to Latin America in 1958 led to a shift in U.S. policy and the establishment of the Interamerican Development Bank in 1960. Previous to that action, U.S. policy toward Chile was largely restricted to fostering Chile's integration into the emerging interamerican security system—especially its military aspects—along with the occasional exercise of good offices in smoothing over difficulties between Chile and the U.S.-owned copper companies. After the 1958 Chilean presidential election, an additional goal that became increasingly important was combating the influence of the Chilean Communist Party (see below).

At the end of the second Eisenhower administration, U.S. policy toward Latin America began to change. The increased emphasis on development symbolized by the creation of the Interamerican Development Bank was accompanied by a greater attention to the development of a democratic response to the challenge posed by the increasing radicalization of the Cuban revolution in late 1959 and throughout 1960. The emphasis on democracy came at a propitious time, since longstanding dictatorships of Latin America in such countries as Colombia, Venezuela, Argentina, and Peru had been overthrown in the last half of the 1950s and had been succeeded by elected civilian governments. A generation of forward-looking reformist leaders had emerged in the social democratic ("*partidos populares*") and Christian Democratic parties, while from Latin America itself were coming reform proposals such as Operacâo Panamerica of President Juscelino Kubitschek of Brazil, which called for an interamerican program of economic and social development in support of democratic government.

The Alliance for Progress

The time was ripe, therefore, for a bold new initiative on the American part, and it came during the 1960 presidential campaign. On October 18, John F. Kennedy proposed an Alliance for Progress with Latin American nations "with a common interest in freedom and economic advance in a great common effort to develop the resources of the entire hemisphere, strengthen the forces of democracy, and widen the vocational and educational opportunities of every person in all the Americas."[4]

In academia as well, now closely linked to Washington policymakers for the first time since World War II, the ideas of development and modernization were being discussed, and books such as Walt Rostow's *Stages of Economic Growth* (Cambridge: MIT Press, 1960), with its arguments for the need for investment as a precondition for "the take-off into self-sustained growth," received wide acceptance. After Kennedy's election, a transition task force on Latin America, headed by Adolph Berle, developed a series of specific proposals that were translated into a highly publicized Kennedy speech on March 13, 1961, calling for an Alliance for Progress with Latin America which would eradicate poverty, illiteracy, and disease from the hemisphere through structural reforms that would "demonstrate to the entire world that man's unsatisfied aspiration for economic progress and social justice can best be achieved by free men working within a framework of democratic institutions." It was to be "a vast cooperative effort, unparalleled in magnitude and nobility of purpose, to satisfy the basic needs of the Latin American people for homes, work and land, health and schools." The speech linked the theme of support for reform and democracy to threats from the left and the right when it spoke of the U.S. hopes that Cuba (under Fidel Castro) and the Dominican Republic (under General Rafael Trujillo) would soon rejoin "the society of free men" and warned of "alien forces which once again seek to impose the despotisms of the Old World on the people of the new."[5]

Kennedy's lofty rhetoric was given more specific content at the meeting of the Interamerican Economic and Social Council of the OAS at Punta del Este, Uruguay, in early August. Secretary of the Treasury Douglas Dillon headed the U.S. delegation and made a speech that promised $20 billion in U.S. public and private aid and investment over the next decade to promote economic growth at an ambitious rate of 2.5 percent per capita per year. Public loans would be at low or zero rates of interest for periods as long as fifty years.

The Charter of Punta del Este, adopted at the end of the meeting, called for "a great cooperative effort to accelerate the economic and social development of the participating countries of Latin America, so that they may achieve maximum levels of well-being, with equal opportunities for all, in democratic societies adapted to their own needs and desires." It specified among its objectives a "substantial and sustained growth of per capita income," the ending of adult illiteracy by 1970, economic integration, the construction of low-cost housing, and "a more equitable distribution of national income . . . at the same time that a high proportion of the national product is devoted to investment." Most important in terms of its impact on Chile, the Charter called for "programs of comprehensive agrarian reform leading to the effective transformation where required, of unjust structures and systems of land tenure and use, with a view to replacing latifundia and dwarf holdings (*minifundia*) by an equitable system of land tenure."[6]

That the goals of the alliance were ambitious and even at times contradictory (could redistribution to low-income groups and reorganization of the system of landholding be combined with an increase in investment?) was evident from the outset. Nevertheless, believing—or hoping—that, in Robert Packenham's words, "all good things go together," the defenders of the alliance argued that democratic reform programs could produce increased economic growth and improved tax collections, which in turn would both reinforce democracy and create demands for participation which would lead to further democratization—thus creating a "virtuous circle."

The U.S. Congress almost immediately voted $500 million for "soft" loans through the Social Progress Trust Fund of the Interamerican Development Bank, and $100 million for earthquake relief for Chile was signed into law in May. But such outlays required visible results to justify the investment of public funds. Almost immediately the search began for a country that could be the "showcase" of the alliance.

Chile as Showcase

A prime candidate for that role was Chile. It had a long history of democracy and a tradition of social reform going back to the 1920s, when it first adopted social security programs and a labor code. In its multiparty system were two allied parties, the Communists and Socialists, that looked to the Cuban revolution as a model for a solution for Chile's poverty and underdevelopment, and in 1958 their joint candidate, Socialist Salvador Allende, had come within 33,500 votes of winning the presidency (in a multicandidate election with a congressional runoff, which by tradition elected the front-running candidate). Its centrist parties, the Radicals and the Christian Democrats, were committed to democratic reforms, and even the rightist parties, the Liberals and Conservatives, had supported social legislation. Its president, Jorge Alessandri, the son of Arturo Alessandri, the social reforming "Lion of Tarapaca" of the 1920s and 1930s, was a conservative businessman, but since 1961 his coalition had included the Radicals, who recognized the need for structural change in the countryside. Santiago was also the headquarters of the United Nations Economic Commission for Latin America (ECLA, or CEPAL for its initials in Spanish), which had developed a number of the concepts that were incorporated into the Alliance for Progress and influenced Chilean political leaders in the direction of more economically oriented solutions to social problems. And it looked as if in the forthcoming 1964 presidential election the Castro-ite left would make another bid for power.

That bid would be a serious one, since Chile suffered from severe inflationary pressures and its principal source of foreign exchange, copper, was subject to rapid fluctuations in international commodity prices. Its agriculture was concentrated in ownership, inefficient, and stagnant, and its manufacturing sector functioned behind high tariff walls that enabled it to produce for a small domestic market of eight million people, a majority of whom could only afford the most basic consumer goods. Its trade unions were politicized and dominated by the left, although there were significant Christian Democratic unions as well, and migration to the cities had produced large shantytowns (called in Chile *callampas,* or "mushrooms") of impoverished, discontented, and often land-hungry poor.

One of the many policy changes involved in the alliance was the review of country development plans by the Interamerican Committee for the Alliance for Progress ("the Nine Wise Men"). At the outset of the alliance, the Chilean government, through CORFO (Corporación de Fomento), the Chilean Development Corporation, produced a plan to promote annual investments of over $600 million, of which $250 million was to come from external funds. The committee's response was favorable to the plan but noted the need for improved tax collection and a reform of the landholding systems. Partly because of the large earthquake relief program, Chile was already the largest per capita recipient of U.S. aid in Latin America, receiving more than $180 million in disbursements in 1961 alone. When Teodoro Moscoso and Richard Goodwin of the Kennedy administration went on an emergency mission to Santiago in early 1962, they were impressed by the Chilean efforts to carry out a stabilization plan and to increase tax collection, and they recommended an integrated system of assistance through "program loans" that gave balance-of-payment support in quarterly payments, or *tranches,* on the basis of preestablished performance criteria. Beginning in 1962 with a $35 million loan, such loans began to go to the Chilean government on a regular basis. They were accompanied by regular reviews of the budget before the release of each quarterly installment, involving the United States closely in Chilean economic policy on a bilateral basis.

Agrarian Reform

There remained, however, the difficult question of agrarian reform—of particular relevance in a country in which 7 percent of the farms occupied about 90 percent of the arable lands, many of them farmed inefficiently or held for social rather than economic purposes. Since the 1950s, there had been pressure for government action to distribute land to the rural poor and to improve agricultural productivity. In 1962, the Alessandri administration had proposed a draft reform law to the Chilean Congress. Signed into law in November 1962, it was principally aimed at the cultivation of idle or unproductive lands, although it gave the government broad powers of expropriation. Arable land that was "badly cultivated" or unused could be taken over by the government upon payment of 10 percent of its value in cash, with the remainder in bonds redeemable over a period of fifteen years. This provision required a constitutional amendment, since the 1925 constitution stated that expropriated property was to be paid for in cash, and the issue of deferred payment almost broke up the coalition of Conservatives, Liberals, and Radicals. Payments in bonds were limited to abandoned and inefficient properties, but the adoption of the constitutional amendment in 1963 set an important precedent for subsequent reform efforts involving compensation in bonds. The Alessandri administration announced a goal of creating 5,000 new proprietors in the countryside between November 1962 and November 1964, but by the time it left office, it had only achieved about 20 percent of its announced goal—between 1,000 and 1,200 families had received land.[7]

Was the alliance responsible for the initiation of agrarian reform in Chile? Clearly it was a contributing factor, and much of the media publicity for the alliance had focused on this aspect of the alliance program as a symbol of change in the socioeconomic structures of Latin America. On the other hand, agrarian reform had long been a highly visible and controversial issue in domestic politics in Chile, and, looking to the 1964 election, when it seemed likely that the Democratic Front—composed of the Conservatives, Liberals, and Radicals—would unite behind a Radical candidate in order to head off challenges from the Christian Democrats and the Marxist left, it was important to present a reformist image to the electorate.

The challenge from the left also contributed to another policy of the Alessandri government which was less pleasing to the designers of the alliance, its resistance to action against Cuba by the Organization of American States. The Chileans opposed the U.S.-initiated moves to exclude "the present government of Cuba" from the OAS and from the Interamerican Defense Board and to establish a special Consultative Committee to collect information on Communist subversion, since they viewed these actions as a violation of the OAS principles of nonintervention and universal membership. The Chileans also voted against a 1964 OAS resolution calling on members to break relations with Cuba after it was discovered that Cuba had been shipping arms to the guerrillas in Venezuela. However, unlike Mexico, which also opposed the action, the Alessandri government obeyed the OAS mandate, arguing that to do otherwise would undermine OAS principles of collective action.[8]

The Chicago Economists

Educational modernization also formed a part of the alliance program, and in this area there had already been cooperation between the U.S. foreign aid program and Chilean universities. In 1956, the Catholic University of Chile in Santiago had signed an agreement with the University of Chicago and the International Cooperation Administration (after 1961, the Agency for International Development, or AID) to send its best students in economics to pursue graduate training in Chicago. The program, which was highly successful and fundamentally influenced Chilean economic policy after the 1973 coup, produced a group of very able young economists strongly committed to free-market economics in Chile who became known as the "Chicago boys" (following, it was reported, the visit to Chile of an American female musical group known as "The Chicago Girls").[9]

In the early 1960s, these programs were expanded to include the University of Chile, and the Ford and Rockefeller foundations began to support training in the social sciences and agricultural development in Chile. With AID support, an agreement on technical and educational cooperation was also signed between Chile and the state of California, and regular exchanges began between the California state universities and colleges and those of Chile. Educational advisers also went to Chile to assist in the establishment of an entrance examination system for higher education, the introduction of a general education program in the initial university years, and in general to move the Chilean universities from the European to the American model (e.g., using the credit and elective systems and replacing faculties with departments).

The United States and the Chilean Military

The changes in the U.S. military relations with Chile and the rest of Latin America under the Kennedy administration were institutionally separate from the alliance but conceptually related to it in its anti-Communist purposes. Arguing that earlier concepts of defense of the hemisphere from external aggression were no longer applicable, the State Department Policy Planning Staff and the Defense Department recommended that the Latin American military receive training in "counterinsurgency" to counteract the threat of Cuban-inspired guerrilla activity. The U.S. Caribbean Command in the Canal Zone was renamed the Southern Command (Southcom), and training programs for the Latin American military were initiated at the newly renamed U.S. Army School of the Americas at the Canal Zone's Fort Gulick. Fort Gulick was also the site of the Special Forces Group, or "Green Berets," which sent trainers to various Latin American nations to teach antiguerrilla "special warfare." Besides the short courses at Fort Gulick, the Latin American officers also took technical courses at U.S. military bases such as Fort Bragg in North Carolina and Fort Ord in Kansas. Colonels and lieutenant colonels who were slated for promotion were also sent to the newly established Interamerican Defense College at Fort McNair in Washington, D.C., for ten-month courses on strategy and the social sciences. Those courses included lectures on the merits of democratic government, since education for democracy was seen by the new administration as one of the goals of the interamerican system. Of particular interest to the Chilean navy was the initiation of Operation Unitas, an annual exercise in which U.S. Navy units sail south along one coast and north along the other and are joined by ships (and sometimes planes) from each country for joint maneuvers.[10]

Chilean participation in these programs was substantial. In 1963 it received $25 million in military aid for training and equipment, all of it in the form of grants rather than loans. Between 1966 and 1973 it sent 1,100 Chilean officers to the Canal Zone and the United States for training, and since initially the military aid was gratis, it was not surprising that the United States became Chile's principal supplier of military hardware. The

Chilean navy had always had close ties with Britain, and the army had been trained by the Prussians beginning in the late nineteenth century, but the air force had always been closely linked to the United States. All three services became more and more closely related to the United States, a relationship that was symbolized by the establishment of offices for the U.S. Military Assistance Advisory Group (MAAG) in the Chilean Ministry of Defense.

The expansion of military ties to Chile in the early 1960s was accompanied by an increase in the covert activities of the Central Intelligence Agency (CIA). The aim of the CIA, which was founded in 1948 as a successor agency to the World War II Office of Strategic Services, was not only the collection of intelligence information overseas but also "such other activities as the president shall direct"—interpreted as a grant of power to engage in covert action ("dirty tricks") to influence other nations. Because of the existence of a large Communist Party in Chile, the country had already become the object of CIA attention in the 1950s. (An early CIA operation described in the memoirs of former CIA agent David Atlee Phillips, *The Night Watch,* involved hiring Phillips in 1950 because he owned the oldest English-language newspaper in Latin America, the *South Pacific Mail.* Phillips' salary was $50 a month, deposited in a Texas bank, plus $12.50 for expenses.) Projects involving peasants, slum dwellers, students, labor, and the media had existed since the mid-1950s, and beginning in 1961, operations were initiated involving key political parties. In 1962, the supervising Special Group approved the extension of financial support to the Christian Democrats ($50,000 and $180,000) and to the Radical Party ($50,000, approved in 1963), which shortly thereafter allied itself with the Liberals and Conservatives in the Democratic Front. Thus, as Chilean politics heated up in preparation for the 1964 presidential election, the CIA was already deeply involved in influencing its outcome.[11]

The 1964 Presidential Election

In Chile, municipal elections are seen as national referenda on the conduct of the government, and the 1963 municipal elections showed losses for the government parties and a spectacular gain for the Christian Democrats, who doubled their electoral percentage. The Christian Democratic Party of Chile had begun as a student-led Catholic splinter party that had split off from the Conservative Party in the 1930s in order to promote a program of social and economic reform. Initially called the Falange, although not out of any admiration for Franco, who established the Falange as the official party of Spain after the Chileans founded their group, it was renamed the Christian Democratic Party of Chile in 1957 after it fused with the Social Christian wing of the Conservatives. Inspired by the social teachings of the Catholic church (e.g., Leo XIII, *Rerum Novarum*, 1891, and Pius XI, *Quadragesimo Anno*, 1931) and the neo-Thomism of the French philosopher Jacques Maritain, the party claimed to offer a third way between capitalism and communism, one that transcended the divisions between left and right. It was also influenced by the postwar success of the Christian Democratic parties of Germany and Italy, and like them it claimed to be pluralistic and nonsectarian, although committed to the "communitarian" social principles of Christianity and to democracy as the political system most in keeping with the Gospel message. In 1958, Eduardo Frei, the Christian Democratic candidate, had come in third, behind Jorge Alessandri, the candidate of the right, and Salvador Allende, the candidate of the Marxist FRAP, the alliance of the Communists and Socialists. Julio Durán, the Radical candidate, had come in fourth, and the Radicals now saw their chance to capture the presidency by allying with the Liberals and Conservatives in the Democratic Front coalition, with Durán as its candidate.

While the left wing of the Radical Party had supported the nationalization of the U.S.-owned copper companies in the past, Durán and his conservative allies did not favor this course. The Christian Democrats argued for greater Chilean control over the copper industry, although without nationalization. The U.S. ambassador, Charles Cole, leaned toward Durán, both as more likely to win and as less threatening to U.S. interests. This was not the view, however, of some of the Kennedy team in Washington, including Robert Kennedy and a close presidential aide, Ralph Dungan, who had been impressed by the lobbying effort that the Christian Democrats had carried out to persuade them that the reforming program of Christian Democrats was more in keeping with the goals of the Alliance for Progress than the conservatism of Durán and the Democratic Front.[12]

The choice between the conservative Democratic Front and the centrist Christian Democrats as most likely to defeat Allende was made in a congressional by-election in Curicó, south of Santiago, to replace a deceased deputy. The candidate of the Democratic Front was easily defeated by the son of the deceased deputy, who was the candidate of the Socialist-Communist FRAP alliance, while the Christian Democratic candidate came in a strong third. The election results led the right to reconsider its election strategy, since the Curicó by-election seemed to indicate that a three-way split in the September presidential elections could lead to the victory of Salvador Allende, the Marxist candidate. The Democratic Front broke up, and the right threw its support to the Christian Democrats in order to stop Allende. Durán withdrew as its candidate and then presented himself as a symbolic Radical candidate in "a salute to the party banner"—and to provide an alternative for anticlerical Radicals who could not bring themselves to vote for the candidate of a church-inspired party. There were rumors that the U.S. embassy actively encouraged Durán to stay in the race, since it was felt that the election would be close enough that a few Radical votes for Allende might tip the balance. Others also argued that Durán's conservatism could reinforce Frei's image as a centrist reformer. The embassy's persuasiveness with Durán seems to have been reinforced by financial incentives, since the 1975 U.S. Senate Committee on Intelligence Activities report, *Covert Action in Chile,* indicates that his campaign continued to receive CIA funds (15).

CIA Involvement

The bulk of the CIA funds, however, went to the Frei campaign, with $3 million authorized and $2.6 million actually spent by the Christian Democrats in the 1964 campaign—an amount the Senate report estimates at half their campaign expenses. This contradicts reports of much larger contributions cited by one reporter (Bernard Collier, "A Revolution without Execution Wall," *New York Times Magazine,* Jan. 17, 1967) and in other press accounts when the CIA financing was revealed in the mid-1970s. (The Senate report also makes it clear that Frei himself did not know of the covert financing.) Smaller amounts were reported also to have gone to two other parties. Whether this included the Radicals, or groups associated with the Liberals and Conservatives now backing Frei, is not clear.

How could the United States intervene in such a massive way in the democratic politics of a small, distant country? To answer this question we must re-create the mind-set of the early 1960s, when Latin America was seen as one of the front-line areas of the Cold War. Guerrilla movements, inspired and in some cases aided by Fidel Castro, had emerged in a number of countries; university students and intellectuals in most of Latin America were mesmerized by Castro's charismatic appeal; and the slums and shanty-towns of the major Latin American cities, swollen by massive immigration from the countryside, seemed to provide a tinderbox for an impending revolution. Books like *The Coming Explosion in Latin America* by Gerald Clark (New York: David McKay, 1963), *The Great Fear in Latin America* by John Gerassi (New York: Macmillan, 1963), and *Latin America: Reform or Revolution?*, edited by James Petras and Maurice Zeitlin (Greenwich, Conn.: Fawcett, 1968), were reinforced by *New York Times* reports describing the northeast of Brazil as the next Sierra Maestra (the mountain range in eastern Cuba where Castro built up his guerrilla army) and a *Look* magazine story about the struggle for the hearts and minds of the poor in Santiago. (The *Look* story was written by Leonard Gross and later led him to write *The Last Best Hope* [New York: Grosset and Dunlap, 1968], which argued that the Christian Democrats in Chile offered the only viable alternative to Castro in Latin America.)

There was also an existing U.S. capacity to fund political parties. Such funding had been initiated in France and Italy after World War II to support democratic socialists and Christian Democrats as alternatives to the large Stalinist Communist parties in those countries. Then in the 1950s a similar capacity involving youth, students, intellectuals, and trade unions was developed as a response to the Soviet-funded international front groups such as the World Federation of Trade Unions, the International Union of Students, and the World Federation of Democratic Youth. Until 1967 this funding remained a well-kept secret, and it led to the development of ties to influential internal groups in many countries, including Chile. And since this support was for "democratic" groups, as a response to similar funding of "totalitarian" groups by Moscow in an ideological cold war, and since, at least until the unsuccessful Bay of Pigs invasion in April 1961, it had been operating effectively in what was seen as the national interest without any significant compromise of secrecy, neither ethical nor pragmatic arguments were made against it.

The CIA election money was used, according to the 1975 Senate Intelligence Committee report, for polling, voter registration, and propaganda, including a scare campaign (dubbed by the left "the campaign of terror") with radio commercials, posters, and pamphlets featuring Soviet tanks, Cuban firing squads, and children with hammers and sickles stamped on their foreheads, as well as a last-minute radio broadcast by the sister of Fidel Castro, denouncing her brother. The election program was coordinated by special committees in Washington and Santiago in addition to the 303 Committee, as it was then called, which reviewed all CIA expenditures.

In view of what took place after the 1970 election, it is useful to note that, according to *Covert Action in Chile* (16–17), on three occasions the United States was approached about supporting a military coup if Allende won, in one case through an intermediary by the Chilean Defense Council. It was made clear to the Chileans that the United States was firmly opposed to a coup. This record is confirmed by the declassified minutes of the meeting of the Interagency Latin American Policy Committee for July 9, 1964, entitled "Chile—Contingency Plans in Connection with September 4 Presidential Elections." They conclude: "The chances for finding a basis for dealing with Allende are remote, but an attempt must be made to wean him away from his extremist supporters. . . . It would be a mistake for the United States to act vs. Allende unless and until he takes decisive steps against us" (Declassified Documents Reference System [DDRS], July 9, 1964, Lyndon Baines Johnson Library, declassified 1977).

Besides Allende's support for Castro, other issues in the campaign included the question of the status of the American-owned copper mines and the intensification of the agrarian reform program. The Christian Democrats proposed an alternative to the nationalization advocated by the left—"Chileanization," the purchase by the Chilean state of majority ownership in the copper mines with the payments to be reinvested in the development of expanded production and refining capacity. Sales decisions were to be determined by a government agency, but the foreign companies were to continue to be associated as minority owners in the development and management of the industry.

On agrarian reform, the Christian Democrats proposed an acceleration and intensification of the Alessandri programs, with ownership based on a mix of cooperatives and individual property rather than the collectivization proposed by the left. They also supported the expansion of peasant union organization as part of a broader program of support for intermediate groups in society entitled Promoción Popular. (Not incidentally, those groups could also constitute an organizational base for Christian Democratic support.)

The ideas behind the Promoción Popular program had been developed by a group of Catholic laymen associated with a think tank, the Center for Research and Social Action (CIAS) at the Jesuit-run Centro Belarmino. Its most influential member and active fundraiser was a Belgian Jesuit, Roger Vekemans, who was particularly effective in raising money from European sources (and through one of its conduits, the Central Intelligence Agency). AID as well as the Ford and Rockefeller foundations also supported specific CIAS development programs, including a low-cost–housing program, production cooperatives, and a central library specializing in social science periodicals, aimed at university students and professionals. While the Roman Catholic church had never been officially linked to the Christian Democrats—and indeed, its predecessor party had often been in difficulty with the hierarchy, which once even considered formally denouncing it—the affinity between the Christian Democrats and the current thinking of the Chilean hierarchy, headed by Cardinal Raúl Silva Henríquez, was apparent. The church had already offered some of its land for use in experimental land reform projects with which Jacques Chonchol, later one of the major architects of the Christian Democratic reform law, was closely associated, and the bishops wrote a pastoral letter calling for structural changes in Chile and specifically endorsing agrarian reform. The influential Jesuit magazine *Mensaje* also published a special issue in mid-1962 entitled "Revolution in Latin America."[13]

A few weeks before the end of the campaign, Alessandri broke relations with Cuba in accordance with the OAS vote, but the left did not react because that might alienate potential voters. The campaign concluded with mass demonstrations in Santiago in favor of Allende and Frei. Years later, witnesses of the Christian Democratic rally recalled the quasi-religious fervor that gripped them as they participated in a candlelight procession down Chile's main thoroughfare and heard the impassioned tones of Frei promising a new society.

Frei won a smashing victory in the election, with 56 percent to Allende's 39 percent and Durán's 5 percent. He received only slightly over half the male votes (Chilean men and women vote at separate polling places) but secured nearly two-thirds of the women's votes. He carried every province except for the three mining areas of the north, the depressed coal mining area near Concepción, and the province of Magallanes in the extreme south. In internal reports, the CIA claimed (*Covert Action in Chile,* 17) that its actions had enabled Frei to secure an absolute majority rather than a plurality, which would have required a congressional runoff. In retrospect, this self-serving statement seems to be wrong, since once a three-way race had been converted into what was basically a face-off between the left and the combined vote of the center and the right, it was inevitable that Frei would win handily. Indeed, in hindsight one might argue that the massive U.S. involvement tarnished the reputation of the Christian Democrats in later years and only marginally helped them in 1964.

Chileanization of Copper

The new administration began in a hurry. Inaugurated in early November, Frei announced in December 1964 that he had reached an agreement with the Kennecott Corporation on the purchase of 51 percent control of their major mine at El Teniente, with the purchase price to be reinvested in expanded production and refining facilities. The speed with which the agreement was worked out was related to Kennecott's earlier doubts about expansion in Chile unless a new source of investment funds was found and political stability was assured. Kennecott was also attracted by the fact that the agreement meant a reduction in its effective tax rate, an upward revaluation of its assets (later to become highly controversial at the time of the 1971 nationalization), and retention of management control for twenty (later reduced to ten) years.

The Cerro Corporation agreed to a 30 percent state participation in its new mining venture at Rio Blanco, but Anaconda, the proprietor of Chile's biggest and most profitable mine, Chuquicamata, flatly refused Chileanization, although it agreed to a 25 percent Chilean share in its new La Exotica mine. Again the purchase price was to be reinvested, and it was understood that the Export-Import Bank in Washington would provide a substantial part of the financing for the scheme.

All of this required Chilean congressional authorization, and Frei sent the copper legislation, along with tax proposals to finance his social programs and the Promoción Popular plan for the organization of shantytowns and the poor, to the Congress, where they were promptly bottled up in committee or defeated. The 1925 constitution provided that the Congress was to be elected on a different schedule than the president, and the next congressional election was in March 1965. Thus Frei argued that having elected him in September 1964, the Chilean electorate should confirm his victory by giving him a legislative majority in March so that he could carry out his program.

The one problem with this scheme was that while the full Chamber of Deputies was elected for a four-year term, only half of the Senate, elected for eight years, was up for election. In the March 1965 election, in which the CIA spent $175,000 (*Covert Action in Chile*, 9), the Christian Democrats won 42 percent, far more than any party had received in recent Chilean history, and they elected 82 out of 147 deputies, or 55 percent of the seats. Twelve Christian Democratic senators were elected, which, added to 1 elected in 1961, gave them a total of 13, 2 seats short of the one-third that, combined with a majority in the Chamber of Deputies, was needed to adopt legislation. The Conservatives elected only 3 deputies and no senators, while the Liberals elected 5 deputies and no senators. The Radicals dropped from 22 percent in 1961 to 13 percent in 1965, but they still had a total of 10 senators. The logical outcome should have been some kind of arrangement with the Radicals to provide the government with a majority in both houses. Yet the very size of the Christian Democratic sweep, plus the fact that they were essentially competing with the Radicals for the same middle-class clientele and had a history of disagreement over church-state issues, meant that both the Radicals and the Christian Democrats were opposed to any agreement or alliance.[14]

Shortly after Frei's election, the Communist-Socialist FRAP alliance had announced that it would "deny salt and water" to the Christian Democrats, that is, refuse to give them any assistance, and relations with the new government were so bad at the outset that the Communists and Socialists boycotted Frei's inauguration. They described Frei as "the new face of the Right" and pointed to the fact that the Conservatives and Liberals had thrown their support to Frei in the 1964 election. The Christian Democratic strategy, however, was to count on the right to vote for Chileanization of the copper mines and the left to vote for the agrarian reform bill, which had been delayed both because of its complexity and because the copper vote was considered more important.

Those (including writers in the United States such as James Petras and Barbara Stallings) who saw the Christian Democrats as dominated by the "bourgeoisie" seem not to have been acquainted with either the Chilean bourgeoisie or the Christian Democrats. On the one hand, the Christian Democrats included a "rebel" faction that made no secret of its anticapitalism and a "third-position" (*tercerista*) group that was almost as ideological in its rhetoric. On the other, the right was outraged at the new taxes that the Christian Democrats imposed to finance their social programs (housing, health, and especially education, the last with the goal of universal primary education by the end of Frei's first year) and fearful of the "confiscatory" aspects of the agrarian reform law. Their fears were intensified when a wealth tax (*impuesto patrimonial*) on all holdings which was supposed to have been adopted on a one-year basis became a permanent part of the tax system, and an amendment to Article 10 of the constitution was adopted in late 1966 which removed most of the earlier limits on deferred compensation for expropriated agricultural holdings.

The right was particularly angry at the public support for the Christian Democratic reform programs—especially the agrarian reform—by the new U.S. ambassador, Ralph Dungan. A longtime aide of John Kennedy during and before the White House years, he had already had a personal relationship with several Christian Democrats before he was appointed ambassador by Lyndon Johnson after Frei's election. The right criticized the fact that the agrarian reform's compensation provisions—payment in long-term bonds that were only partially readjustable for inflation—did not apply to the U.S.-owned copper companies and argued that Ambassador Dungan was responsible for Chile's increasingly conflictive politics. A businessman is said to have told him at a Santiago dinner party, "This country is being led to social chaos, and you are to blame" (*New York Times,* Nov. 7, 1966).

The Dominican Intervention and Project Camelot

Not long after his arrival, Dungan was faced with two crises in U.S.-Chilean relations. When President Johnson landed fourteen thousand marines in the Dominican Republic in late April 1965, the Chilean foreign minister, Gabriel Valdés, issued a statement denouncing the unilateral intervention as a violation of the OAS charter, and the Chilean ambassador to the OAS introduced a resolution calling for an immediate end to the intervention. Student demonstrators threw red paint at the U.S. consulate, and Johnson sent W. Averell Harriman as a special emissary to explain the U.S. position to President Frei. When the intervention received dubious legitimation from the Organization of American States, which appointed a Brazilian commander, sent in a few Costa Rican and Brazilian troops, and established an Interamerican Peace Force, Chile, along with Mexico, Peru, Ecuador, and Uruguay, voted against it.

Since the American intervention had led to the defeat of a group of military rebels which had been sympathetic to Juan Bosch, the democratically elected president who had been overthrown two years earlier, the Chilean view was that the U.S. action violated the principles of both democracy and nonintervention. They also suspected that the Johnson administration had abandoned the ideals of the Alliance for Progress, particularly its support for democracy. Their suspicions had been aroused by a *New York Times* report a year earlier that Johnson's assistant secretary of state for Latin America, Thomas Mann (a fellow Texan), had held a briefing for U.S. ambassadors in March 1964 at which he had downplayed the differences, from the point of view of U.S. interests, between elected and military governments, arguing that the latter were often more effective agents of reform and development (*New York Times,* Mar. 19, 1964). The impression was reinforced when the Johnson administration seemed to welcome the military coup that overthrew the Goulart government in Brazil at the end of the same month.

The Chilean outrage at the U.S. intervention in the Dominican Republic led to a boycott by the left of the opening of Congress on May 21, 1965, because of the presence of the U.S. ambassador. It was intensified by the revelations by *El Siglo,* the Communist Party daily, that a Chilean professor at the University of Pittsburgh was attempting to recruit Chilean academics to participate in a multinational study ("Project Camelot") which was to measure the potential for revolution ("internal war") using a "social systems" approach. Concealed from the Chilean academics had been the fact that the study had been commissioned by the U.S. Army. The resulting uproar in Chile produced the cancellation of the project, a protest by Ambassador Dungan that he had not been informed of its existence, an investigation by the U.S. Senate, and widespread discussion in the American social science community on the ethical issues involved in government-sponsored research.[15]

Yet cooperation between the United States and Chile continued in many fields. Educational experts promoted curricular and structural reforms on the primary, secondary, and university level; farm credit programs and loans for the importation of machinery and fertilizer were aimed at increasing Chile's lagging food production; health programs included family planning initiatives (despite the Catholic inspiration of government ideology); and innovative tax reforms including the use of computers and occasional jail sentences for tax evaders were initiated with American assistance. Behind it all was the close U.S.-Chilean cooperation on budgetary matters which was implicit in the program loan quarterly disbursements for budget support.

Budget control was important, since a prime government objective had been lowering Chile's chronic inflation rate while expanding social spending. This delicate juggling act worked for the first three years of the Frei administration, despite pressures from a militant left-dominated trade union movement, and inflation dropped from 80 percent in 1964 to 17 percent in 1966.

Program lending played a role in the complicated negotiations between the United States and Chile relating to Chilean efforts to raise the international price of copper. In 1965, when the Chileans attempted unilaterally to increase the price by two cents a pound over the agreed producers' price, they were forced to lower it again in response to U.S. pressure and a promise to increase program lending by an equivalent amount. The Chileans gave notice, however, that after the expiration of the current contracts, Chile was determined to sell its copper at the world price, which had been increased because of the escalation of the U.S. involvement in the Vietnam War.

Increasing the world market price of copper was only possible if there was some way of limiting production either by commodity agreements or by the establishment of a producers' cartel. The Christian Democrats took the lead in establishing CIPEC (the International Council of Copper Exporting Countries), composed of Chile, Peru, Zambia, and Zaire, the Third

World producers, but as long as the group did not include the United States and Australia, two other major producers, it could not raise the price. The United States was hostile to interference with world market prices—although not to marketing agreements such as those in World War II and the Korean War which kept the price down. It did support Chilean efforts in the late 1960s to create an Andean Common Market involving the countries along the west coast of South America, and later Venezuela, as a way to create economies of scale and larger markets as well as to promote efficiency by bringing down tariffs within the Common Market area. The Alliance for Progress had been encouraging similar programs in Central America since the middle 1960s, and in 1967 President Johnson went to Punta del Este to announce his support for an ambitious plan for the economic integration of all of Latin America.

Agrarian Reform

Once the Chileanization of copper had been adopted, the main goal of the Frei administration was the adoption of its agrarian reform bill. In late 1965 it proposed what was the strongest agrarian reform law ever adopted under democratic auspices. It established a size limit of 80 hectares (about 200 acres) of "basic irrigated" land or its equivalent and authorized the government to take over "abandoned" and "poorly worked" land. Compensation would be based on tax assessments, with 10 percent in cash (less for abandoned and poorly worked land) and the balance in twenty-five-year bonds at 3 percent interest with 70 percent of the face value of the bonds adjustable for inflation. The "reformed" sector was to be made up initially of cooperatives for a transitional period of three to five years, after which the members of the cooperatives would decide whether to divide the land into individual plots.

It took from November 1965 until July 1967 for the agrarian reform law and the necessary constitutional amendment liberalizing compensation requirements to be adopted. It was undoubtedly the most controversial and difficult part of the Frei program, and it deeply embittered the right against him and the Christian Democrats for many years to come. In theory the large landowners were a small group, but many members of the urban industrial class also owned rural *fundos* or had relatives that did so. In addition, the reform was portrayed as a general attack on "property," and rumors were circulated that the government intended to follow up with an urban reform that would take over middle-class property in the cities for the benefit of the poor. A Catholic group, Fiducia, devoted to "Tradition,

Family, and Property," began to publish attacks on the bill, and *Frei, el Kerensky Chileno,* a translation of a Brazilian book attacking the Revolution in Liberty for preparing the way for a Communist takeover, began to circulate in Chile—until it was banned by the government.

The Frei government had been using the agrarian reform law passed by the Alessandri administration to carry out expropriations, mainly of unused or abandoned land, but the process was slowed by the lengthy legal appeals written into that law and the limited number of cases in which payment could be made in bonds. The new law, however, was much less rigid on deferred compensation, allowed immediate expropriation with possible court appeals later, and set a relatively low upper limit (with certain exceptions for "efficiently farmed" landholdings, which could be up to four times as large). Only about 1,000 families received land under the earlier law, but between mid-1967 and September 1970 another 27,000 families were incorporated into the program. This was far below the 1964 goal of 100,000 family farms, but that goal had been set on the assumption that there would not be a lengthy delay in the adoption of the law.

Agrarian reform formed an important part of the Alliance for Progress. Programs of distribution of agrarian land were supposed to promote the creation of medium-sized holdings ("the family farm") and result in the creation of a rural middle class while reducing revolutionary pressures from the landless. They obviously could not solve the problem of rural poverty (in Chile there were an estimated 400,000 families in the countryside), but the hope was that they would both increase efficiency, because more intensive methods would be used, and decrease the concentration of ownership of rural land.

These arguments were not imposed on Chile by the United States. Land reform and improvement of agricultural productivity had been discussed since the end of the 1950s, but the combination of pressures from the left, reinforced now by the example of Cuba, which had carried out two agrarian reform programs, with U.S. offers of technical assistance, surplus food programs ("Food for Peace") to ease the transition to agricultural self-sufficiency, and loans for fertilizer, farm machinery, and technical assistance (supplemented by active programs of the Ford and Rockefeller foundations) made agricultural change a high priority.

Were there other alternatives to a politically costly and administratively difficult agrarian redistribution program? The Frei government encouraged the establishment of rural worker unions, which had been legal before but were almost nonexistent, and competition between the Communists and the Christian Democrats led to the establishment of several rural trade union organizations and an increase in the number of agricultural unions from 24 with a membership of 1,863 in 1964 to 510 with a membership of 114,000 in 1970.[16] The government also began to enforce the minimum wage laws and social legislation and to require wage payments in cash rather than in kind in order to raise the standard of living of the rural poor.

Another alternative to direct redistribution might have been the use of the tax system to encourage breakup of rural lands, with special incentives to cooperatives and intermediate-level farmers. With American advice and technical assistance, agricultural production was also increased, but all the media publicity was given to the expropriations and accompanying rural unrest. Production increased but not dramatically—and not enough to reduce Chilean reliance on food imports, despite U.S.-encouraged efforts to raise the prices paid to farmers, which had been set low and made subject to price controls in order to keep urban food prices down.[17]

1967: The Turning Point

At the end of 1966, after just a little over two years in office, the Revolution in Liberty looked like a success story. It had "Chileanized" much of the copper industry, reduced inflation, increased production, redistributed income in favor of middle- and lower-income groups through tax and wage policies, and expanded education, especially on the primary school level; a strong agrarian reform law was on the verge of adoption; and the most recent by-election (in the Christian Democratic stronghold of Valparaiso) had shown continued popular support for the Christian Democrats.

Yet 1967 turned out to be the year in which the Frei program began to come apart. It began with a humiliating vote in the Chilean Congress by a combination of the right and left opposition to veto a trip by President Frei for a scheduled meeting with President Johnson in Washington (using a nineteenth-century requirement of congressional approval for foreign trips which had been designed to prevent presidents from absconding with the national treasury). Earlier the Radicals, who were now moving to the left, had joined with the Socialists and Communists to elect Salvador Allende as president of the Senate. In February 1967, stories of CIA infiltration of student, youth, and labor groups in Chile, published in the United States, revealed the involvement of several Christian Democratic organizations (although not the party as such). In April the highly politicized municipal elections resulted in a comeback for the right and a drop in the Christian Democratic vote from 42 percent in 1965 to 36 percent.

Although an analysis of the election reveals that the principal losses of the Christian Democrats were to the right, after the election the Christian Democrats appointed a committee, chaired by Jacques Chonchol, to draw up a report entitled "The Non-Capitalist Way of Development." As presented to the party in July, it attacked "developmentalism" and called for more nationalization and the "democratization of the Chilean economy" through the extension of worker control. In the vote on party officers which followed, the leftist ("rebel") sectors of the party defeated the pro-Frei *oficialistas* to win complete control of the party leadership.

The Radical Party now moved more decisively to the left. In April the Radicals voted to support a Socialist candidate in a forthcoming senatorial by-election, and at the Radical convention in June they moved to continue to oppose the Christian Democrats and to work "to achieve a grouping of all the collectivities and popular forces of the left." In the election of officers, the candidates of the party's right wing were defeated, and the editor of a right-wing journal of opinion, *PEC* (later revealed to be receiving a CIA subsidy), was expelled from the party. Shortly thereafter, the rightist minority left the party and formed the Radical Democratic Party, headed by Julio Durán. It received financial support ($30,000) from the CIA (*Covert Action in Chile*, 18).

Even the left moved to the left. The Socialists had been moving left ever since the late 1950s, but that process culminated in their Chillán congress in November 1967, which defined the party as a "Marxist-Leninist organization" and declared that "revolutionary violence is inevitable and legitimate," while "peaceful and legal forms of struggle are limited instruments of action incorporated in the political process which leads to armed struggle." Thus the Socialists placed themselves on the extreme left of the Chilean political spectrum, rejecting the peaceful way (*vía pacífica*) to socialism which the Communists had supported since the 1950s.[18]

As if his political problems were not sufficient, Frei also began to run into economic difficulties. The inflation rate began to rise, reaching 28 percent for the year. Domestic private investment dropped 23 percent. Whether this was due to the political radicalization, the upsurge in inflation, or government restrictions on credit is not clear. Unrest increased in the countryside and the universities, and a new revolutionary group committed to the use of violence to change the system, the Movement of the Revolutionary Left (MIR), was organized in Concepción. By the time that Ralph Dungan left his ambassadorship in August to become chancellor of higher education in New Jersey, it was clear that the Frei "revolution" was in serious trouble.

The policymakers in the Frei administration attributed much of the inflationary pressure to sharp increases in wages as a result of pressure from the left-controlled trade unions. When they attempted to promote unions more favorable to the government, the left wing of the party accused them of weakening the trade union movement by creating "parallel unions." The most controversial effort to control inflation was a proposal that wage settlements in excess of the inflation rate for the previous year be paid in government-guaranteed bonds and the proceeds used to finance the government's social programs.

The proposal was voted down in committee by the opposition-controlled Senate, and it also was opposed by the top officers of the Christian Democratic Party, leading to an emergency meeting of the party in January 1968 which replaced the leftist leaders with officers from the *oficialista* faction. (Years later, in an interview with this writer, Frei claimed that one of his errors as president had been to return to his home for lunch with his wife instead of using presidential luncheons as a way to exert more influence over his fractious party.) As inflation increased, and as Santiago was subjected to a series of nocturnal bomb explosions at such places as the American consulate, the headquarters of the Christian Democratic Party, and the office of the major conservative newspaper, *El Mercurio,* polls began to show increasing support for the candidacy of former president Jorge Alessandri in the next presidential election, scheduled for September 1970. (Frei was still much more popular than his party, but the 1925 Chilean constitution forbade the president to succeed himself.)

In November 1968, Richard Nixon was elected president of the United States, and it became clear that Chile was no longer the darling of U.S. policymakers. There had already been some disillusion with the Alliance for Progress, as congressional hearings revealed the limits of U.S. capacity to promote reform, the incompetence or ignorance of some of its administrators, and occasionally the misuse of U.S. funds. A 1966 Senate hearing had made all of these criticisms and focused on a case in which earthquake relief funds had been used to build vacation houses for a landowner. The Senators also criticized the confusion of political and economic objectives and the excessive use of program loans, which relieved pressure to make hard policy choices.[19] Nixon had visited Chile in 1967 and seemed to have developed an intense dislike for the Christian Democratic Party, both as too closely linked to the Democrats in the United States—especially its Kennedy wing—and as destabilizing to Chilean politics in its efforts to press for radical reform. AID loans declined, and the cozy relationship between the Frei government and the United States began to sour. Ralph Dungan's successor as ambassador, Edward Korry, had already determined that the United States was too closely tied to the Christian Democrats and too involved in the internal politics of the country. Although an appointee of Lyndon Johnson, Nixon allowed him to remain as ambassador, and he wrote a policy memo on the need for developing a "low profile" in Latin America which closely paralleled Nixon's own thinking on the subject.

The divisions within the Christian Democratic Party continued to manifest themselves during 1968, culminating in the resignation of Jacques Chonchol in November as head of the Agrarian Development Institute (INDAP) because of the lack of progress in the agrarian reform program. Radomiro Tomic, who under an informal agreement with Frei made many years earlier was slated to be the next presidential candidate, resigned his post as ambassador to the United States and returned to organize his campaign. He soon made it apparent that he agreed with many of the criticisms by the left factions of the party. However, those divisions had to be muted because legislative elections were scheduled for March 1969.

Congressional Elections

As the congressional elections approached, the CIA covert action program became more active. It had been supporting anti-Communist groups of women, slum dwellers, and students since the mid-1960s (although the student support had ended in 1967), and it promoted the development of peasant and labor groups to compete with those controlled by the left. In July 1968, the committee that supervised the covert activity of the CIA approved the expenditure of $350,000 ($200,000 was actually spent) to influence the March 1969 legislative elections. Presumably the bulk of it went to the Christian Democrats and the rightist National Party (which had been created in 1966 as a fusion of the Liberals and Conservatives) as well as to the Radical Democrats, who had broken with the Radical Party after its move to the left. Funds also went to a dissident Socialist group headed by Raúl Ampuero in an effort to divide the votes of the left. Between the presidential elections of 1964 and 1970, the CIA spent a total of nearly $2 million on twenty covert projects in Chile (*Covert Action in Chile*, 17–20.)

The 1969 congressional elections took place at a time when inflation had accelerated, spurred by the effects of a disastrous drought in 1968, and they revealed a pattern of increasing political polarization. The Christian Democrats' percentage dropped from 42 percent to 30 percent, while the rightist National Party received 20 percent in comparison with the 14 percent that its predecessor parties had received in 1965, making it the second largest party in Chile. On the left, women in lower-class areas voted for the Marxist parties rather than the Christian Democrats, although many of them also turned to the National Party. Jorge Alessandri's nephew was the top vote-getter in the country, and his niece received the fourth largest number of votes.[20]

Nationalization by (Forced) Agreement

The result was a surge of confidence within the National Party that Alessandri would win in 1970 and a deepening of the internal divisions of the Christian Democrats. In April, the National Party voted not to repeat the 1964 pattern of support for the Christian Democrats. In May, when in a close vote the Christian Democrats defeated an attempt to ally the party with the left and another *oficialista* was elected as head of the party, the leftist *rebelde* faction seceded from the party and formed the Movement of Popular Action (MAPU).

Frei attempted to demonstrate his continuing nationalist credentials by a last-minute addition to his May 21 State of Nation Address to the Congress which served notice on the Anaconda Company that it would be compelled to join the Chileanization program of mixed ownership of Chile's copper mines if it wished to avoid nationalization. He also noted that copper prices on the international market had stabilized at a price (62 cents) which was considerably higher than projected earlier, and "this obliges the government of Chile to reevaluate the share of the state in that vital activity" by increasing its tax share. Chile then imposed a sliding scale of increasing taxes on income generated by any "overprice" (*sobreprecio*) in excess of 40 cents a pound, and it embarked on negotiations with Anaconda on the sale of 51 percent control of its two major copper mines, which it had refused to include in the earlier Chileanization agreements. After a short period of negotiations in which Ambassador Korry exerted strong pressure on Anaconda to yield, it was persuaded to agree. Frei announced that Chile would purchase 51 percent ownership immediately, with payments to be made out of profits over the next twelve years, and that once 60 percent of the purchase price had been paid, it would have the option to buy the remaining 49 percent at a price depending on recent earnings. Until that point, Anaconda would have management control, and it also received a three-year marketing contract at a fee of 1 percent of sales.[21]

Predictably the agreement was attacked by the left for not breaking the relationship with the American companies entirely by immediate nationalization. Radomiro Tomic also insisted that if he were elected president, he would nationalize. However, in retrospect, it seems to have made good sense to retain the management and marketing skills of the companies rather than engage in confrontational tactics.

Radicalization and Polarization

One of the reasons for the pressure for nationalization was the influence of Marxism in Chile, particularly, but not only, in academic and union circles. Another, however, was the emergence and broad appeal of the theory of *dependencia,* which held that the underdevelopment of the Third World countries was due to their dependence on the developed countries. Widely influential in Latin America and among academics in the United States and in Europe, *dependencia* was largely a Chilean invention. It emerged in the late 1960s among those associated with the Santiago-based Economic Commission for Latin America of the United Nations. It was possible to argue for a strategy of increasing the bargaining power of less-developed countries through economic integration, producers' cartels, and use of international organizations—and this was the approach that the Christian Democrats had been taking. However, a more radical prescription was to break the links with the capitalist world (for reasons that were never explained very convincingly, *dependencia* was supposed to be an exclusively capitalist phenomenon) by a socialist revolution in order to end *dependencia.* This is the view that influenced many Chileans, including Tomic himself, making a Christian Democratic rapprochement with the right impossible.

An additional radicalizing influence in the late 1960s was the religious radicalism that became known as liberation theology. Among the Jesuits who edited *Mensaje,* in the Catholic University sociology department, among young priests and nuns who worked among the slum dwellers (and who briefly occupied the Santiago cathedral in August 1968 to protest the church's involvement with the structures of power), it seemed that Latin American bishops' denunciation of "institutionalized violence" in many parts of Latin America at their 1968 Medellín Conference applied to Chile as well, despite the existence of a facade of democratic institutions. They led land seizures, university occupations, and protests of slum dwellers which contributed to the atmosphere of disorder and accentuated the polarization of opinion in Chile—increasing the appeal of Alessandri as a "law and order" candidate.

Anti-*dependencia* feelings and Latin American nationalism were evident at the meeting of a new organization, the Latin American Coordinating

Commission, held in Viña del Mar in May 1969. The meeting was held outside the framework of the Organization of American States and point-edly excluded the United States. It developed "the Consensus of Viña del Mar," which was presented to President Nixon by the Chilean foreign minister, Gabriel Valdés, the following month. It attacked U.S. tariff barriers against Latin American products, criticized the "buy American" features of the U.S. aid program, and blamed foreign investment for distorting competitive conditions domestically and internationally and for creating net losses in financial flows because more money left the Latin American countries in profits and technology payments than entered as new investment.

The consensus was presented to President Nixon in June, shortly after Nelson Rockefeller, sent as Nixon's personal emissary to do a report on Latin America, had been "disinvited" by the Chilean government (on the grounds that public disturbances were likely to occur). Valdés told Nixon that Latin America was sending back 3.8 dollars for every dollar it received in aid, and when Nixon interrupted, Valdés cited a report by a U.S. bank. Henry Kissinger as national security adviser was present at the meeting, and Valdés later recalled, "As I delivered my speech, he was looking at me as if I were a strange animal." Kissinger then asked for a private lunch with Valdés the next day. Kissinger is quoted by Valdés as saying at the lunch, "Nothing important can come from the South. History has never been produced in the South. The axis of history starts in Moscow, goes to Bonn, crosses over to Washington, and then goes to Tokyo. What happens in the South is of no importance. You're wasting your time."[22]

Nomination of Candidates

The turmoil within the Christian Democratic Party finally subsided in August, when it assembled to nominate a candidate. There had been a few halfhearted attempts to find a candidate more acceptable to the right than Tomic, and he offered those who sought this course an opportunity when he pressed for an alliance with the left in early 1969 and withdrew his candidacy when that effort failed. However, after his initial critical reaction to the agreement with Anaconda, he toned down his criticisms and in August announced his availability once more. On August 15 he was nomi-nated unanimously by the party assembly.

Allende had a good deal more trouble securing the nomination of his Socialist Party. The Socialist Central Committee cast 13 votes for him with 14 abstentions on the first round, and in the second round, the withdrawal from the vote of two of the abstainers permitted him to be nominated by a vote of 13–12. The other parties on the left, the Communists and the Radicals, also nominated candidates with the understanding that all the parties of the left would meet and name a single candidate.

In the meantime, however, Chilean party politics was interrupted by what Chileans referred to as "the rattling of the sabres." The Chilean military had been complaining of low wages for a year, and Frei had named a general as minister of defense in April 1968 to respond to their complaints. In October 1969, the Tacna Regiment in Santiago engaged in a two-day rebellion in support of higher wages. All the political parties except the Socialists rallied to the defense of the government, and a settlement that involved the retirement of General Roberto Viaux, the leader of the revolt, was quickly reached.

In response to the threat to civilian government posed by the "Tacnazo" and anticipating the annual demonstration in his support on the anniversary of the end of his administration on November 4, 1964, Jorge Alessandri formally announced his candidacy. It was thus clear that the 1964 scenario of a coalition of the center and right against the left candidate was not likely to be repeated. The Christian Democrats had named their most vociferously anti-rightist candidate, and in turn the right had named someone who was anathema to the Christian Democrats. The left was still divided and had not produced a single candidate who might frighten the other two members of the "three-thirds" into joining together. The actual creation of the Popular Unity coalition behind Allende, including the Communists, Socialists, Radicals, and three smaller parties, seems to have been mainly the work of the Communists. Allende was much more their candidate than that of the squabbling Socialists. The Communists had never been serious about their candidate, the poet Pablo Neruda, and the Popular Unity program was lifted almost directly from that of the Communist Party.[23]

CIA Involvement

The development of dissent within the military had led the CIA to establish a program to monitor coup plotting beginning in mid-1969. The question of organizing a CIA program in connection with the 1970 presidential election similar to that of 1964 had been raised with the covert action review group, now called the Forty Committee, in April 1969, but no action had been taken. In December the ambassador and the CIA station in Santiago proposed a program against Allende, but they disagreed on whether to give direct financial support to Alessandri, a course that was favored by the CIA but opposed by Korry. Finally, in March, $135,000 was authorized for an anti-Communist "spoiling" campaign, with no money to go to the campaigns of either Tomic or Alessandri.

In his memoirs, Henry Kissinger describes the $135,000 figure as "a negligible sum" and blames the delay on divisions between the CIA and the State Department and on ideological prejudice in the Latin American Bureau of the State Department which opposed direct support for Alessandri "ostensibly for being too old, in reality because he was considered insufficiently progressive."[24] In June, Ambassador Korry proposed approval of $500,000 for the spoiling campaign and to "influence" the likely congressional runoff. The State Department opposed the bribery proposal as "stupid and immoral," and it was postponed, but $300,000 was approved for the anti-Communist program with the understanding, Kissinger insists, that nothing was to go to Alessandri's campaign. It was at the June 27 meeting of the Forty Committee that Kissinger made his oft-quoted observation, "I don't see why we need to stand by and watch a country go Communist because of the irresponsibility of its own people."[25]

According to *Covert Action in Chile* (21–22), the spoiling campaign consisted of six projects involving the production of anti-Communist booklets, posters, editorials (*El Mercurio* published at least one editorial a day "based on CIA guidance"), radio programs, and "black" propaganda attributed to other groups. Some of the 1964 materials portraying Cuban firing squads and the persecution of religion were recycled, along with posters of Soviet tanks rumbling into Prague in 1968. No money went to the candidates or for polling and getting out the vote, as had been done in 1964, although the Radical Democrats, who dissented from the Radical Party's leftist line, received a subsidy.

In July 1970, John McCone, former head of the CIA and now a member of the board of directors of the International Telephone and Telegraph Company (ITT), arranged for a meeting between Harold Geneen, head of ITT, and William Broe, chief of the CIA Western Hemisphere clandestine operations. The meeting had been suggested by Henry Heckscher, the CIA station chief in Santiago, who was in close touch with the ITT representative there. Geneen offered a substantial amount of money to the CIA to be passed to the Alessandri campaign, but the CIA rejected the plan. However, the CIA station in Santiago put ITT representatives in touch with the Alessandri campaign, and $350,000 was passed to his campaign and to his party by ITT, as well as another $350,000 from other U.S. businesses.

Chileans quickly found out about the passing of the money to Alessandri's campaign, since on July 21 five masked men entered Alessandri's advertising agency and at gunpoint forced it to turn over the financial records of the campaign. Those records were given to a Chilean congressional investigating committee in August by two journalists who claimed they had received them from "anonymous sources." They showed that Alessandri's campaign had received funds from *El Mercurio* and two U.S. banks, $5,000 from Anaconda Company, and a total of $600,000 from a mysterious "Charlie" who seems to have been a conduit for the American business contributors.[26] This was all publicized in late August, but how many votes it affected is not clear, although there is no doubt that the kinds of scare tactics employed in 1964 were less effective in the altered atmosphere of 1970.

How much did the propaganda paid for by the CIA and the campaign funds donated by the American corporations influence the outcome of the election? This writer was in Chile for several weeks at the end of the campaign, and at least by that time the propaganda messages were lost in the din of the campaign. There were many polls, but each seemed to predict the victory of the candidate who sponsored the poll. The right was overconfident about its chances of victory and did not create as effective an electoral organization as the Christian Democrats and the left, relying instead on the charismatic appeal of "Don Jorge." That appeal was diminished by a new factor that was far more influential in 1970 than at any previous time—television. (Chile had 30,000 televisions in 1964 and 500,000 sets in 1970.) Alessandri's health and age were a campaign issue, and during a television program early in the campaign, after a tiring campaign trip to the north and a night without sleep, the television camera focused on a tremor in Alessandri's hand, just as he spoke of the need for strong government in Chile. Polls showed a drop of 4 percent in his support the following week.

The Allende Victory

Yet all these factors were only marginal compared with the fundamental structural division in Chilean public opinion into three different camps, the right, the left, and the center. The center had been eroded (what Chileans call *desgaste*) by the inevitable costs of governing for six years, especially its failure to control inflation. The right was making a comeback, but it had suffered a serious defeat in the middle of the decade. The left began with 30 percent of the vote, represented by the Socialists and

Communists, and had now added most of the Radical Party and what turned out to be a relatively small sector of the Christian Democrats. Add to that the worldwide movement to the left in the late 1960s and the large increase in electoral participation in Chile, and it is not difficult to explain why Allende won the election.

It was close, however. Allende received 36.1 percent of the votes to Alessandri's 34.9 percent and Tomic's 27.8 percent, a margin of 39 thousand votes out of 3 million. As in 1964, Allende ran much more strongly among men than women. He held the traditional leftist areas in the copper mines in the north, the nitrate and coal mines around Concepción, and the working-class communes of Santiago. Overall he had a lower percentage of the vote than in 1964 (when he received 39 percent of the vote in what was essentially a two-way race with Frei), but because the opposition was divided and Chile was more polarized than it had been in 1964, he won a plurality.

Would a 1964-style U.S. involvement in support of Alessandri as advocated by the CIA and (after the fact) by Kissinger have changed the result? In view of the narrowness of Allende's victory, it is possible that increased electioneering combined with a targeted effort to persuade Tomic voters to cast their ballots for Alessandri might have had an effect. It is a demonstration of how deeply the United States had been involved in Chilean domestic politics that we can even speculate on this subject.

Whether it was because of ideological considerations, as Kissinger maintains, or the Nixon shift to a "low profile" to which Korry was committed, the United States failed to get as deeply involved. Moral considerations also seem to have played a role in the opposition of the State Department to Korry's proposals to bribe the Congress in the constitutionally prescribed runoff between the top two winners.

Moral considerations did not seem to have been operative on the broader question of the propriety of deep U.S. covert involvement in the democratic elections of an independent country. William Colby, in *Honorable Men: My Life in the CIA*, calls the decision not to get directly involved "rather foolish" (302) and attributes it to the decline of "the covert action culture" in the late 1960s. For him financial support for anti-Communist parties in Chile was no more immoral than was a similar support program that he ran at the time of the Italian elections in 1948. The Cold War logic was that democratic parties needed help to counterbalance that given by the Soviet Union and Cuba. (*Covert Action in Chile* cites a CIA estimate of $350,000 from the Cubans and an undetermined amount from the Soviets, who were known to subsidize the Chilean Communist Party in ways that had been analyzed in the Chilean press.) What was missing from the logic, as later debates demonstrated, was an effective rationale for that support being covert and not subject to democratic controls.

Conclusions

1. What can one say about U.S. economic support for the reforms of the Frei government through the Alliance for Progress? Critics on the left argue that from the beginning there was a contradiction between structural reform through the democratic process and U.S. interests in maintaining political stability and economic cooperation with Latin America. For them it should have come as no surprise that the democratic content of the alliance became diluted fairly early in the game as military governments took over, often legitimizing their destruction of democracy with doctrines of counterinsurgency and national security derived from, or strongly influenced by, the United States. Liberals, on the other hand, argue for a fundamental compatibility between the United States and Latin America in the promotion of democracy and modernization of social and economic life, and they attribute the declining enthusiasm for the alliance and the lack of reforms in Latin America to personal factors such as the death of President Kennedy or the pursuit of short-term anti-Communist interests rather than a longer-term commitment to democratic development. Conservatives, like their counterparts on the left, are impressed by the contradictory elements in the U.S. support. Robert Packenham has argued that the fundamental error of the alliance was the belief that "all good things [social, economic, and political] go together," when in fact rapid social and economic changes place great strains on fragile democratic political systems. Chilean conservatives go further and argue that the alliance reforms mobilized the population and raised impossible expectations that produced a combination of radicalization and polarization which led to the election of Allende (Frei as "the Chilean Kerensky").[27]

How does the experience of the Frei government (1964–70) in Chile help us in evaluating these claims? As to the charge of the left that the United States could not promote reform, the alliance did in fact foster a strong agrarian reform, the modernization and expansion of Chilean education, the beginnings of a population policy, the creation of 470,000 low-cost houses or equipped building sites for the poor, a large increase in tax collections and in the technical capacity of the central government, significant economic growth, and a negotiated solution of the copper question which benefited both sides.

As for the conservative criticism, it is true that there are often tradeoffs involved in development, notably between investment for the long term, and short-term increases in income and consumption, often inflationary in character. The Frei government recognized this but was not able for political reasons (lack of support in the Congress) to pursue policies that would reduce inflationary wage increases and persuade private investors to continue investment.

What frustrated the Revolution in Liberty—and with it the showcase of the Alliance for Progress in Chile—was not the inherent contradictions of democratic reform, but the peculiar characteristics of the Chilean political system. Popular presidents such as Alessandri in 1964 and Frei in 1970 could not succeed themselves, nor could they transfer their charisma to their parties or successor candidates. Staggered elections and an electoral system based on proportional representation made it highly unlikely that a president would have a working majority in the legislature, but a fixed term forced him to remain in office despite a hostile Congress. Worst of all, a multiparty system of election of the president without a second runoff round (a runoff proposal was made by a MAPU senator in early 1970, but it got nowhere because of calculations of political advantage by each presidential candidate) made the election of a minority president almost a certainty.

The conservative criticism has some merit if it is directed at the agrarian reform, since this seems to have produced considerable instability and uncertainty in the countryside and made the question of stable property guarantees a central focus of Chilean conservative concern for decades to come. Between 1965 and 1973, 5,809 farms were expropriated, amounting to 40 percent of the farmland of Chile and 67 percent of the irrigated lands.[28] Given the urgency of the need for increased agricultural production, a tax program based on efficiency and productivity might have been preferable to land redistribution, which, even if it had reached its goal of 100,000 families, would not have assisted a majority of the estimated 400,000 rural families or made a large political difference in a country that by 1970 was 70 percent urban. So much political capital was invested in the agrarian reform that more important changes, such as the organization of rural unions and better wages for the rural workers, received less attention than they should have.

The particular form and context of the agrarian reform made it more controversial and threatening than it need have been. Some of its more radical proponents frightened the Chilean middle class with more general attacks on property, and the compensation provisions, which included a percentage that was not readjustable for inflation and thus would amount over time to confiscation, reinforced this fear. The defenders of the reform argued that it succeeded in breaking up the inefficient traditional landholdings (latifundia), thus paving the way for the modernization of Chilean agriculture which took place in the late 1970s and early 1980s, but the social cost of this change was considerable.

More generally, the aid relationship to Chile in the mid-1960s, involving as it did general budget support through "program loans," was a demeaning one, as quarterly installments were doled out by AID after consultation on the government expenditure program. Performance criteria are difficult to administer, as the international aid agencies have discovered. Because both sides recognized the unsatisfactory nature of the relationship, the program loan system was phased out in 1968 as Chile received higher receipts from international copper sales.

This is not to argue, as Jerome Levinson and Juan de Onis did in their Twentieth Century Fund study of the alliance, that all U.S. aid should go through international agencies. There are programs that the United States may want to promote which can be carried out more effectively on a bilateral basis. For example, it is difficult to see how the Food for Peace program could be carried out other than bilaterally, since it depends on a complicated set of financial mechanisms and storage and supply facilities that are specifically American. The alliance experience, however, did show the virtues of multilateral advisory organizations involving representatives of other countries of Latin America—for example, the Interamerican Committee for the Alliance for Progress (CIAP—its Spanish-language acronym). When Latin American finance ministers had to justify their programs to experts from other Latin American countries, the process achieved some of the same goals as U.S. review but without the stigma of "imperialism."

2. On the issue of covert financing, its disadvantages, which became shockingly evident in the Allende period, were also present in the Christian Democratic administration. There was no control by the U.S. Congress, and executive oversight was limited to a small number of people. It was used to subsidize some fringe groups (for example, the far-right journal *PEC*) which would not have received open funding from public or private sources. It required knowledgeable people, including the U.S. ambassador, to lie in denying the U.S. relationship when asked. And in the Chilean case, it involved the establishment of a separate and divergent policy-making center that, although theoretically under the control of the ambassador, could undercut and even counteract him. When the covert subsidies

to student, youth, and labor groups were revealed in 1967, it was proposed that the United States set up publicly supported political foundations for international aid similar to those that the German Federal Republic had established to assist kindred groups abroad, but nothing came of it until the creation of the National Endowment for Democracy in the mid-1980s.

Aid programs and support for political parties, unions, and the like were denounced in the 1960s and later as illegitimate intervention in violation of national sovereignty. However, if they are publicly known and accepted as legitimate assistance by elites in the recipient countries, they are more appropriately called instances of the exercise of U.S. *influence* rather than *intervention*. Particularly if the programs are similar to the type of support which is carried out by large private foundations such as Ford and Rockefeller, promoting the modernization of the economy and society, they are more likely to be considered legitimate international aid, even if there are also political reasons related to U.S. security for extending the aid.

3. The Chilean experience shows that there are problems of continuity and consistency in government aid programs. Thus, when Lyndon Johnson became president, there was a shift away from the more idealistic elements of the alliance, and with Richard Nixon a deliberate move was made away from what was regarded as a Kennedy initiative. This was accentuated by the earlier too-close public relationship between Ambassador Dungan and the Christian Democrats, which hurt the programs both in Chile and in the United States.

4. The relationship between the United States and the Chilean military became much closer during the early 1960s as grant and training programs expanded, and low-interest loans for military purchases encouraged increasing reliance on U.S. weapons. However, by the mid-1960s the Congress was already beginning to place conditions on military aid (reducing the aid, for example, if the Latin Americans bought high-tech planes or detained U.S. fishing boats). It was in the U.S. interest to have a close relationship with the Latin American military, but it sometimes involved the United States in areas that when publicized were seen as opposed to U.S. ideals—for example, brutal interrogation techniques and repression of legitimate protest. The police training program was phased out in 1974, but the general problem of excessive involvement with the military was present throughout the 1960s. Those relationships could be used in positive ways, such as promoting the peaceful settlement of border disputes, but there were arguments—not persuasive in this writer's view—that the U.S.

aid indoctrinated the Latin American military with an extreme form of anti-Communism which contributed to the wave of coups which swept across Latin America from 1964 to 1976.

5. The actions that the United States took in defense of the copper companies in the 1960s have also been seen as yet another instance of the subordination of the U.S. national interest to the economic interests of the multinationals. The AID Investment Guarantee Program, and later the Overseas Private Investment Corporation (OPIC), have also been criticized for using public funds to eliminate the risks for U.S. companies investing in the developing countries. However, the Chilean case gives us at least one example, the "nationalization by agreement" of the Anaconda Company in 1969, of the use of U.S. government pressure in support of a program that was seen as politically advantageous for the U.S. government at the expense of the economic interests of a major U.S. company.

6. What of U.S. support for democracy? This was clearly spelled out in the Charter of Punta del Este, which established the Alliance for Progress, but often undercut by subsequent developments. The covert manipulations of the democratic process by massive secret funding and efforts to divide and weaken political parties clearly violated the principle of popular sovereignty (although there would be less objection to helping to establish a "level playing field" for the opponents of authoritarian governments through public financial support, as in a number of cases in the 1980s). When military governments took over most of Latin America, it was difficult to place the same emphasis on support for democracy, and the intensity of U.S. opposition to the extension of Cuban, and therefore Soviet, influence often operated to favor improved relationships with military regimes. Given a choice between a "friendly tyrant" on the right and a Castroite regime on the left, it was clear how American policymakers would decide.[29] Yet the principle of U.S. support for democracy had been enunciated and embodied in a program for Latin America. The vagaries of Chilean politics and the election of a conservative president in the United States made the U.S. commitment weaker by the end of the 1960s. U.S. policy has always vacillated between pragmatism and idealism in its relationship with Latin America, with the Republicans often leaning to the more pragmatic side. With the victory in the September 1970 popular election in Chile of a Marxist candidate, the U.S. commitment to democracy in Chile was put to the test. It failed that test.

3

The United States and the Allende Government (1970–1973)

T HE 1925 CHILEAN constitution provided that if no presidential
candidate received a majority of the popular votes, there would be
a runoff in the Chilean Congress between the top two candidates fifty days
after the popular election, and the victorious candidate would take office
ten days later. By tradition, but not by law, the Congress had in the past
voted for the front-running candidate, who in this case would be Salvador
Allende. Chile therefore faced a revolution—in the sense of the election of
a candidate committed to a Marxist program of social and economic
change—with two months' notice.

Furious activity aimed at preventing an Allende victory went on during
these two months in Washington and in Santiago. Thanks to a leak to
columnist Jack Anderson of the confidential papers of the International
Telephone and Telegraph Company (ITT), the full-scale investigation by
the Senate Intelligence Committee, headed by Senator Frank Church, in
1975, and the release of a number of relevant documents under the Freedom
of Information Act, we know as much about U.S. policy making toward
Chile for the period from September to November 1970 as we do about
policy making in any period in recent American history. It is a controversial
period and one that does not do credit to American ideals, since it includes
an effort to prevent a freely elected president from taking office by fomenting a military coup; the assassination of a Chilean general, for which
the United States was indirectly responsible; authorization, although not
execution, of efforts to bribe the Chilean Congress; subsidization of a
quasi-fascist extreme rightist group; and improperly close relationships
between the U.S. government and a major corporation.[1]

Besides the State Department, the principal players in the bureaucratic
politics of U.S. policy toward Chile were the CIA, the national security
adviser (Henry Kissinger), and President Richard Nixon, and in Santiago
Ambassador Korry, the head of the CIA station (Henry Heckscher), and

the army military attaché, Colonel Paul M. Wimert, Jr. Deeply involved as well were the head of ITT, Harold Geneen; his senior vice president for Latin America, W. J. Gerrity; and two ITT representatives in Santiago, who sent back frequent reports on developments between September and November.

The maneuvering leading up to the congressional runoff in Chile began with a visit the day after the popular election by Radomiro Tomic to Allende's residence, where he said to journalists, "I have come to greet the President-elect of Chile, my old friend, Salvador Allende." When he met Allende, he said, "You finally have won." These actions were taken in accordance with an informal agreement between the two that if either won by more than 30,000 votes, the other would support him in the runoff. (Allende won by 39,000 votes.)

As Alessandri supporters immediately made clear, Allende was not president-elect, but only one of the two candidates in the congressional runoff on October 24, the other being Alessandri. Four days later, Alessandri made a clear bid for Christian Democratic support when he announced, "In case of my election by the Congress, I would resign the post, which would give rise to a new election. I can state categorically, of course, that I would not participate in that election under any circumstances" (*El Mercurio,* Sept. 10, 1970). Since there would have been an intervening president (if only for a short time), Eduardo Frei would then be eligible to run, and given his continuing popularity and the assured support of the right, he would clearly win in a two-way race against Allende.

The Christian Democrats had 75 votes in the two houses of Congress, to Allende's 80 and Alessandri's 45, so that their vote was crucial. On September 14, the National Council of the Christian Democratic Party met and rejected the Alessandri offer, opting instead to condition their support of Allende on his acceptance of a series of constitutional amendments, to be known as the Statute of Democratic Guarantees, which would guarantee the free functioning of political parties, trade unions, private education, and the mass media and the independence of the armed forces from political control. Once Allende had accepted this proposal, it was impossible to prevent Allende from taking power, but the U.S. government made a massive effort to do so.

Track I and Track II

The Forty Committee met to discuss the Chilean situation on September 8, and Richard Helms, head of the CIA, reported that the Chilean Congress was likely to vote for Allende and that a military coup "would have very little chance of success unless organized soon." Both Ambassador Korry and the CIA station cabled that there was no possibility of a military coup. Thus, when the Forty Committee met again on September 14, it decided on a massive anti-Allende propaganda campaign and economic pressure on Chile. Over State Department objections, it also approved a contingency fund of $250,000 for "covert support of projects that Frei or his trusted team deem important," including bribery of members of Congress. Korry was instructed to try to persuade Frei to accept the Alessandri proposal, and he or other "appropriate members of the Embassy mission" were asked to approach the military about their possible reaction if Frei turned over power to them and called new elections. The problem, as Korry reported a week later, was that General René Schneider, the army commander in chief, had publicly committed himself to strict observance of the constitution, and thus for "the Frei gambit" to work, Korry said, quoting a leading Christian Democrat, Schneider "would have to be neutralized, by displacement, if necessary." That Korry did not favor this course, however, is clear from his cables, in which he repeatedly referred to an attempt to provoke a coup as a potential Bay of Pigs failure and "an unrelieved disaster for the U.S. and the President."[2]

Yet the covert promotion of a military coup in what later became known as "Track II"—as distinct from "Track I," the "Frei gambit" program endorsed by the Forty Committee—became U.S. government policy as a result of the direct decision of Richard Nixon. Agustín Edwards, the publisher of *El Mercurio*, left Chile almost immediately after the election and flew to the United States to be the house guest of Donald Kendall, the president of Pepsi-Cola. Through Kendall, he secured a private meeting with Nixon on September 14; with Attorney General John Mitchell and Kissinger, the national security adviser, on September 15; and with CIA director Richard Helms on the following day. That same day, Nixon, Kissinger, Mitchell, and Helms met, and the president informed Helms that $10 million was available for a secret program to prevent Allende from taking power. He was told to "make the economy scream." As Helms testified to the Church committee in July 1975, "The President came down hard. He wanted something done and he didn't much care how. . . . If I ever carried a marshal's baton out of the Oval Office, it was that day." A few days later, the CIA station in Santiago received a "back-channel" message, "Parliamentary legerdemain has been discarded. Military solution is objective. . . . This authority granted to CIA only to work towards a military solution to the problem." The message also indicated that the State

Department, the Forty Committee, the ambassador, and the embassy were not to be told of the effort. The CIA station replied that there was no possibility of securing the support of President Frei and General Schneider and that work would have to be done with lower officers. The cable specifically mentioned General Camilo Valenzuela, the commander of the Santiago garrison.[3]

Seymour Hersh's biography of Henry Kissinger argues—on the basis of statements by a navy enlisted man who worked in the National Security Council—that one of the options under consideration by the CIA was the assassination of Allende (258–59). There is evidence that the CIA was in touch with retired General Arturo Marshall, who talked openly about assassination plots, but the agency considered him unstable.[4] (When the CIA station learned that he had been behind the blowing up of power stations, it passed the information to Ambassador Korry, who in turn told President Frei, who had Marshall arrested.) When Helms was asked by the Senate Select Committee whether the marshal's baton included authorization of Allende's "physical elimination," he replied that from the time he had taken over as CIA director, he had made his position clear: "We weren't going to have any of that business when I was Director."

Track I did not seem to have any likelihood of success insofar as it involved the election of Alessandri, or Frei's resignation in favor of the military, but its economic side soon began to take effect. Possibly as a result of U.S. pressure, Finance Minister Andrés Zaldivar told the nation on September 23 that since the election there had been a run on the banking system and industrial production had dropped in a catastrophic fashion. The ITT papers indicate that on September 11 its representatives once again offered to assist the U.S. government financially in preventing an Allende victory, but nothing had come of it before the White House meetings. After Helms' meeting with President Nixon, the CIA itself took the initiative in getting ITT's help in a program "aimed at inducing economic collapse in Chile," but initial inquiries indicated that the other U.S. companies contacted were not interested in endangering their Chilean investments. On October 7, the ITT Washington office reported that "repeated calls to firms such as GM, Ford, and banks in California and New York have drawn no offers of help."[5]

On September 24, a mass rally to oppose the election of Allende was held by Patria y Libertad (Fatherland and Freedom), a movement organized by a young Chilean lawyer, Pablo Rodríguez. He called on the Congress not to give power to "a third of the electorate" and, referring to coup rumors, declared, "Freedom will not be defended by a coup d'etat [*golpe de estado*] but by a blow [*golpe*] for patriotism . . . in which youth, men, and women go out into the streets to offer their lives if necessary because freedom must exist in Chile" (*El Mercurio*, Sept. 25, 1970). Patria y Libertad continued to promote, at least verbally, violence against the government in the next three years. *Covert Action in Chile* revealed (31) that in the initial period it received $38,500 from the CIA.

Ambassador Korry had forbidden embassy personnel to make contacts with the Chilean military, but in violation of his order (and an earlier order aimed specifically at General Roberto Viaux after the October 1969 revolt) the CIA was in touch with General Viaux, who had been retired and was known to be plotting a coup. An ITT memo reported on September 17, "One retired general, Viaux, is all gung-ho about moving immediately, reason or not, but General Schneider has threatened to have Viaux shot if he moves unilaterally," and evidence later presented at General Viaux's trial refers to an offer of arms by a mysterious Chilean-born Venezuelan named Reyes who claimed to have resources of $1 million. The CIA station lacked direct contact with military officers on active duty, however, and therefore began to use Paul Wimert, the U.S. military attaché, to reach Chilean officers on active duty. On October 5, the first of twenty-one such contacts were made. By October 8, the CIA could inform the White House of two groups of plotters, associated respectively with retired General Viaux and with General Valenzuela, commander of the Santiago garrison. At this point Ambassador Korry, suspicious that the CIA was "up to something behind my back," cabled his continuing opposition to U.S. support for a coup and his suspicion that the CIA was plotting with Patria y Libertad. The cable was sent on Friday, October 9. Korry was summoned immediately to Washington, and on Monday, October 12, he met Kissinger and Nixon. To Kissinger he said that "only an insane person would deal with a man like Viaux" and described him as "a totally dangerous man," while he told Nixon that Allende's election was "an absolutely foregone conclusion" and described Viaux as a "madman." He repeated his claim that there was no chance for a military coup and this time was backed up by the CIA representative, who described Viaux as "unpredictable" and the chances of his mounting a successful coup as "slight."[6]

The result was a White House decision on October 15 to "defuse" the Viaux coup plot while instructing Korry to "preserve your assets" and "stay in touch." The next day the CIA station in Santiago was instructed to warn Viaux against precipitate action, while encouraging him to join forces with other plotters, since "there is great and continuing interest in Valenzuela et al." and "It is firm and continuing policy that Allende be overthrown by a coup."

Henry Kissinger in his testimony to the Church committee argued that the decision to turn off Viaux was the end of Track II, and President Nixon in his written response to committee questions agreed. In his memoirs Kissinger interprets the continued CIA plotting and aid to the coup plotters as well as the explicit messages promoting a coup as a misunderstanding of the White House order—which is not likely, given what would have been bureaucratic punctiliousness of the CIA on such a sensitive matter. The Valenzuela group tried on October 19 and 20 to kidnap General Schneider as the prelude to a coup, but in what Kissinger calls "a comedy of errors worthy of the Keystone cops" they failed both evenings.[7]

The Murder of General Schneider

According to the Church committee, the Valenzuela plan was to fly Schneider to Argentina and demand that Frei resign and leave the country and dissolve the Congress. Valenzuela was also promised $50,000 by Wimert. For reasons not clear from the Church committee report, he also asked for three submachine guns, which were delivered by Wimert at 2 A.M. on October 22. At 8 A.M. that same day, the Viaux plotters, who were young right-wingers not associated with the armed forces, attempted to kidnap General Schneider on his way to work. When he resisted, they wounded him mortally. The conclusion of the Church committee report was that there was no direct connection between those who killed Schneider and the CIA, since Viaux and his coconspirators had been advised on October 17 not to act, advice they immediately rejected, although Colonel Wimert had remained in touch with the Valenzuela group.

What was the degree of U.S. responsibility for the death of Schneider? While the United States had opposed the Viaux action a few days before it occurred, it had continued to support Valenzuela and other top officers (Admiral Hugo Tirado and *Carabinero* General Vincente Huerta and their group), who made two unsuccessful attempts to kidnap Schneider and were planning a third. Despite Kissinger's and Haig's denials of support for further action after the October 15 meeting that decided to "turn off" Viaux, the Church committee found that the CIA man in charge of the operation had met with General Haig on October 19 (a meeting that General Haig later testified he did not recall) and that Santiago station had been sent a cable, citing "queries from high levels" as to events that may have occurred on October 19, the day of one of the failed attempts at a kidnapping. The Senate Intelligence Committee was denied access to the Nixon and Kissinger calendars, so that there is no way of knowing whether either of them was kept informed of the progress (or rather, lack of progress) of the armed forces plot, although the denial of access raises serious suspicions. On the question of whether Track II—in the sense of encouraging an anti-Allende coup—was formally ended on October 15, there is again conflict between the CIA representative in charge, who testified to the committee, "As far as I was concerned, Track II was really never ended," and Kissinger's testimony, "After October 15th there was no separate channel by the CIA to the White House [and] all the covert operations in Chile . . . were directed at maintaining the democratic opposition for the 1976 election."

President Frei decreed a state of emergency and strict curfew and placed the armed forces on maximum alert. Those involved in the attack were quickly identified, and those who had not fled the country were arrested. The overall effect of the assassination was to intensify the Chilean commitment to the constitutionalism that Schneider had repeatedly asserted it was his duty to defend. Alessandri asked his supporters not to vote for him, but the National Party congressmen were determined to do so. On Saturday, October 24, Salvador Allende was elected president of Chile by a joint session of the Congress with 153 votes in favor (the left and the Christian Democrats), 35 votes against (the National Party), and 7 abstentions (the Radical Democrats). General Schneider died the next day, and three days of national mourning were declared. At his funeral, the honorary pallbearers included the outgoing and incoming presidents of Chile.

How does one explain the blatant intervention by the U.S. government into the free electoral process of a country of which it was an ally and friend? The earlier electoral involvement through subsidies and propaganda had become part of the normal battery of instruments of U.S. Cold War policy since the late 1940s in Europe. Economic pressures had also been used, especially in cases involving expropriation of U.S. property, but those actions had been in accordance with preexisting laws. Bribery of legislators was also not unknown, the best-known case being the former Belgian Congo (Zaire) in the early 1960s, but the ambassador's proposal to do so in one of the oldest legislatures in the world shocked some of those involved, especially the State Department, which voiced its opposition—and in fact, events in Chile rapidly made that proposal irrelevant.

Most difficult to reconcile with American ideals was Track II, the effort to promote a military coup to short-circuit the democratic processes. Here personal and institutional factors seem to have combined. Richard Nixon had achieved political success through exploiting the Communist issue, and his visceral anti-Communism was reinforced by predictions from the CIA station and the ambassador (who had served as a journalist in Eastern Europe in the 1940s) that Chile would soon become a "popular democracy" on the Eastern European model. Those predictions were confirmed by Agustín Edwards and Nixon's personal friend, Don Kendall. There seems to have been more to Nixon's anti-Communism than the concern for the assets of American companies, which Hersh and many others see as his primary motive. In *The Price of Power,* Seymour Hersh quotes Korry's account of Nixon at the October 12 meeting smashing his fist into his hand and repeating, "That S.O.B., that S.O.B.," adding, "Not you, Mr. Ambassador. I know that this isn't your fault and you've always told it like it is. It's that son-of-a-bitch Allende" (284).

The defense of American economic holdings seems to have been even less central to Kissinger's motivations. His geopolitical outlook on world politics was well known from his books and articles, and his balance-of-power approach to world politics was clear in a speech he gave to midwestern newspaper editors on September 16. Stating "I have yet to meet somebody who firmly believes that if Allende wins, there is likely to be another free election in Chile," he argued that "an Allende takeover" would "present massive problems for us, and for democratic forces and for pro-US forces in Latin America." Kissinger cited Chile's geographical location next to unstable neighbors, arguing that a major Latin American country "with a Communist government, joining for example Argentina, which is already deeply divided, along a long frontier, joining Peru, which has already been heading in directions which are difficult to deal with, and joining Bolivia which has also gone in a more leftist anti-U.S. direction" would endanger U.S. security. In private conversations with staff members at the National Security Council, he also alluded to the impact of a freely elected Marxist government in Chile on the Eurocommunists' bid for power in France and Italy (Hersh, 270–71).

The issue of respect for the democratic process does not seem to have been considered by either Nixon or Kissinger. In Kissinger's case this was because of his own view of the world, which held that interests and power are more important than ideals; in Nixon's case it was because in his view a "Communist" (Allende was a Socialist, of course, but had always worked closely with the Communists) could not himself be a democrat.

Did opposition to Communism extend to the assassination of those who might put them in power? Despite the hearsay evidence that Hersh cites—which also includes an undocumented assertion that one of the CIA agents sent to Chile under a false name slipped a large sum of money to a "Chilean desperado whose sole goal at the time, as the Agency knew, was to assassinate Allende" (262)—the Church committee conclusion that there was no link between the CIA and assassination plots in Chile still seems to stand.

The hysterical reaction of Nixon and Kissinger differed sharply from the view articulated by the foreign policy bureaucracy and the CIA. An interdepartmental Group for Interamerican Affairs, made up of representatives of the CIA, the departments of State and Defense, and the White House, concluded shortly after Allende's election that the United States had no vital interests within Chile, the world military balance of power would not be significantly altered if Allende was elected, and an Allende government would not threaten the peace of the region, although it would represent a psychological defeat for the United States and an advance for Marxism (*Covert Action in Chile,* 48). An earlier CIA National Intelligence Estimate prepared in July had predicted that Allende would carry Chile far down the Marxist road during his six-year administration but would first have to overcome important obstacles, including the armed forces, the Christian Democratic Party, some labor unions, the Chilean Congress, and the Catholic church (*Covert Action in Chile,* 44).

U.S. Policy toward Allende

By mid-October, the State Department was preparing memoranda on the future course of U.S.-Chilean relations after Allende's election. President Nixon decided on October 21 that there was to be no congratulatory message after Allende was elected by the Chilean Congress and that a small, low-key delegation would be sent to the inauguration on November 3. He also ordered the resumption of U.S. aid to the Chilean military, which had been suspended as one more way to discourage Allende's election. An options paper was prepared for the newly constituted Senior Review Group on Chile on October 29, which forwarded a revised version of the paper to the National Security Council meeting of November 5. The result of that meeting was the issuance of NSDM (National Security Decision Memorandum) 93, sent on November 9 to State, Defense, the CIA, and the Office of Emergency Preparedness, establishing the basic U.S. policy toward the new government. It called for a "correct but cool" posture on the part of the United States combined with an effort to "maximize pressure on the Allende government to prevent its consolidation and limit its ability to implement policies contrary to U.S. and hemisphere interests." Those pressures were to include the termination of new Export-Import Bank guarantees, as well as efforts to terminate and reduce existing programs, the exercise of "maximum feasible influence" to limit credits from international financial institutions, an effort to make private businesses aware of U.S. concern about investments in Chile, the termination of all new economic aid programs, except for humanitarian aid such as the Food for Peace program, and examination of ways to "reduce, delay, or terminate" existing aid programs. The memorandum also mandated a study of the impact of the world copper market and U.S. copper stockpiles on the Chilean economy. A Special Interagency Working Group was established to prepare options for U.S. actions, which were to be presented to monthly meetings of the Senior Review Group.[8]

It is thus clear that the program that Allende later called "the invisible blockade," and which many observers, including this writer, initially believed to have been initiated in response to the takeover of American companies and industries in Chile, actually antedated any hostile action by Allende. It did not go as far as a blockade, since trade and private bank lending were not cut off and existing aid and investment programs were continued, but it was designed to make life difficult in Chile and to lessen the possibility of a successful transition to socialism under Marxist auspices. In the first volume of his memoirs (*The White House Years,* 681), Kissinger argues that this program was less drastic than that later pursued against Pinochet or Somoza, but that is doubtful. He also says that the policies pursued by the Allende government itself destroyed Chile's creditworthiness over the next three years, but despite the nationalization policies in the Allende program, it was not clear at the time of Allende's inauguration, when the economic squeeze was decided upon, that this would be the case.

In his inaugural address, Allende quoted from a reference by Friedrich Engels to the possibility of "a peaceful evolution from the old society to the new in countries where the representatives of the people have all the power and in accordance with the constitution can do what they desire when they have the majority of the nation behind them." Allende announced that the destruction of latifundia (large landholdings) and monopolies and the nationalization of foreign-owned mines and factories would be carried out "in [the] Chilean way (*vía chilena*) . . . the way to socialism in democracy, pluralism, and liberty." In a private meeting at that time with Charles Meyer, the U.S. assistant secretary of state for Latin America, Allende emphasized his desire to maintain good relations with the United States and not to allow foreign (i.e., Russian) bases on Chilean soil.[9]

Nationalization Issues

Allende also assured Meyer that the projected nationalizations of foreign-owned companies in Chile would be carried out in a nondiscriminatory fashion and in accordance with Chilean law, as interpreted by an independent judiciary. The emphasis that Allende's program had given to nationalization as well as the extent of American holdings in Chile made it evident that this would be one of the first areas of tension between the two governments. U.S. investments in Chile were valued at over $1 billion and included a partial share in three copper companies, a minority interest in a nitrate company, three iron mines, and ITT's majority interest in the Chilean telephone company and its cable company, telephone equipment plant, and hotels, as well as subsidiaries of major automobile and petroleum and chemical companies along with branches of two banks. The Hickenlooper Amendment to the Foreign Assistance Act of 1963 provided that all foreign aid be suspended to any country that has nationalized a U.S. company and has not within six months "taken appropriate steps, which include arbitration, to discharge its obligations under international law . . . including speedy compensation in convertible foreign exchange." In addition, a number of companies had taken out investment insurance guaranteeing them against losses from expropriation. The policies were taken out with the Agency for International Development (AID) under a program that was in the process of becoming semiautonomous—but still U.S. government funded—with the creation of the Overseas Private Investment Corporation in January 1971. The Allende government had inherited a reserve of $343 million in foreign exchange from the Frei government, but if the ideologues in his own party had their way, the foreign imperialists would receive "not one centavo" of compensation for decades of "exploitation and greed."

A major issue was the status of the remaining U.S.-owned shares in the newly Chileanized copper mines, and Allende decided that they would be nationalized by constitutional amendment, which required absolute majorities in both houses of Congress. Since the Tomic campaign had committed itself to nationalization, and because a takeover of the American companies had wide popular support, this seemed feasible. An amendment would also avoid conflicts about violating earlier contract laws relating to Chileanization and would limit and structure legal appeals.

Another way to avoid international controversy was to buy out foreign holdings with bonds as an alternative to expropriation. This method was used in the cases of the iron mines, the nitrate interests, and the banks. A more dubious method of takeover was the use of what the Chileans called "legal loopholes" (*resquicios legales*), such as Decree Law 520, issued by a short-lived Socialist government in 1932, which authorized "requisition" of enterprises that failed to produce "articles of basic necessity" or, alternatively, "intervention" of firms that were paralyzed by labor disputes. In both cases compensation was not necessary, since the seizures were supposedly only temporary. Requisition or intervention, often following labor troubles stimulated by government-related unions, was used to take over several hundred companies beginning with Ralston Purina on November 20, 1970, and followed by Ford, General Motors, and the ITT telephone company.

The ITT papers indicate that at the end of October its representatives in Washington sent Henry Kissinger a proposal for a program to protect U.S. investments in Chile by threatening Allende with reprisals if U.S. companies were expropriated without speedy compensation. After the election, an Ad Hoc Group on Chile, made up of companies with substantial Chilean investments, was formed and began to coordinate strategy. However, the Chilean government had still not done anything to trigger U.S. action, and in a number of cases, the U.S. investors, including the copper companies, were awaiting the results of action by the Chilean Congress.

The effects of NSDM 93 were also slow to be felt. In public, the "cool but correct" policy was maintained when President Nixon said in his State of the World message for 1971, "We are prepared to maintain the relationship with the Chilean government that it is prepared to have with us." Credits were not cut off, although there was a long-term downward trend in private bank credits. (One bank had short-term credits of $28 million still outstanding at the time of the September 1973 coup.) There was a minor furor when an impending visit of a U.S. aircraft carrier was abruptly canceled at the end of February 1971, reportedly after a thirty-six hour debate pitting the navy against Henry Kissinger, the national security adviser (*New York Times,* Feb. 28, 1971). In January 1971, the Forty Committee approved the expenditure of $1,240,000 by the CIA to finance opposition radio stations and newspapers (including the new Christian Democratic paper, *La Prensa*) and to support the candidates of the anti-Allende parties in the April 1971 municipal elections, which were viewed as a test of the popularity of the Allende government. In March and May 1971, support for the Christian Democrats totaling more than $500,000 was approved, and in July another $150,000 went to opposition candidates in a by-election that was won by the left.[10]

There does not seem to have been any Forty Committee hesitancy about supporting the opposition parties and media, since there were already reports concerning government pressures on their financial resources. The Edwards Bank was "intervened" and later dissolved for financial irregularities; *El Mercurio* and other opposition newspapers lost their government advertising; and large wage increases were granted to the workers in the largest publishing house in the country, producing bankruptcy and a government takeover. A similar but unsuccessful effort was made with the paper company owned by the Alessandri family.

The effort to keep the opposition parties and media alive financially is the only aspect of the CIA program in Chile alluded to in Richard Nixon's memoirs. In slightly over a page devoted to Chile, he argues, "In Chile we sought to help non-Communist parties have at least the same resources as the lavishly-financed pro-Allende forces," citing Cuban money that came in to support Allende, and observes, "It is a peculiar double standard that would require us alone to stand abjectly aside as democracies are undermined by countries less constrained by conscience."[11]

If the aid given to the opposition parties in March 1971 was intended to bolster their chances in the April municipal elections, it does not seem to have been that useful. Seen as a referendum on the new government, the election was a triumph for Allende. Government deficit spending had produced a miniboom, inflation had not risen, and there was no evidence of the restrictions on civil liberties which the opposition had predicted would result under a Marxist government. In January 1971, Allende had given an interview to the French revolutionary theorist Regis Debray in which he described the observance of bourgeois legality as a "tactical necessity" with the ultimate objective the same as that of Debray's friend, Che Guevara, the overthrow of capitalism and the establishment of scientific Marxist socialism, but Debray's book containing the interview had not yet appeared in print.[12]

The election resulted in a considerable victory for the candidates of the Allende coalition, who received 49.7 percent of the votes—if one includes 1 percent for the dissident Popular Socialist Party, which was not a member of Popular Unity coalitions—compared with 48 percent for the opposition. Allende's Socialist Party increased its vote by 10 percent—an indication of the "presidentialism" of the Chilean voter which had also helped the Christian Democrats in 1965—and the Communists gained 1 percent. In a by-election later in the year in the impoverished extreme south, the Socialist senatorial candidate won a three-way race with 51 percent of the vote.

At this point it seemed that Allende's hopes for a peaceful transition to socialism (the *vía chilena*) might be realized. Inflation was down, employment up, and the most important political issue was the nationalization of the remaining American copper mines, an issue on which there was a broad national consensus.

The United States had always accepted the right of sovereign governments to nationalize enterprises within their boundaries but had insisted that under international law "prompt, adequate, and effective compensation" must be paid in freely convertible currency. Nationalization had become a major issue for U.S. policy as a wave of expropriations in such countries as Argentina, Peru, Bolivia, and Ecuador had taken over American companies, usually with only token compensation. The Hickenlooper Amendment, adopted in 1963 in reaction to the nationalization of an ITT subsidiary in Brazil, cut off U.S. aid to countries that nationalized without compensation. Now the U.S. Congress was debating the Gonzalez Amendment requiring U.S. representatives to international lending agencies to vote against international loans to such countries. As the dollar ran into increasing difficulties, Richard Nixon had established a Council on International Economic Policy, which included among its duties "protecting and improving the earnings of foreign investment." Thus, as the Allende government moved the copper nationalization amendment through Congress, the compensation issue became a major irritant in U.S.-Chilean relations.[13]

It had been assumed that Ambassador Korry would be replaced after Allende's election, but he remained in Santiago because of his expertise on the copper issue, which was acquired at the time of the 1969 negotiations with Anaconda. As the Allende government systematically went after the American-owned companies in Chile, Korry was instrumental in getting a long-term compensation agreement with Bethlehem Steel and Northern Indiana Brass Company. In May he attempted to work out a similar arrangement for the new Rio Blanco copper mine being developed by the Cerro Corporation, which he hoped could be used as a model for the nationalization of the Anaconda and Kennecott holdings. Korry's interest was to avoid a confrontation between Chile and the United States and a major drain on the resources of the new Overseas Private Investment Corporation (OPIC).

As finally adopted by the Chilean Congress in July, the compensation provisions of the constitutional amendment on copper provided for payment in thirty-year bonds at book value less "depreciation[,] . . . exhaustion of the mines," and "all or part of the excess profits which those enterprises may have obtained." The controller general, a permanent civil servant responsible for the maintenance of proper administrative and legal procedure, was to make the overall evaluation, but the amount of the deduction of all or part of the excess profits since 1955 was to be determined by the president. The companies could appeal the controller general's evaluation to a Special Copper Tribunal, but the excess profits decision was not subject to appeal. In September 1971, Allende announced the amounts he intended to deduct as excess profits. When matched against the controller general's evaluation, they left the Anaconda Company owing the Chilean government $78 million, and Kennecott received a bill for $310 million.

According to testimony by Ambassador Korry to the Senate Intelligence Committee, backed up by a declassified cable dated October 1, 1971, Korry attempted to secure Chilean approval of an arrangement whereby the Overseas Private Investment Corporation would guarantee Chilean twenty-year bonds as compensation. In negotiations before Allende's excess profits announcement, he felt that he had persuaded the government copper specialists, but when he met Allende himself, the day before the announcement, he was told that opposition within the Popular Unity coalition (presumably from the left wing of the Socialist Party, headed by Senator Carlos Altamirano) made it impossible for him to accept.[14] The copper companies had agreed to the proposal in August because the U.S. guarantee would permit the bonds to be resold at a relatively low discount. The U.S. government, despite its hostility to Allende, favored the arrangement as a way to maintain the principle of compensation as well as OPIC's reserves. After the 1973 coup, members of the Allende government interviewed by this writer expressed regrets that the proposal had not been adopted. But ideology and Allende's deference to his own party dictated intransigence against the "imperialists."

The compensation issue produced a new series of actions by the United States. In August, after the adoption of the copper amendment, the Export-Import Bank attempted to pressure Chile by announcing that a projected loan for the purchase of three Boeing jets by the Chilean national airline was being postponed, although "it was still under consideration," and on August 11, the president of the bank noted that there was a relationship between the postponement and the copper compensation question. (The Export-Import Bank had continued to give loan guarantees to Chile despite the November 1970 decision not to do so.) In September, the ITT majority-owned Chilean Telephone Company was "intervened" on the grounds of deficient service, and ITT wrote to the presidential assistant for economic affairs to protest the continuation of "pipeline" AID aid and previously unused Interamerican Development Bank (IDB) funds for earthquake relief. In January 1971, two private universities had also received an IDB loan, with the explicit approval of President Nixon.

ITT proposed an eighteen-point program "to make sure that Allende does not get through the next six months," including a cutoff of U.S. imports from Chile and a delay or embargo on exports, possibly including fuel to the Chilean military. Secretary of State William Rogers issued a statement deploring "the unprecedented retroactive application of the excess profits concept" and called a meeting of the U.S. companies with interests in Chile. According to the ITT memo on the meeting, the response was "quite mixed" when Rogers raised the question of whether there should be an informal embargo on shipments to Chile, with ITT taking the hardest line in favor of strong measures. Anaconda also urged strong pressures, but Ford and other companies as well as the bank representatives were for a low-profile policy, although they said that they had reduced their lines of credit with Chile. Another ITT memo noted that since Chile owed substantial amounts to U.S. lenders, an embargo could do considerable damage to U.S. interests.[15]

No such action was taken, leading the ITT observers to complain that Secretary Rogers had adopted the "soft line low profile policy for Latin America" of Assistant Secretary of State Charles Meyer. However, the copper companies sued in American and European courts to recover their losses and attempted to seize copper shipments in Europe and Chilean assets in the United States. Chilean copper production dropped owing to strikes, absenteeism, inexperienced management, and difficulty in securing replacement parts. In November 1971, Chile suspended all debt payments except for those to international agencies and for military purchases, leading to further doubts about Chile's creditworthiness.

In January 1972, President Nixon issued a formal statement that new U.S. bilateral aid would not be extended to countries expropriating American companies without taking "reasonable steps" toward compensation and that U.S. representatives in international lending institutions would be instructed to vote against aid projects to such countries. The World Bank also had a policy against lending to countries with expropriation disputes and terminated consideration of one loan in October 1971 when Allende announced that the major copper companies would not be compensated. No new Chilean projects were considered by the World Bank during the Allende period, although a project for fruit and vineyard development was being prepared for presentation at the time of the September 1973 coup. The Interamerican Development Bank lent $11.5 million to the two Chilean private universities, and as the ITT representatives indicated, an earlier earthquake reconstruction program was reactivated, while projects for electric power and natural gas were "under study"—that is, indefinitely postponed. The Allende government was able to get substantial credits from European governments as well as from Brazil and Argentina—a total of nearly $1 billion. It also received $82.3 million in loans from the International Monetary Fund. Total Chilean indebtedness rose by $1 billion during the Allende period. U.S. aid, except for military assistance, was negligible, although the Food for Peace program distributed $10 million worth of food during the Allende period, including 10 million pounds of milk to fulfill an Allende campaign promise.[16]

CIA Programs

The CIA program of support for the opposition was continued in the last part of 1971. In September, the Forty Committee approved the expenditure of $700,000 for support of *El Mercurio,* which was supplemented by another $965,000 the following April. (The Allende government repeatedly examined *El Mercurio's* books but was not able to detect these transfers.) An additional $815,000 was approved in November for the opposition parties and $160,000 in December to help the opposition candidates in an important by-election in January 1972.

It is difficult to assess the impact of these expenditures. *El Mercurio* was and is the most respected and comprehensive newspaper in Chile, and it controls a chain of other newspapers in the country. Opposition radio stations were widely listened to and had an impact. (Two of the three television stations were controlled by government sympathizers, and the Catholic University television station was divided.) Opposition books and pamphlets were widely published. A split in the Radical Party in July led to the creation of the Left Radicals, who joined the opposition in early 1972, an action that may have been related to the activities of the CIA. In the January 1972 by-elections to replace a deputy and a senator, the Christian Democrats and the rightist National Party began to cooperate for the first time, and the opposition won both seats, while the government percentage dropped by 4 to 7 percent in comparison with the April municipal elections.

It is hard to ascribe causality in these cases because there had clearly been a process of polarization under way in the last months of 1971. The remaining members of the left wing of the Christian Democrats had joined Popular Unity as the Christian Left, but the *terceristas,* led by Senator Renán Fuentealba, were now highly critical of the Allende government.

Inflation was beginning to rise, shortages appeared for the first time (leading to the December "March of the Empty Pots" protest in which the government used tear gas for the first time), and a month-long visit by Fidel Castro exacerbated feelings on both sides. Allende did not help things by proposing a constitutional amendment to replace the Congress with a unicameral legislature, while the opposition reciprocated by impeaching the minister of the interior for not maintaining order in the March of the Empty Pots. The conflict was intensified by a dispute over a congressionally initiated constitutional amendment to limit takeovers of industry, which Allende then vetoed. By April 1972, the constitutional deadlock had reached the point that the military began for the first time to discuss whether there was a likelihood of a complete breakdown of the institutional order.[17]

According to *Covert Action in Chile* (38–39), in mid-1971 the CIA station had been monitoring reports of coup plotting in the armed forces through a new network of informants. After much discussion a packet of documents on Cuban activities in Chile, including a fabricated letter on Cuban infiltration, was passed to a Chilean military man outside Chile in December 1971, but when the CIA station in Santiago suggested that the ultimate objective of such actions might be a military coup, it was told by CIA headquarters that there was no Forty Committee approval of such involvement, and no further packets were passed. However, the CIA was in touch with the leader of a group of plotters through an intermediary by January 1972. It also subsidized an antigovernment news pamphlet directed at the armed forces.

There was no real danger of a coup at this time. As the new American ambassador, Nathaniel Davis, noted in a dispatch in December 1971: "The prospects for military intervention for the foreseeable future are extremely small unless discontent becomes so great that military intervention is overwhelmingly invited. It is held that military will wait for this public repudiation to become more clear and more open than it is likely ever to be."[18]

One reason that Ambassador Davis could be so certain that the armed forces were most unlikely to intervene was that the commanding general of the army, the most important of the services, General Carlos Prats, had moved from an initially critical position to one of general support for the government—in keeping with the doctrine enunciated in 1970 by General Schneider that as long as the government respected the law and the constitution, the army would be "obedient and non-deliberating" as the constitution required. There were occasional movements of opposition in the armed forces, most notably the organization of a mass "sickout" by the cadets at the military school by its commander, Colonel Alberto Labbé, and the continual criticism of the army's support for Allende by General Alfredo Canales. Both officers were forced into retirement by Prats in 1972.[19] (Canales may have been the January 1972 leader mentioned in *Covert Action in Chile*.) Labbé was forced out quickly, but Prats only moved against Canales in September 1972 after there were reports of a "September Plan" to overthrow the government.

Part of the criticism of U.S. policy toward Chile in the Allende years has centered around the continuation of military aid when other types of economic assistance dropped so dramatically. In fact, military aid declined in comparison with the Frei years (see table in *Covert Action in Chile*, 37), although the number of Chilean officers receiving training in the School of the Americas in Panama rose to 197 in 1972 and 275 in 1973. In 1972, a loan of $10 million was approved, mostly for C-130 transport aircraft, and in 1973, Chile bought training aircraft and landing vessels and contracted for F-5E fighters.[20] The economic deterrents to regular loans did not apply to military purchases, since a secret Chilean law (*ley reservada*) allocates 10 percent of hard currency income from sales of Chilean copper to military purchases.

The Cuban Arms Issue

Aside from disturbances caused by the seizure of large landholdings in the south, there had been little violence since Allende had come to power. But in early 1972, as the tension increased, there were reports that regular flights from Havana to Santiago were bringing in illegal arms. When a customs officer reported to the opposition that thirteen uninspected crates had been rushed onto trucks from an Air Cuban plane by the Ministry of the Interior, a congressional uproar ensued. The government said the *bultos cubanos* contained "works of art" and gifts to Allende, but the press reported that a dropped crate had revealed that it contained automatic weapons. After the 1973 coup, the junta White Book published an inventory of over a ton of armaments said to have been contained in the shipment. The incident also led to the adoption of an arms control law by the opposition-dominated Congress which was to be used as legal authorization for raids and searches by the armed forces in the last days before the coup.

The Cuban arms incident, the deteriorating economic situation, and the increasing polarization were sapping the dynamism of the government, when it received a boost from the publication in the United States by Jack Anderson of ITT files on Chile which had been leaked to him by a disgruntled employee. The full files were a striking insight into the close relations between ITT and the CIA in 1970, as well as ITT's extraordinary—but unsuccessful—efforts in 1971 to organize a blockade against the Chilean government. The files were immediately translated and published by the Allende government (and, separately, by *El Mercurio*), and they resulted in the termination of the lengthy negotiations between the government and ITT on compensation for its intervened telephone company and the initiation of expropriation procedures. Their publication also led to the creation of a Subcommittee on Multinational Corporations by the U.S. Senate Foreign Relations Committee. The subcommittee carried out a full-scale investigation a year later, revealing additional details that were recycled in Chile by the Allende government—among them the first clear indication that there had been, in CIA director Helms' words, "a minimal effort" by the CIA against Allende in 1970; an evasive answer by former CIA director John McCone as to whether there had been CIA involvement in the 1964 election; and McCone's unconvincing claim that the $1 million offered by ITT to the CIA (and rejected) after the September 1970 popular election had been intended for "housing, . . . technical assistance, assistance in agriculture . . . so badly needed in Chile."[21]

Invisible Blockade?

In April 1972, when Chile's creditor countries met in Paris, they agreed to postpone payments on 70 percent of Chile's 1971–72 debts, with payments only of interest on the remaining 30 percent. The United States brought up the issue of compensation for expropriated properties, but the Chilean reply was that the disputes would be settled in accordance with Chilean and international law. The details of repayments were supposed to be worked out in later meetings between Chile and the individual countries. The U.S. meetings with the Chileans did not begin until mid-1973 and almost immediately were stymied by the expropriation issue. The result was that the Allende government paid nothing on its official debt to the United States in 1972 and 1973. It had defaulted on its Export-Import Bank loans in January 1972, but in June it signed an agreement with the private banks on a deferred payment program similar to that with the Club of Paris. As a result, despite all of Allende's talk of "the invisible blockade," Chile still had lines of credit with two American banks at the time of the 1973 coup.

In May 1972, the Chilean embassy in Washington and the residences of three Chilean officials in New York were broken into. Later investigations in connection with the Watergate break-in a month later revealed that the

Chilean entries were the work of the Watergate "plumbers," and Ambassador Davis in his memoirs connects the incident with earlier efforts to "bug" the Chilean embassy which became involved in a "turf war" between the CIA and the FBI. However, the full purpose of acting in such an obvious fashion is still not clear.[22]

The problem was not the invisible blockade but an increasingly sharp decline in foreign exchange. By the end of 1971, Chile's international reserves were almost nonexistent; there had been no devaluation, so that the currency was overvalued by at least 22 percent; and it was difficult to secure imports because short-term credits from American (but not European) banks had declined. There were shortages of spare parts which affected production in the copper and other industries, as well as, increasingly, the fleet of buses and taxis. Because farmers were paid low controlled prices, their production was diverted to the black market, and the instability in agriculture due to land seizures and hastily collectivized holdings further contributed to shortages. In 1972, food imports doubled in comparison with 1970, and in 1973 they quadrupled, and by the end of the Allende regime subsidies to the nationalized firms (paid simply by printing more money) amounted to 55 percent of the national budget—although they were not part of that budget. Further inflationary pressures were produced by income redistribution in 1971 which increased total wages and salaries 53 percent while inflation went up 22 percent. With uncertain property relations, labor unrest, and price controls, there was no inducement to invest. Thus it was not the invisible blockade—or, better put, the credit squeeze induced by the U.S. government—that caused the dramatic worsening of the economy in 1972 but Allende's own politically motivated "consumerist socialism."

In June 1972, Allende removed his economics minister, and in July he announced a series of austerity measures, but by now the government had lost control of the economy. Henceforth, each month the inflation rate increased and production dropped. Wages were increased by 50 percent but failed to keep up with inflation. By September, inflation had reached triple digits, and a year later the official rate was 300 percent, with unofficial figures much higher.[23]

Leaders of the Allende coalition attempted to make up for their incompetence with revolutionary rhetoric. As the lines for food grew longer, the government talked of initiating a rationing program and appointed local Supply and Price Committees to monitor distribution and observance of the price controls. Like everything else in Chile in the last year of the Allende government, attitudes toward these measures became polarized.

The Supply and Price Committees were feared as the basis for Cuban-style Committees for the Defense of the Revolution, and the proposed rationing was seen as an instrument for political control. The Neighborhood Committees (*Juntas de Vecinos*), which had been elected in the Frei period, suddenly took on a new life and became a principal organizational base for the opposition. The professional and trade organizations, which had always been important lobbies in the centralized politics of Chile, also became centers of antigovernment activity—and it was these organizations that provoked the next great crisis of the Allende government, the truckers' strike of October 1972.

The Truckers' Strike

It was a mark of the degree of political polarization in Chile in October 1972 that the strike was described by the government as "the employers' lockout" and by the opposition as "the national strike." It began in an unlikely location, the province of Aysén in southern Chile, in response to the government's announcement that it intended to set up a state trucking firm in order to compensate for the inadequacies of privately owned trucking. Blaming the government for shortages of replacement parts, the private truckers of the province announced an indefinite strike on October 11. The National Truckers Confederation supported them, and soon the country was paralyzed, since, given its geography, it was dependent on the truckers for most of its transport. Within two days, the Shopkeepers Confederation and the Central Chamber of Commerce had joined the strike, citing the government closing of an opposition radio station and its effort to bankrupt the privately owned paper company by refusing to allow price increases to compensate for wage boosts. On October 14, the Christian Democrats supported the strike, denouncing the arrest of the strike leaders as a violation of the Statute of Democratic Guarantees. Two days later the engineers, bank employees, gas workers, lawyers, architects, and taxi and bus drivers joined. Most of the trade unions, including those sympathetic to the Christian Democrats, did not join, but the middle class, the professionals, including doctors and dentists, and 100,000 peasants struck. Strike leaders estimated that 100 percent of transport, 97 percent of commerce, 80 percent of professionals, and 85 percent of the cooperatives had joined, with about 600,000 to 700,000 Chileans on strike.[24]

Did the CIA play a role in orchestrating the rapid spread of the strike movement? This is a significant question because the 1972 strike and a similar action in July and August 1973 were important in exacerbating the polarization that brought on the September 1973 coup. *Covert Action in Chile* tells us that on September 24, $46,500 was approved for "emergency" support of a businessmen's organization (either the Sociedad de Fomento Fabril [SOFOFA] or the Confederation of Production and Commerce) but that other organizations did not get support "because of possible involvement in anti-government strikes" (30). (There had been protest demonstrations, shopkeeper closings, and strikes since mid-August.) The striking occupational and professional groups (*gremios*) formed a National Defense Command and coordinated their actions on a national level. The strike lasted twenty-six days.

In an article in the *New York Times* of September 20, 1974, after the initial revelations of the CIA role in Chile but before the Church committee investigation, Seymour Hersh claimed that "the majority of the $7 million authorized for covert action in Chile went to support the strikers in 1972 and 1973." However, *Covert Action in Chile,* the Senate Select Committee report, says that "the Forty Committee did not approve any funds to be given directly to the strikers" (31), although it notes that $2,800 was diverted to the strikers in October 1972 "contrary to the Agency's ground rules." In his memoirs, *The Last Two Years of Salvador Allende,* Ambassador Davis concludes, "I am confident that no element of the U.S. Mission in Chile extended financial support to the strike movements of October 1972 and August–September 1973" (327). He says that he avoided contacts with the strike leaders and quotes the Church committee argument that "the pattern of U.S. deliberations suggests a careful distinction between supporting the opposition parties and funding private sector groups trying to bring about a military coup. However, given turbulent conditions in Chile, the interconnections among CIA-supported political parties, the various militant trade associations (*gremios*), and paramilitary groups prone to terrorism and violent disruption were many." Davis also says that he rejected a suggestion to bail out the paper company—although this writer can attest that many Chileans thought that outside money was being given to the Fund for Freedom, which had been organized to keep it from being taken over.

The extreme right-wing Patria y Libertad (Fatherland and Freedom) group was reported to have been active during the strike, distributing "Miguelitos," boards with three-pronged nails, on the highways to prevent travel. According to *Covert Action in Chile* (31) the CIA had remained in contact with the group after the September–November 1970 period in which it had been most active, and it received about $7,000 in additional small disbursements through third parties, but those payments had ended in 1971. However, it was still possible that sums given to conservative political parties such as the National Party could have reached them after that time. The truckers' strike was still in force but nearing a resolution when, on October 26, the Forty Committee approved the largest covert expenditure in Chile since the 1964 election—$1,427,666, which was to go both to the opposition political parties and to the newly mobilized private sector organizations. The money was intended to be used in the forthcoming political campaign leading up to the March 1973 elections.

Allende was only able to end the strike by appointing General Prats as minister of the interior along with navy and air force officers as mining and public works ministers. The direct involvement of representatives of the armed forces in the cabinet pacified the opposition, but it also involved a new stage in civil-military relations in Chile. Earlier General Prats was able to appeal to the Chilean military tradition of professionalism to restrain the politicization of the army, although it was no secret that several generals were close to the Christian Democrats or to the National Party. Allende had given the army wage increases and control over the border areas and had developed a personal relationship with Prats and with the head of the *carabineros* (national police). Prats now argued for supporting Allende to control extremists of left and right in an increasingly polarized system. He also appealed to those military men with Christian Democratic sympathies, arguing that with the aid of the armed forces Allende might be able to arrive at an understanding with the Christian Democrats and break with the more extreme elements of the left, including Senator Carlos Altamirano of his own Socialist Party.[25]

The appointment of General Prats to the politically sensitive post of interior minister shortly before the opening of the congressional election campaign sharply reduced the political tension in Chile. Allende was able to leave the country for visits to several countries—and to the United Nations, where he denounced the U.S. "invisible blockade"—leaving, in accordance with the constitution, General Prats, his interior minister, as acting president. (There is no vice president in Chile.)

The 1973 Congressional Elections

Attention now focused on the congressional candidates. The government and the opposition had agreed to allow the establishment of joint tickets, and the two sides organized the Federation of Popular Unity and the Democratic Confederation (CODE), respectively. The opposition was encouraged by a series of victories in the Chilean university elections, even in the University of Concepción, traditionally a hotbed of radicalism. The right even spoke of the possibility of gaining two-thirds of the seats in the Congress, which would give them a possibility of impeaching President Allende. (Only a majority is required to impeach cabinet ministers, and a number of ministers had been impeached. Allende normally responded by simply appointing them to a different cabinet post. Chileans referred to those actions as "castling" (*enroque*)—a chess move to keep the king from being captured by exchanging places with a castle.) However, achieving a two-thirds majority in both houses was almost impossible under the Chilean system of proportional representation, particularly since only half of the Senate was up for election.

The basic issues were inflation (the official figure for 1972 was 163 percent); food shortages; the government proposal to establish a monopoly on the distribution of basic food items through the Price and Supply Committees, seen as de facto rationing; and the deficits incurred by the government and the nationalized industries and agriculture. It was the first congressional election in which illiterates and 18-year-olds could vote—with the latter group, in particular, considerably increasing the electoral rolls. Two-thirds to three-fourths of the radio stations favored the opposition—thanks presumably to CIA money—but two of three television chains were blatantly progovernment, although the third, that of the Catholic University, now leaned toward the opposition.

On the first Sunday in March, 3,666,898 Chileans turned out to vote, a figure that was 26 percent higher than the number who had voted in the 1971 municipal elections. The CODE opposition received 56 percent of the vote to the government's 44 percent, if we exclude the 1.6 percent abstention and a negligible vote for the breakaway Popular Socialist Party. Former president Frei received the largest senatorial vote in Chilean history, followed by strong votes for the Communist and Socialist leaders, Volodia Teitelboim and Carlos Altamirano (who had campaigned with the slogan "Hit them again harder"), with Sergio Onofre Jarpa, head of the National Party, in fourth place. In comparison with the last congressional election in 1969, the results were almost identical, with government increases in rural votes balanced by opposition gains in Santiago and Valparaiso. Because of the overrepresentation of the rural areas, the government gained 2 seats in the Senate and 6 seats in the Chamber of Deputies, reducing the opposition majority to 30 (out of 50) in the upper house, and 87 (out of 150) in the Chamber. The unusually large number of new voters was the basis of a study published in July 1973 by members of the Catholic University law faculty, which claimed a progovernment fraud involving 200,000 to

300,000 votes. The report turned up a few cases of vote fraud, but its statistical analysis was unconvincing, and its partisan purpose and sponsorship made its conclusions doubtful.[26]

How much difference did the U.S. covert aid make? Probably not much, if any. The traditional ideological division between the right, the center, and the left ("the three-thirds") still operated, with some increase in government support related to the mobilization in factories and in the countryside. The one area in which CIA support may have made a difference was in keeping *El Mercurio* and its chain from going bankrupt—and, if it was indeed involved, preventing a government takeover of the major paper company. As is customary, each side claimed victory, with the Allende apologists comparing their 44 percent with the 35 percent he had received in 1970 and the opposition comparing it with the nearly 50 percent the government candidates had received in 1971.

After the election, Allende again considered appointing a cabinet that would include representatives of the armed forces, but the generals presented a list of conditions that were unacceptable to Allende, including adoption of the opposition constitutional amendment limiting property takeovers, and stronger enforcement of the arms control law adopted in 1972. In his account of the background to the coup, *The Crucial Day*, General Pinochet emphasizes the concern of the top military about the growth of paramilitary groups during 1972, when he was chief of the army general staff, and the increasing opposition to the government, which he detected as acting commander in chief while General Prats was interior minister. After his return to the chief of staff position, he says that he commissioned a study of the postelection political situation which concluded that a constitutional solution was no longer possible.[27]

The National Unified School

The military opposition to Allende intensified dramatically when the Allende government announced its intention to establish a National Unified School (ENU—Escuela Nacional Unificada) curriculum, which would be based on the principles of "socialist humanism," as required instruction in all schools, including the private and Catholic schools to which the generals sent their children. Rear Admiral Huerta, the former minister of mines, who had resigned over the rationing program in January, submitted a hostile memorandum to the minister of education, and eight hundred officers met with General Prats at the military academy to express their opposition to the program. The Christian Democrats ordered the mobilization of their bases against the decree, the Secondary School Students Federation engaged in violent demonstrations against it, and the Catholic church, which had not been openly critical of the government at any previous time, expressed strong reservations. The plan was withdrawn, but it had produced a mobilization of the military which would escalate until September.[28]

The apparent breakdown of law and order was dramatized by *El Mercurio* when it published a picture (which continued to be reproduced down to the 1989 presidential elections) of a helmeted left-wing militant clubbing a Chilean policeman. The political polarization was not reduced when the government announced that it was introducing a bill to nationalize the paper company and to make permanent the takeover of all firms that had been intervened or requisitioned before April 30, 1973. At the national assembly of the Christian Democratic Party on May 12, Senator Patricio Aylwin was elected president of the party under the slogan "Don't let the government get away with one more thing," and his resolution was adopted calling on the party to "use all legitimate means to assure respect for the constitution and the laws."[29]

General Prats was out of the country for most of the month of May, and General Pinochet again became acting army commander. In his book on the coup, Pinochet says that a revised Internal Security Plan was distributed on May 28 at a meeting of the army generals which was designed in such a way that it could be used to take simultaneous control of all key points in the country and to seize radio stations and communications facilities. David Phillips, CIA Western Hemisphere chief at the time of the coup, wrote in his memoirs and testified to the Church committee that in May the CIA felt that a coup was likely in the near future and, fearing that the CIA would be blamed, sent the CIA station in Santiago a cable ordering it to keep clear of any plotting and to avoid actions that might be construed as support for a coup.[30]

In May and June, the Supreme Court wrote open letters to President Allende complaining about the refusal of the government to obey court orders and the abuse of legal loopholes, leading to the "imminent breakdown of the judicial order." Allende's response, according to his Catalan political adviser, Joan Garcés, was to call a meeting of the representatives of his Popular Unity coalition and predict that there would be a coup within three months unless he called a plebiscite. Aware of the probable results, based on the March 1973 vote, the party representatives rejected the proposal.[31]

The Tank Rebellion (*Tancazo*)

Air force sources have said that they began plotting a coup in June, but there is no evidence of a coordinated effort to overthrow the government at this point, despite what postcoup writers on the left, like Robinson Rojas Sandford (*The Murder of Allende*), assert. General Prats continued to support the government, and no one knew where his next in command, Augusto Pinochet, stood. The confusion in the military was dramatized by a bungled coup attempt made by the members of the Second Armored Regiment on June 29 as they attempted to rescue a captain of their regiment who had been imprisoned for plotting with Patria y Libertad. The tanks and armored cars proceeded from their headquarters to La Moneda, the presidential palace, and the Ministry of Defense, stopping for red lights on the way. Allende was not at the palace, and he spoke on the radio urging the workers to defend his regime. They seized several hundred factories but did not march to the center of the city as Allende had suggested. General Prats, after making sure of the loyalty of the other Santiago units, went to La Moneda and personally persuaded the tanks to surrender. The takeovers of the factories further complicated the economic situation and demonstrated to the military that the stories about the left controlling industrial belts (*cordónes industriales*) around Santiago were correct. However, the rebellion also appeared to indicate that there was little likelihood of a mass uprising to defend the government in the event of a coup.[32]

Allende had already been negotiating with the armed forces to persuade them to rejoin his cabinet. After the failed coup, a joint committee of representatives of the three branches drew up a list of twenty-nine demands for policy changes, which they presented to Allende on July 2. The next day he announced an all-civilian cabinet. Pinochet ordered a new draft of the Internal Security Plan, directing particular attention to the left's control of factories, shantytowns, and communications. The question of the possible military organization of the left was being publicly debated following Allende's reference to popular power (*poder popular*) in his speech after the *tancazo* was put down. The presidents of both houses of Congress also issued a joint statement that denounced the creation of "a parallel army in which numerous foreigners are involved."

There was considerable public discussion of the emergence of a parallel set of organizations to that of the government, organized by the left wing of the Allende coalition. The workers had demonstrated organizing ability at the time of the October strike, when the first references were made to left-directed industrial belts around Santiago. A number of shantytowns had created their own governmental and police units and refused to allow the regular *carabinero* force to enter. The national television chain was completely under left control. At this time, too, the military intelligence services discovered that in addition to the paramilitary brigades of the Communists and Socialists, the MAPU and the Radicals were beginning military training, and the Movement of the Revolutionary Left (MIR) was using worker-controlled factories to manufacture and distribute arms. As this writer can testify from a visit in July 1973 to the middle-class area where he had lived earlier, the polarization of the country had extended to the acquisition and storing of arms by the Supply and Price Committees (JAPs) on the government side and by the Neighborhood Committees (Juntas de Vecinos) on the part of the opposition. On the extreme right, Patria y Libertad, having been compromised by its involvement in the tank uprising, began a series of bombings and blackouts which further contributed to the atmosphere of tension. On July 25, the truckers, dissatisfied with the government's response to their complaints, began another strike, to which the government responded much more forcefully than in the preceding October, requisitioning trucks and forcing open shops that had closed in sympathy. The other *gremios,* including taxi drivers, bus owners, shopkeepers, and professionals, joined in. The strikes did not end until September 11.[33]

Following unsuccessful negotiations with Patricio Aylwin, head of the Christian Democrats, which had been organized by the cardinal, Allende appointed another military cabinet on August 9. General Prats did not take the post of interior minister because of army opposition but became minister of defense, and the heads of the navy and air force took finance and public works and transport (involving negotiations with the striking truckers). The cabinet lasted only ten days when there was a reshuffling of the air force command, which put General Gustavo Leigh, who had been actively plotting a coup, at its head.

The next day a demonstration by several hundred officers' wives—including the wives of several generals—in front of Prats' house, ostensibly to present a letter critical of her husband to Prats' wife, escalated into violence and was broken up by *carabinero* tear gas. When Prats asked for support from his generals, it became evident that only a few of them were behind him. Faced with a choice between removing fifteen of the top generals—an action that he felt might precipitate civil war—and resignation, he chose the latter. Assured by Prats of the loyalty of his chief of staff, who was next in the line of succession, Allende appointed Augusto Pinochet as commander in chief.[34]

Just as all this was going on, and contributing further to the atmosphere of crisis, the Chamber of Deputies on August 22 adopted an *acuerdo* ("Sense of the Congress") resolution accusing the Allende government of "habitually" violating the constitution and the laws, attempting to impose a totalitarian system on Chile, and encouraging the establishment of "parallel powers" that threatened democratic institutions. It urged the members of the armed forces who were ministers to "put an immediate end to all the de facto situations listed above which violate the constitution and the law" or be guilty of violating the professional and nonpolitical character of the armed forces.[35]

Did the United States Foment the Coup?

What was the U.S. role in all of this? For the left, as represented, for instance, by Robinson Rojas Sandford's book *The Murder of Allende*, it was deeply involved at every stage. He accuses the CIA of organizing an attack on government electronic jamming equipment in March (250); advising Brazilian right-wingers on support of their counterparts in Chile (160); organizing a street incident to discredit General Prats in June (162); and provoking the June 29 aborted coup (173). These actions were carried out, according to Rojas, by the CIA through Patria y Libertad. Rojas also claims that the U.S. military mission was informed in the first week of July that General Pinochet had agreed to join the conspirators in the navy and the air force, who were headed by Admiral José Toribio Merino and General Gustavo Leigh (both later members of the junta). A third claim is that the United States supported and encouraged the truckers to begin their strike again at the end of July and gave them financial support that enabled them to persist in their action until the September 11 coup. The best-known source for this last claim is the article by Seymour Hersh in the *New York Times* of September 20, 1974, which asserted that CIA money had been used "to provide strike benefits and other support for anti-Allende strikers and workers. . . . Direct subsidies were also provided for a strike of middle class shopkeepers and a taxi strike among others that disrupted the capital city of Santiago in 1973."

The Senate Select Committee on Intelligence Activities, chaired by Senator Church, made a special effort to examine the CIA relationship to Patria y Libertad. Besides the $38,500 passed to the group in September and

October 1970 and $7,000 in 1971, its report can only speculate as to whether funds were passed through other groups, but there is no claim of direct contact of the sort that Rojas asserts. There is also no evidence that Pinochet agreed so early with the conspirators, even in his own apologia, *The Crucial Day,* and there is considerable evidence that he finally "signed on" for the coup only two days before it occurred (see discussion below). Thus, if the U.S. military mission received such information, as claimed by Rojas, it was false.

The question of support for the strikers is more complex. Again the Church committee gave this question special attention. It noted that the CIA proposed that the strikers receive $25,000 in support but that Ambassador Davis specifically opposed it (30). As Davis notes in his book, *The Last Two Years of Salvador Allende* (324–25), he saw such support as tantamount to fomenting a coup, since this was the clear intention of the strikers. David Atlee Phillips also says he opposed the idea, as head of the CIA Western Hemisphere Division in Washington (*The Night Watch,* 253–54). In any case, *Covert Action in Chile* explicitly states that "the 40 Committee did not approve any funds to be given directly to the strikers." It adds, however, that "it remains unclear whether or to what extent CIA funds passed to opposition parties may have been siphoned off to support the strikers" (31). *Time* magazine ran a story (Aug. 27, 1973) which included an interview with the striking truckers, who claimed—perhaps facetiously—that their meals of steak and wine were paid for by the CIA.[36]

With the resignation of General Prats, the nonparticipation in the cabinet of General Leigh as air force commander, and pressures against Admiral Raúl Montero, the navy commander, Allende feverishly reconstructed his cabinet at the end of August to include minor military men in cabinet posts. His new interior minister, Carlos Briones, was like Allende a Socialist but on favorable terms with the Christian Democrats (his appointment was opposed by the Socialist Party), and he made a last-ditch effort to work out a compromise with the Christian Democratic Party (PDC). The shopkeepers, professionals, taxi and bus drivers, and truckers were on strike, and health care services were almost paralyzed by the doctors' and nurses' strike. The navy admirals kept trying to force Admiral Montero out, and Allende kept demanding more time. Pinochet seems to have planned a coup for September 14 using the preparations for the annual National Independence Day and Days of Glory of the Armed Forces as a justification for moving troops to the outskirts of Santiago. The navy was scheduled to join the U.S. fleet in the annual Unitas maneuvers on September 10, but the admirals sent Pinochet and Leigh a message that they planned to move against Allende at 6 A.M. on September 11. Pinochet and Leigh signed a written commitment to join them at a birthday party for Pinochet's daughter on Sunday, September 9. (The navy had sent two officers from Valparaiso with a note asking for their collaboration.)[37]

The End of Chilean Democracy

On the morning of September 11, in an operation that was remarkable for its effectiveness of execution, Chilean democracy was overthrown. Valparaiso, Chile's second city, was seized by the navy by 7 A.M.; Concepción, its third urban center, was occupied by 8:15 A.M.. Santiago took a little longer, mainly because of resistance in and around the presidential palace, to which Allende had gone when he first heard about the coup. After unsuccessful negotiations by telephone with the leaders of the coup across the street in the Defense Ministry, the presidential palace was bombed at 11:55 A.M.; at 1:30 P.M. most of the defenders of the palace emerged from a side door behind a white flag; and at 4 P.M. the armed forces announced that Allende had committed suicide at the time of the surrender of the other defenders.

Many questions were subsequently raised about the circumstances of Allende's death. They were based on (1) the delay until early November in the publication of the medical report on Allende's death and of the testimony from a physician who witnessed the suicide; (2) the change in Mrs. Allende's view from an initial statement while she was still in Santiago that he had committed suicide, to her assertion that he had been killed, made after she arrived in exile in Mexico City; (3) the fact that the immediate family could not see the body but was only allowed to accompany the sealed coffin to the Grove family plot in Viña del Mar; and (4) the argument in chapter 1, "The Artful Staging of a 'Suicide,'" of Robinson Rojas Sandford's book, *The Murder of Allende,* which maintains that Allende's clothes were changed to conceal the bloodstains from his murder, following which he was propped up on a couch and his suicide staged. The single account that had the most impact on readers in the United States was the cover article in the March 1974 *Harper's* by the Colombia novelist Gabriel García Marquez, entitled "The Death of Salvador Allende": "He resisted for six hours [and] died in an exchange of shots with that gang. Then all the other officers, in a caste-bound ritual, fired on the body. Finally a noncommissioned officer smashed in his face with a rifle."[38]

There is compelling counterevidence against the Rojas–García Marquez thesis. Immediately after his death, Chileans recalled that Allende had frequently referred to President Balmaceda's suicide after he was defeated in the 1891 civil war, and he was quoted as saying, "If I leave La Moneda [the presidential palace] before 1976, it will be feet first." In January 1974, this writer interviewed Carlos Briones, Allende's last interior minister, who said that the doctor who had witnessed the suicide told him the story the night of the coup, leaving no time for the concoction of a cover story. Since 1973, the recordings—made by private "ham" radio operators—of the military communications at the time reporting Allende's suicide have been broadcast and published. His private secretary and close friend, "La Payita," interviewed in 1988, said she saw his body immediately after his suicide. Most persuasive of all were the reports of participants in the exhumation of Allende's body before his reinterment in the Santiago General Cemetery on September 4, 1990 (the twentieth anniversary of his election), which indicated that his skull had been blown away and that there were no bullet holes in his body.[39]

It was widely believed internationally that the United States had much to do with the coup. The U.S. news broadcasts on September 11 noted darkly that Chilean navy ships had been scheduled to rendezvous with a U.S. Navy detachment in Operation Unitas—although in fact, the U.S. ships were a thousand miles to the north near the town of Arica on the Chilean-Peruvian border and were immediately ordered to turn around. Stories circulated of U.S. "acrobatic pilots" (in British Hawker Hunters!) carrying out the rocket bombing of the presidential palace. A Socialist news agency in Buenos Aires reported that U.S. weather planes had coordinated the coup from the (Argentine) city of Mendoza on the other side of the Andes (repeating a similar story about the 1971 military coup in Bolivia). It was observed that Ambassador Davis had flown to Washington the Thursday before the coup and returned on Sunday—and the conclusion was drawn about U.S. complicity. The fact that the trip was made to discuss his appointment as director general of the U.S. foreign service was not mentioned. Both Davis and Henry Kissinger note that in their meeting on Saturday, September 8, they discussed the likelihood of a coup, but both refer to the notes taken by a State Department official on the conversation which indicate that the United States was not involved.[40]

The most important medium through which the American public was persuaded of U.S. involvement was the book *The Execution of Charles Horman: An American Sacrifice* by Thomas Hauser (New York: Harcourt Brace Jovanovich, 1978) and the film based on the book, *Missing,* starring Jack Lemmon and Sissy Spacek. (The book was later reissued as *Missing: The Execution of Charles Horman.*) Beautifully acted and persuasively filmed (the scenes of postcoup Chile, although filmed in Guadalajara, Mexico, coincide with this writer's impressions in a January 1974 visit to Santiago), it argues that an American leftist journalist, Charles Horman, was killed by the Chileans on orders from the U.S. embassy "because he knew too much." The book reports that Horman heard a navy engineer, Arthur Creter, boast on the day after the coup, "We came down to do a job and it's done." (The scene is repeated twice in the film.) Horman was in fact picked up and killed by the Chileans, but the book and film argue that this was because an embassy staff member had reported that he knew about the U.S. role in the coup.

Ambassador Davis has effectively refuted the main thesis of the film. He has reviewed the relevant statements and documents, including U.S. Navy records that reveal that the quoted remark was made by a retired navy engineer who "couldn't really speak Spanish" and had been sent to Chile to repair firefighting equipment for the Chilean navy.[41]

The U.S. media never reported this, and while *Missing* was not a very successful film in its initial commercial showing, it was later seen by many Americans on video. (In my Latin American Politics classes, about half the students each year indicate that they have seen it on video.) It reinforced the sense of culpability which many Americans felt after the coup. That sense of culpability had an important effect on U.S. policy, since the U.S. role in Chile was probably the single most influential case leading the American public and policymakers to make important changes in their view of the goals of American foreign policy. Specifically, it led to a different concept of the place of covert action and the need for democratic controls upon it, and more fundamentally it was a major factor in making the defense of human rights a major aim of American foreign policy.

Conclusions

1. The Allende example has been exhaustively analyzed and discussed by writers in many languages. For the left, it proves that any attempt to create a socialist system that threatens U.S. companies will be undermined and overthrown by an unholy alliance of the Pentagon, the CIA, the State Department, and the White House with the major U.S. multinational corporations. For moderates, it reveals the need for democratic restraints on a president and intelligence agency that were so obsessed with the Cold War that they were willing to destroy democracy to save it, and to contribute to the establishment of the most brutal dictatorship in Chilean history. For the right, the coup was a necessary evil in opposing a regime

that was bent on undermining Chilean democracy and replacing it with a Marxist-Leninist regime. While the three groups may disagree about the legitimacy of covert support of the opposition, and about the degree of U.S. responsibility for the end of Chilean democracy, all would probably agree that the U.S. role in 1970—revealed in 1974 and 1975—in fomenting a military coup against a freely elected government violates the most basic ideals that the United States stands for in the world.

Part of that effort also involved direct U.S. support for a plan to kidnap the Chilean army commander. While U.S. support was cut off from the group that actually carried out the kidnapping (and in the process murdered General Schneider), the two groups were closely related, and the entire plan would probably not have been carried out without knowledge that the U.S. government was behind it. Thus the U.S. government bears a share of the responsibility.

There was also a problem with the passage of money to extremist groups. Along with the plans, never put into execution, to bribe the Chilean Congress, the CIA support for extremists committed to the use of violence suggested that there was a need for a much improved process of oversight of covert operations by the legislative branch. New procedures were later adopted, and their effectiveness is evaluated in subsequent chapters.

2. The subsequent revelations also provoked a continuing public debate on the legitimacy of other forms of covert aid—in particular, to opposition parties and media. The justification given was the need to counteract the Allende government control over communications. There was some evidence of the use by the Allende government of economic pressures on newspapers and magazines and of government assistance to the left in taking over television. The struggle for control of Chile's only paper company was also seen by both sides as important in its impact on the media. However, it is hard to believe that without *El Mercurio* and the opposition radios the left would have been able to suppress its critics, at least as long as it did not control the armed forces. And again, an open U.S.-financed support program would have avoided the dangers of the covert effort that actually took place—the planting of false stories, subsidizing of pamphlets that were aimed at promoting a coup, and manipulation of the opposition media.

3. The accusation that the United States organized an "invisible block-ade" of the Allende government raises questions of the legitimacy of economic warfare and the role of multinationals in the U.S. policy. Clearly

some efforts were made to persuade U.S. banks and companies to deny credit to the Allende government—and those efforts antedated the Allende government's confiscatory nationalizations. However, those efforts were only partially successful, both because not all companies and banks were willing to follow the government suggestions and because the Chileans had other sources of foreign loans. The harassment that the Allende government suffered from the copper companies was the predictable result of its decision not to make any meaningful effort to compensate for nationalizing the cooper mines, and the U.S. support for the companies' position was in keeping with both U.S. and international law. Moreover, Ambassador Korry's effort to arrange a U.S. Treasury guarantee for compensation bonds, if successful, would have avoided the difficulties that followed.

The ITT papers reveal a close relationship between its operatives and the CIA, but the U.S. government twice turned down offers of ITT funding for anti-Allende operations. The CIA later tried to use ITT to organize economic pressures by American corporations, but those efforts failed. So close a relationship, however, does not seem to have been characteristic of the general pattern of contacts between U.S. overseas corporations and the U.S. government but was due more to personal contacts, especially those of John McCone, as well as the highly organized overseas reporting system of ITT. The U.S. program against Allende undertaken in September 1970 at the behest of President Nixon does seem, however, to have been the direct result of lobbying by the president of Pepsi-Cola, who was able to utilize his personal friendship with the president to give Agustín Edwards direct communication with the president and the national security adviser.

4. The U.S. relationship with the Chilean military has been seen as an important contributory factor to the 1973 coup. Yet the relationship and its direct use by the CIA in 1970 did not produce a coup that was desired by the United States, and the termination, or at least limitation, of such relationships in May 1973 considerably antedated the September coup. Despite the articles, books, and films that have claimed the contrary, there is no evidence of U.S. participation in, or direct encouragement of, the coup.

5. What of U.S. support for democracy? President Ford and Secretary of State Kissinger have insisted that support for opposition media and parties was in the interest of the maintenance of democracy. They also emphasize the Soviet and Cuban aid that was being given to the Marxist groups. Others, like Assistant Secretary of State Jack Kubisch, also later

argued that it was more in the U.S. interest for the Allende government to continue until 1976 and be defeated at the polls. Yet it seems that the U.S. government made no clear distinction between the maintenance of democracy and combating the Allende government with all means at its disposal. Anti-Communism in the defense of the free world was equated with the defense of democracy even if antidemocratic groups were given money and a coup indirectly (or in 1970 directly) promoted. U.S. policy continued to be dominated by anti-Communism even after the Soviet Union had indicated at the outset of the Allende government that it was not interested in subsidizing another Cuba in Chile.

The fact that the United States had a role in the overthrow of a freely elected government by a brutal military regime created a widespread sense after the coup that American values had been distorted and perverted by official malfeasance—a sense that was reinforced by the investigation of the Watergate break-in and the winding down of the Vietnam War. These factors combined to create a powerful force in the country and in the U.S. Congress calling for a basic change in the conduct and direction of U.S. foreign policy. Chile had an important role in bringing about that change.

4

Chile and U.S. Human Rights Policy

THE COUP in Chile produced a reaction of horror and revulsion in the United States and in Europe. In contrast to the mild public response to U.S. interventions in Cuba in 1961 and in the Dominican Republic in 1965, the Congress received what Senator William Fulbright described as an "unprecedented number of telegrams, letters, and phone calls" expressing opposition to the coup, concern for its victims, and strong suspicion of U.S. involvement. From the day of the coup when General Gustavo Leigh of the air force spoke of the need to extirpate "the cancer of Marxism" and General Augusto Pinochet of the army declared the Chilean Congress "in recess", which had functioned with only one interruption since 1833, stories continued to come out of Chile which fueled the fire of public protest. The leaders of the Allende government were rounded up and shipped to detention on windswept Dawson Island in the extreme south of Chile; thousands of suspected leftists were detained, questioned, and in a number of cases shot in the National Stadium in Santiago; and the headquarters of the Socialist and Communist parties were attacked and burned and the pro-Allende parties outlawed. A strict curfew was imposed, and censorship was imposed on the publications that were allowed to appear. The armed forces staged raids on residences of pro-Allende functionaries and burned leftist books. The country's major labor union confederation was dissolved, and the universities, including those under church control, were put under the direction of military "delegate-rectors." With the complicity of the judiciary, which supinely endorsed all its actions, the new junta, made up of the commanders of the three services plus the national police (now transferred from the Interior Ministry to the Defense Ministry), issued a series of "decree-laws" that in an Orwellian note both promised to respect the constitution and laws and decreed a state of siege (according to the 1925 constitution, only possible with the approval of Congress), which allowed detention and summary trials and executions and forbade judicial appeals from the military courts.[1] Four days after the coup the Santiago Court of Appeals rejected a habeas corpus (*recurso de amparo*) petition, presented on behalf of those detained, arguing that the country was under a state of siege. The appeals court decision was confirmed by the Supreme Court. In succeeding years, thousands of such petitions were rejected for similar reasons or because the minister of the interior denied that the named persons were in detention.

The junta defended its actions on the ground that Chile was at war with 10,000 leftist foreigners (the number seems to be based on the tourist visas issued at Chilean entry points that had not been turned in on exit) who had been allowed to enter Chile, as well as with their Marxist Chilean collaborators.

Plan Z

Five days after the coup the new government announced that it had discovered a document in the safe of the undersecretary of the interior which described an Allende government plan to murder the top military commanders and opposition leaders at the time of the national holidays in mid-September. Dubbed "Plan Z" from the code name beneath its title, "Plan for the Mobilization and Operations for a Coup d'Etat," it was dated August 25, 1973, and reproduced in the *White Book of the Change of Government in Chile,* published a few weeks after the coup. Its tentative date of implementation was set for September 19, 1973, and it outlined plans for the president's private bodyguard—the GAP (Allende called them his Grupo de Amigos Personales)—to carry out the "physical elimination" of the high command and the principal military leaders and "annihilation" of disloyal units and right-wing bastions.[2]

It seems extremely unlikely that the Allende government would seriously contemplate a coup by the presidential guard against the top leadership of armed forces numbering 87,000 men. It is an indication of the surrealistic quality of the Chilean politics of the time, however, that some of the more extreme leftist groups might conceivably have been thinking along these lines at the end of August. Nevertheless, the possibility of a forgery cannot be excluded. An American writer, Fred S. Landis, has argued in *Liberation* magazine that "a 35 man U.S. military mission on the seventh floor of the Chilean Defense Ministry" forged Plan Z and, "sometime after August 25, 1973," gave it to Chilean Naval Intelligence "across the hallway." No source is given for this information, and Landis also claimed that individualized copies of Plan Z containing their names and those of their children were given to top officers. Later in a collaborative book he attributed Plan Z's authorship to the head of the CIA Western Hemisphere Division, David

Phillips. According to Ambassador Davis, both Phillips (who was in Washington, not Santiago) and the CIA station chief in Santiago personally denied to him that CIA officers had anything to do with the plan, and he suggests that it is possible that it was a forgery that was Brazilian in origin, citing similarities to documents circulated earlier in Brazil.[3]

The issue of CIA involvement is relevant because the existence of Plan Z or a similar plan to assassinate top military and civilian leaders was repeatedly used by the junta to justify the massive repression that followed the coup and the wholesale killing that took place over the next six weeks. Before the coup, signs had appeared on walls in Santiago stating "Djakarta is Coming," referring to the murder of thousands of Communists when the Indonesian military took over after a leftist coup attempt in 1965, and although the numbers were not comparable, there was a similar sense of outrage, hatred, and reprisal on the part of the Chilean military. In the late 1980s, a series of articles, books, and exhumations in various parts of the country focused Chilean attention on the atrocities committed after the coup. In 1989 and 1990, a work of investigative reporting on the atrocities, *Los zarpazos del puma* by Patricia Verdugo, led the best-seller lists for many months and was available at every kiosk. It gave a detailed account of the October 1973 trip to the north of Chile in a Puma helicopter by General Sergio Arellano Stark to review the sentences by military courts of collaborators of the Allende regime, in many cases taking those serving sentences out of prison, shooting them, and burying them in unmarked graves. The justification frequently given was that they knew about, or were involved in, the Plan Z program for the execution of the military.[4]

As was the case in Indonesia, there is also a question that is still debated concerning the role of the U.S. embassy in providing lists of leftists to be rounded up. *Covert Action in Chile* states that the CIA prepared "arrest lists" before the coup but claims that they were never turned over to the Chilean military (38). It also notes that "two CIA collaborators"— presumably Chileans—assisted in the preparation of the *White Book* (40). (Pamela Constable and Arturo Valenzuela in *A Nation of Enemies* overstate the CIA connection, citing *Covert Action* to prove that the CIA itself "assisted in preparing the White Book" [37]).

Congressional Involvement

In the United States the question of CIA involvement in Chile had not reached this degree of detail, but it had already become an issue because of the information about CIA activities in 1970 which was contained in the

ITT papers revealed in 1972 and further explored in the March 1973 Senate hearings. Already in February 1973, during former CIA director Helms' confirmation hearings as ambassador to Iran, he was asked whether the CIA had tried to overthrow the Allende government or passed money to its opponents. Helms replied "No Sir" to both questions—answers that led to his being fined and given a suspended sentence for perjury in 1977.

The coup took place while Senate confirmation hearings were being held on Henry Kissinger's nomination as secretary of state. On September 17, in reply to questions about U.S. involvement in the coup, Kissinger admitted that the CIA had been involved "in a minor way" in the 1970 elections, but he stated, "Since then we have absolutely stayed away from coups." He added, "To the best of my knowledge and belief [the CIA] had nothing to do with the coup" (*New York Times,* Oct. 5, 1973)—an answer that was able to survive the scrutiny of the Church committee two years later (as that of Helms was not).

There was fuller discussion at hearings held on September 20 by the Subcommittee on Interamerican Affairs of the House Foreign Affairs Committee. In his opening statement, Assistant Secretary of State Jack Kubisch stated categorically, "We were not involved in the coup in any way." But when asked about U.S. financing of the opposition, he replied that this should be discussed in executive session. He also alluded to the reported plan to murder the military leaders and reaffirmed, "We were not involved in any way in the overthrow of President Allende or his government; not the U.S. government and not any element of the United States Government, including the Central Intelligence Agency."[5]

The subcommittee began to press Kubisch on the nature and extent of CIA involvement, but Kubisch argued that the CIA itself should discuss the subject in executive session. Although it was not customary for the CIA to come before congressional subcommittees, William E. Colby, the CIA director, agreed to testify to the Subcommittee on Interamerican Affairs in executive session on October 11. According to Colby's account in his memoirs, the session amounted to "little more than a fencing match" between Colby and Congressman Michael Harrington of Massachusetts, since Colby refused to discuss actual CIA operations except with the Intelligence Subcommittee of the House Armed Forces Committee (which had earlier been informed of Track I but not of Track II, the effort to promote a military coup in 1970 between the popular election and the congressional runoff).[6]

In the Senate the most active participant in the debate on Chile policy was Senator Edward M. Kennedy. Encouraged and briefed by one of his aides, Mark Schneider, a former Peace Corps member who had returned from Latin America convinced that human rights should be at the core of U.S. foreign policy, Kennedy used his position as chairman of the Refugee Subcommittee of the Senate Judiciary Committee to hold hearings on Chile on September 28, 1973. Following the hearings he denounced the U.S. decision to grant the new government a credit of $24 million for the purchase of wheat to replace shipments from the Soviet Union and Eastern Europe which had been turned around on the high seas on the day of the coup. Kennedy called it "the latest symbol of our willingness to embrace a dictatorial regime that came to power in a bloody coup and which continues to conduct summary executions, to burn books, to imprison persons for political reasons, and to deny the right to emigrate." A week after the coup, he and Congressman Don Fraser proposed a sense of Congress resolution on human rights in Chile. On October 2, he proposed an amendment to the Foreign Assistance Act which urged the president to cut off all aid to Chile other than humanitarian assistance, "until he finds that the government of Chile is protecting the human rights of all individuals, Chilean and foreign."[7] The amendment was not adopted, but the Foreign Assistance Act as finally adopted in December 1973 called on President Nixon to urge the Chilean government to respect human rights and to request an investigation of "recent events in Chile" by the Interamerican Commission on Human Rights. Kennedy's efforts were the beginning of a series of increasingly vigorous congressional efforts to cut off military aid to Chile which finally resulted in a complete ban in 1976 on all aid and sales to the Chilean military, a ban that was to remain in effect in one form or another until the early 1990s.

The Latin American Subcommittee of the Senate Foreign Relations Committee also held hearings in early November during which Ambassador Davis testified in closed session. As reported by Davis (*The Last Two Years,* 384–86), they were concerned mainly with the Horman case, since Senator Jacob Javits, a friend of Horman's father, was a member of the subcommittee and because there had already been accusations that the embassy had been nonresponsive in seeking Horman's whereabouts for reasons related to Horman's leftist ideology. (Horman's body had not been located until mid-October.) According to Davis, the Chilean morgue registered Horman's body on September 18, the day after he was picked up and the same day that the embassy was informed of his disappearance. Davis argues (381) that the embassy took action to locate him the same day and that the consul went to the National Stadium to search for him the next day. He does not discuss CBS newsman Frank Manitzas's report of the cold treatment Horman received at the embassy and consulate earlier in the day on which he was arrested (see Hauser, *Missing,* 90–95).

One other American, Frank Teruggi, was arrested for violating the curfew on September 20, and his body was found in the morgue on October 2, dead of bullet wounds. The consul, Frank Purdy, was strongly criticized in the *New York Times* by an American academic, Richard Fagen of Stanford University, for "lies, contradictions, and ineptness in aiding American citizens."[8]

In contrast to the hesitancy of the U.S. embassy, the Swedish ambassador, Harold Edelstam, traveled around the city contacting those he felt were in danger from the new government and arranging for them to be given asylum at the Swedish embassy. Before he was declared persona non grata in December 1973, he was able to save hundreds of Chileans from torture and possible murder. No one asked for asylum at the U.S. embassy, but many European embassies were crowded with refugees. Sweden, France, Holland, and West Germany took hundreds of refugees (West Germany announced that it would accept 1,000). The United States received 140 requests for visas and granted 25, arguing that the others were not subject to the "well-founded fear of persecution" which the relevant legislation demanded.

Congressman Harrington continued to press his attack on the U.S. role. He flew to Chile for a three-day visit in late October, and despite efforts by the ambassador to arrange a private meeting with him, he only saw Davis at a meeting that the embassy arranged with members of the military junta—later complaining that his only opportunity to talk with the ambassador was in the presence of "three or four Chilean generals" (Davis, 385). On December 7, the Subcommittee on Interamerican Affairs of the House Foreign Affairs Committee met in joint session with the Subcommittee on International Organizations and heard testimony from Harry Shlaudeman, the deputy assistant secretary of state for interamerican affairs, who had been deputy chief of mission at the U.S. embassy in Chile from 1969 until 1973. Congressman Harrington asked Shlaudeman whether "the Committee of 40" had approved a State Department–CIA effort to influence the vote of the Chilean Congress in 1970, to which he replied, "No such effort was made." When Harrington asked him about "authorization of funding in August for continued effort toward political destabilization of the Allende regime," he answered, "There was no such funding." This is the first recorded use of the term "destabilization" to describe the U.S. anti-Allende program in Chile. Harrington used it again when he asked Shlaudeman,

"Have we spent, to your knowledge, from any source that would be U.S. funding, any moneys that were directed towards either the support of policies or individuals which had as a purpose political destabilization?"— to which Shlaudeman replied, "For political destabilization, no; not to my knowledge." When Harrington rephrased his question as "support of political activity," Shlaudeman suggested that what was done in Chile should be discussed in executive session.[9]

As the Church committee report indicates, Shlaudeman's replies were technically correct, since the Forty Committee did not approve the plan to bribe the Chilean Congress in 1970, nor were CIA programs aimed directly at the overthrow of Allende. However, his responses were somewhat less than completely candid as Harrington began to zero in on the programs that were finally exposed in 1974. Most of those programs had been discontinued after the coup, although *Covert Action in Chile* revealed (40) that a major propaganda effort aimed at improving the image of the junta was initiated, involving the sending of anti-Allende trade unionists to Europe.

Los Chicago Boys

Before the coup most political observers believed that if the armed forces took over, they would pursue a statist economic policy not unlike the developmental nationalism of the neighboring military regime in Peru. In fact, almost from the outset the new government undertook a very different program. The way the "Chicago boys," as the exponents of free-market Chicago-style economics were known, succeeded in dominating the economic policy of the new regime has been described in detail by Arturo Fontaine Aldunate in his book *Los economistas y el Presidente Pinochet.*[10]

The Chicago-trained economists had established themselves at the School of Economics of the Catholic University of Chile in the late 1960s under Sergio de Castro as dean of the Faculty of Economics and Social Sciences. In the Allende period, a group of them, headed by de Castro, wrote for the economic page of *El Mercurio* and for a new news magazine, *Qué Pasa,* founded by Hernán Cubillos. Cubillos, the son of a distinguished navy admiral, and a former navy officer himself until he resigned for economic reasons, was a member of an aquatic sports group in Valparaiso which also included Agustín Edwards, publisher of *El Mercurio;* Roberto Kelly, another former navy man; and José Toribio Merino, the admiral who became the navy representative on the junta in 1973.

In 1972, the navy asked Kelly to ask sympathetic economists to produce a plan to resolve Chile's increasing problems of inflation, price distortions, and declining production. In May 1973, the ten economists involved held a meeting to draft a comprehensive plan. On September 11, the day of the coup, Cubillos's printing plant's photocopiers produced multiple copies of their several-hundred-page plan. The next day the relevant military officers had copies of "the brick" (*el ladrillo*), as its authors referred to it, on their desks.

In the allocation of responsibilities after the coup, the navy, headed by Admiral Merino, was put in charge of the economy. He in turn asked Kelly to take charge of the planning office (ODEPLAN) and named de Castro as principal adviser to the general who had been appointed minister for the economy. ODEPLAN under Kelly was dominated by the Chicago-trained economists, who, after some initial disputes with more socially oriented Christian Democrats and generals, succeeded in persuading the military that the only way to resolve Chile's economic problems was to reverse the statism of the Allende regime. Citing the need to reduce inflation and remove market distortions, they eliminated price controls on most items, lowered tariff rates, and moved toward a market-related exchange rate through a sharp devaluation. (At the time of the coup, the Chilean escudo ranged from 25 to the dollar for imported food to 3,000 to the dollar on the black market.) Seized factories and farms were returned to their owners; state farms and cooperatives were divided into individual landholdings; and foreign investment was invited to reenter Chile. The regime announced that it planned to sell off money-losing state enterprises, and it sold fifty in the first year.

The price increases caused by the removal of price controls and the currency devaluation caused considerable hardship among the poor, leading to criticisms of the economic policy by the other generals. However, there was near unanimity among the economic team and total support by Admiral Merino, General Pinochet, and the general in charge of the Finance Ministry. When that general resigned in April 1974, he was replaced by a civilian, Jorge Cauas, who had been at the World Bank. Trained at Columbia University and formerly a member of the Christian Democratic Party (PDC), Cauas agreed with the policies of the Chicago economists and formally resigned from the PDC, which since January 1974 had moved into opposition to the government, both because of its economic policies and because of human rights abuses. Most of the cabinet was still composed of military men, but the two posts dealing with economic policy were now under the direction of civilian technocrats.

The Declaration of Principles

Political analysts were already identifying two different philosophical approaches among the civilian advisers to the junta. On the one hand, a group of conservative corporatists with strong Catholic ties were critical of democracy and favored a restructuring of Chilean political institutions to give representation to functional groups and avoid the "demagoguery" of mass democracy. On the other, there was also a libertarian group that saw the military government as an opportunity to reorient Chilean politics in the direction of a market-dominated decentralization of decision making to maximize individual choice and sharply reduce the role of the state. The tensions between the two approaches were already evident in the junta-appointed Committee on the Revision of the Constitution, but that group, although it met frequently, made very little progress in the first years after the coup. A clearer indication of the ideological orientation of the new regime came in March 1974 with the publication of the Declaration of Principles of the Government of Chile. Written mainly by Jaime Guzmán, a brilliant young Catholic lawyer who had been a leader of the rightist *gremialista* movement at the Catholic University in the late 1960s and a well-known opponent of the Allende government on television panel shows, it used the "principle of subsidiarity" enunciated by Pope Pius XI in his 1931 encyclical, *Quadragesimo Anno*—"by virtue of which no higher group can arrogate to itself the area which lower entities can satisfy"—to link the two opposed philosophies. Ignoring the substantial limits the pope had placed on the property right ("the social function of property" to which the Christian Democrats had appealed in arguing for agrarian reform), the declaration said that from the principle of subsidiarity comes "as its natural form the right to private property," as well as respect for and encouragement of lower "intermediate groups between the individual and the State" and "functional decentralization" of politics and society. The declaration also stated that although the government respected human rights, it could not allow, "in the name of a misunderstood pluralism, a naive democracy [to] permit organized groups within it, . . . pretending to accept the rules of democracy, to support a doctrine or morality whose objective [was] the construction of a totalitarian state. Consequently Marxist movements and parties will not be admitted again to civic life." Again combining contradictory philosophies of democracy and authoritarianism, the declaration concluded that although the government would not set a date (*plazo*), in due time it would give power to those elected by a "universal, free, secret, and informed vote," but only after the mentality of Chileans had been changed and decentralized and regional "vehicles of participation" had been created making possible a democracy that was "organic, social, and participatory."[11]

Guzmán did not speak English, and only General Gustavo Leigh of the members of the junta had spent time in the United States. The new regime had an American-influenced component—the economic team—and others in the business community and in the media who had strong U.S. connections, but to regard the junta as an American creation, as some foreign observers did, was to be ignorant of its background and orientation. General Leigh himself became more and more isolated and suspicious of the increasing influence and centralization of power on the part of Augusto Pinochet. According to the best "insider" account,[12] originally the junta had talked of a rotation in its presidency, and as late as the end of September 1973 Pinochet still indicated that a rotating presidency was planned (*Qué Pasa*, no. 127, Sept. 27, 1973, 7), but it soon became apparent that such a system would be unworkable. In June 1974, Pinochet was named "Supreme Head of the Nation," and in December, over the objections of Leigh, he was designated "President of the Nation."

Beginning to operate in January 1974, but formally announced only in June, a single Directorate of National Intelligence (DINA) was created to centralize the uncoordinated efforts of the intelligence branches of the four services and to carry out the fight against real or imagined opposition. It was reported to have four thousand military and civilian employees and sixteen thousand informants.[13] Its head, Colonel—later General—Manuel Contreras created a powerful instrument of terror which until its dissolution in 1977 engaged in a ruthless campaign of torture and murder against "subversives."

Congress and Human Rights

Human rights groups and a steady stream of delegations that visited Chile reported that there had been no decrease in the repression but that it had become more systematic. An increasing concern with human rights on the part of the U.S. Congress found in the Chilean case a prime example of the need for legislative action to give a greater humanitarian orientation to U.S. foreign policy—now directed by a secretary of state who was noted for his commitment to Realpolitik in international relations.

Since August 1973, Congressman Fraser's Subcommittee on International Organizations had been holding hearings on violations of human rights in various countries with a view to gaining support for U.S. ratification of a number of international human rights conventions and to establishing a Bureau of Humanitarian Affairs in the State Department to deal with such matters. In December 1973, Fraser's subcommittee and the Interamerican Affairs Subcommittee held joint hearings on the status of human rights in Chile. The principal witness was Professor Frank Newman of the University of California, chairman of the American Bar Association's Committee on International Aspects of Human Rights, who had gone to Chile in October for the human rights organization, Amnesty International, to urge the Chileans to respect the freedoms guaranteed in the Universal Declaration of Human Rights. Newman testified that there were two thousand Chileans held in indefinite detention and another thousand awaiting trial on political charges. He noted that the Chilean government had promised to observe the procedures guaranteed in international law but that there was evidence of detention without charges, torture, and arbitrary killings, which led him for the first time to favor using U.S. foreign assistance as a lever to aid human rights. He also argued that the Chilean case offered a rare instance of an international consensus in the United Nations and that in the early 1970s the United Nations had established formal procedures for the consideration in the U.N. Human Rights Commission of instances of government violations of human rights.

The two subcommittees held further hearings on Chile in May and June 1974 and heard reports from U.S. and international delegations on the repression in Chile, as well as arguments for a cutoff of U.S. aid. Harry Shlaudeman, deputy assistant secretary of state for interamerican affairs, appeared on June 12, 1974, to defend U.S. policy. He noted that the U.S. embassy had not been aware of the presence in Chile of the two Americans who were killed in the first days after the coup, argued that the military government had improved its procedures for dealing with detainees, and defended the continuing U.S. program of assistance and training to the Chilean military as a contribution "in a balanced and nonpartisan way to stability in the area." Dante Fascell, chairman of the Interamerican Affairs Subcommittee, pressed Shlaudeman on whether "representation had been made to the Chilean Government" that respect for fundamental human rights was important for the continuation of military aid, to which Shlaudeman replied, "I can say quite confidently that they are indeed aware of the concern of the Congress in these matters and the relationship between these matters and the assistance." Fascell's response, reflecting rising congressional pressures to cut off military assistance to Chile, was that while there was consensus on continuation of humanitarian economic aid, "There certainly is not a similar consensus with respect to either military sales or military grant assistance to the government of Chile."[14]

After Fascell completed his questioning, Congressman Fraser began to ask Shlaudeman about U.S. covert activities in connection with the 1970 election. He replied that U.S. policy toward Chile had been one of nonintervention, but when asked about U.S. covert support of opposition parties after 1970, he was evasive, leading Fraser to point out that the latter activities clearly involved intervention. Congressman Harrington then leapt into the fray with a repeat version of his earlier question concerning the "Committee of 40" and efforts to bribe or change the result of the 1970 congressional runoff, as well as the August 1973 appropriation "for continuing efforts towards political destabilization of the Allende regime." Having again been answered with a denial by Shlaudeman, Harrington concluded, "I at this point quit, Mr. Chairman" (128–29). After noting that a recent U.N. vote calling on Chile to respect human rights had been 42 in favor, none against, with only 2 abstentions—the United States and Chile—Fraser concluded the meeting, "I hope that some day the Department (of State) will undertake a greater expression of concern for the human rights of the people in the conduct of foreign policy . . . [and that] the American people will get the full story some day as to exactly the kind of intervention we did practice during the tenure of President Allende" (135).

CIA Involvement Revealed

Thanks to Congressman Harrington, that story began to be told. There had always been a semblance of congressional review of CIA covert activities, lodged in the chairman of the Intelligence Subcommittees of the House and Senate Armed Services committees. When Congressman Harrington failed to receive an answer to his questions about CIA covert activities in Chile in October 1973, he urged the chairman of the House Intelligence Subcommittee, Lucien Nedzi, to hold a hearing with Colby in executive session. At that hearing, held on April 22, 1974, Colby gave full details on the Track I efforts in 1970 as well as the subsequent support for the Chilean opposition between 1970 and 1973. Following the hearing, Colby approached Nedzi individually and gave him a summary of the heretofore secret Track II. Harrington was not a member of the subcommittee, but he requested, as any House member was entitled to do, the transcript of the Colby testimony. After some hesitation he was given access to it, with the understanding that, as was customary, he would sign a written promise that he would honor the subcommittee's rule that such testimony remain secret. Although he signed the statement, he then wrote the chairman of the House Foreign Relations Committee summarizing Colby's report and urging public hearings on the U.S. role in Chile.[15] On September 8 the contents of the letter were published in the *New York Times*. The result was an uproar over the U.S. role in Chile, a series of news articles by investigating reporters from the *New York Times* and the *Washington Post,* and a press conference question to President Gerald Ford (Nixon had resigned in disgrace a month earlier) concerning CIA covert action during the Allende years. To a reporter's question on the U.S. role, Ford replied that the CIA had attempted "to help and assist the preservation of opposition newspapers and electronic media, and to preserve opposition political parties." He added, "I think that this is in the best interest of the people of Chile and certainly in our best interest." Ford noted that the "Communist nations spend vastly more money than we do for the same kind of purposes" and promised to meet with congressional committees to determine whether changes were needed in the process of review of CIA activities (*New York Times,* Sept. 17, 1974). Initially there was some sentiment to abolish the covert action capability of the CIA entirely, and a bill to this effect was introduced in October in the Senate but was defeated 68 to 17. However, in December, the Senate and House both adopted the Hughes-Ryan Amendment to the Foreign Assistance Act, which prohibited CIA clandestine operations for other than intelligence-gathering purposes "unless and until the President finds that each such operation is important to the national security of the United States and reports, in a timely fashion, a description and the scope of such operations to the appropriate committees of the Congress."[16]

Throughout the fall of 1974—the period, one should note, just after the end of the Watergate investigations and the resignation of President Nixon—the Congress continued to be concerned with the two issues of human rights and controls on the CIA, both of them involving Chile. On September 29, a letter signed by 104 members of the House was sent to Secretary of State Kissinger stating, "We do not believe that long-term U.S. foreign policy interests are served by maintaining supportive relationships with oppressive governments, especially in the military field"; it urged that "U.S. foreign aid policies—especially military assistance policies—more accurately reflect the traditional commitment of the American people to promote human rights." A week later, the *New York Times* reported that Kissinger had reacted to a cable from the U.S. ambassador to Chile, David Popper, reporting on his expression of concern about human rights in a discussion of military aid with the Chilean defense minister, by writing on the cable, "Tell Popper to cut out the political science lectures!"—which had led to a formal State Department reprimand of Popper. Congressman Fraser demanded an explanation from Kissinger, in view of the congressional mandate contained in the 1973 foreign aid legislation directing the president to discuss the human rights issue with the Chilean government. The assistant secretary of state for congressional affairs replied, arguing that there had been an improvement in the human rights situation in Chile and defending the abstention by the United States in several U.N. votes on human rights in Chile. In response Congressman Fraser held hearings on the status of human rights in Chile and published the entire correspondence, as well as reports on torture in Chile by the International Commission of Jurists and the Interamerican Commission on Human Rights of the Organization of American States.[17]

That same month, the Senate Foreign Relations Committee sharply cut the administration request on economic aid to Chile and placed a total ban on military assistance, including military sales. After negotiation with the House, the amount of economic aid was further reduced to $25 million, and the ban on military aid (but not on commercial sales) was reaffirmed "unless the president reports to Congress that Chile is making fundamental improvements in the observance of human rights."

President Ford had raised the question of the structure of congressional oversight of the Central Intelligence Agency and attempted to preempt Congress's action in the area by appointing a committee, headed by Nelson Rockefeller, to evaluate the agency. That committee restricted its mandate, however, to examining the extent to which the CIA had violated the legislative prohibition in its authorization act against carrying out domestic activities. In any case, in the post-Watergate atmosphere, the Congress was not willing to leave the question to the executive branch, and both houses voted to establish select committees to investigate the conduct and organization of U.S. intelligence.

The Senate Select Committee on Intelligence Activities was established in January 1975, and Chile was mentioned as one of the cases to be investigated. On January 22, 1975, the day after the resolution authorizing this committee was introduced, the Senate Foreign Relations Committee held a hearing to review the testimony it had received in 1973 from Richard Helms, now ambassador to Iran but then director of the CIA. Helms argued that in his denials at that time that the agency had passed money to Allende's "opponents" in 1970 he had meant by "opponents" the opposition parties and that there was no U.S. effort to influence the Chilean Congress directly. However, he admitted for the first time, and in contradiction to the testimony of all administration witnesses until that time, that he had understood that the objective of the Nixon administration was the overthrow of the government of Allende.[18]

The Church Committee

When the Senate Select Committee on Intelligence Activities, headed by Senator Frank Church, began its activities in March, it turned its attention first to the question of U.S. involvement in the assassination of foreign leaders. This had a Chilean component, since one of the foreign leaders discussed was General René Schneider, who had been killed in the kidnap attempt in October 1970. This in turn led the committee to Track II, the heretofore secret effort by the United States to promote a military coup, which was publicly revealed in July 1975 and fully described in the select committee's *Assassination Report,* published in November.

The select committee had 135 employees, of whom about half were investigators, and concerned itself with many aspects of CIA activities since its establishment after World War II. Chile was a central area of interest, both because of the Schneider assassination and more importantly because it was considered to be paradigmatic of the problem with which the committee was concerned, the control of covert action. It was decided, therefore, to prepare a special report on the Chilean case.

The committee heard testimony on Chile in executive session from CIA director Colby in May and in August from Henry Kissinger and General Alexander Haig, who had been Kissinger's assistant at the National Security Council in 1970. Later in the year there were negotiations with Kissinger and with Richard Nixon's lawyer concerning possible subpoenas to compel their testimony on the Chilean case. Faced with a refusal by Kissinger to testify in public and a series of crippling conditions put on his testimony by Nixon, the committee held only one public session on Chile, on December 4, with testimony from two former ambassadors, Ralph Dungan, who had been ambassador from 1964 until 1967, and Edward Korry, who had succeeded him and remained until late 1971. The committee later also heard in executive session from Ambassador Nathaniel Davis and once again in February 1976 from Korry, who insisted that he had not been permitted to tell his side of the story—specifically his ignorance of, and opposition to, any plan involving an attempted military coup. Korry also insisted (versus Kissinger's earlier testimony, which Korry described as "hogwash") that Track I and Track II were quite distinct, since the latter had been directed at a military coup and the destruction of the constitutional process. In written answers to committee questions in March, Nixon denied all knowledge of U.S. efforts to promote a coup in 1970 or to pass arms to the conspirators.[19]

The two reports involving Chile, the *Assassination Report* and *Covert Action in Chile,* were published in November and December 1975. In their published testimony Dungan called U.S. actions "a national disgrace," while Korry attacked the *Assassination Report* as a "pornflick" and *Covert Action* as "a morality fable in which American officials were all Nazi-like bully boys cuffing around decent social democrats . . . although Dr. Allende, as the embassy reported for many years, had personally been financed from foreign Communist enemies."

As staffers described the millions of taxpayer dollars spent on elections in Chile involving two or three million voters, Senator Walter Mondale asked about the nature of "the threat that Mr. Allende posed to this country." The response was a lengthy silence, and then a staffer replied that it involved the possible use of Chile as a base to subvert other Latin American countries, as well as concern that Allende would transform Chile into a Marxist totalitarian state.[20]

Controls on the CIA

The committee also heard proposals for the abolition or substantial modification of the covert activities of the CIA. The committee decided that the way chosen by the Congress in December 1974, a presidential finding on each covert action and formal notification of the committees involved, was the course to be recommended. Over the opposition of Senators Tower and Goldwater ("This is a report that probably should never have been written"), the senators made ninety-seven recommendations for improved congressional control of intelligence activities. In May the Senate, again over Republican opposition, established a permanent Senate Intelligence Committee and strengthened the provisions of the 1974 Hughes-Ryan Amendment, which called for informing Congress "in a timely fashion," demanding that the committee be kept "fully and currently informed" of "any significant anticipated intelligence activities." Besides full briefings for the Intelligence Committee (and its counterpart in the House of Representatives), subcommittee or committee chairmen of the Appropriations, Armed Services, and Foreign Relations committees were also to be kept informed. The requirement of notification of those committee chairmen was eliminated in the Intelligence Oversight Act of 1980—still leaving the members and some of the staffers of the House and Senate

Intelligence committees, totaling about 35 people. The 1980 act also allowed the president in "extraordinary circumstances affecting the vital interests of the United States" to limit those informed to the chairs and minority ranking members of the Intelligence committees, the speaker and minority leader of the House, and the majority and minority leaders of the Senate.[21] Further changes were made in 1991 (see Chapter Eight).

The establishment of strong congressional oversight structures was important for the future conduct of U.S. foreign policy. While the Intelligence committees could not forbid any projected covert activities, the very fact that they had to be informed acted as a deterrent—especially since a CIA operation to which legislators strongly objected was likely to "leak" and provoke a hostile reaction from the media and the public. In the 1980s, for example, the CIA funding of the contras in Nicaragua became public knowledge very soon (in November 1982, the cover of *Newsweek* headlined "The Secret War in Nicaragua"), and congressional resistance led to the Iran-contra efforts to bypass congressional controls by using Lieutenant Colonel Oliver North of the National Security Council rather than the CIA to pass money to the contras. An even earlier example of the effect of the congressional desire to limit the CIA was the congressional cutoff of funds for covert support of the anti-Marxist groups in the Angolan civil war in December 1976.

Institutionalizing Human Rights Concerns

The Angolan cutoff was one of the last acts of the liberal post-Watergate Ninety-fourth Congress, which was elected three months after President Nixon's resignation. This was also the Congress that took the most active role in institutionalizing a concern for human rights as an important objective of U.S. foreign policy. Part of the impetus for that concern was the continuing repression in Chile—for which Americans felt a sense of culpability, now heightened by the revelations concerning the CIA role in Chile. In the House in particular, Congressman Don Fraser used his chairmanship of the Subcommittee on International Organizations of the House Foreign Affairs Committee to focus attention on human rights and to press for human rights conditions on U.S. international assistance.

Those conditions were both generic and country specific, and in both cases Chile played a role. Besides the December 1974 ban on military aid to Chile, mentioned above, the Ninety-third Congress had also approved Section 402B of the foreign aid legislation calling on the president to "reduce or terminate security assistance to any government which engages in a consistent pattern of gross violations of internationally recognized human rights." An escape clause was provided that "in extraordinary circumstances" aid could be furnished, but the president was required to submit a report to Congress advising it of the circumstances that dictated the exception.

In November 1975, the State Department submitted to the Senate Foreign Affairs Committee and the House International Relations (Foreign Affairs) Committee a report on the implementation of Section 402B which complained of the difficulty of making "inherently subjective" determinations as to "gross violations." The congressional response was the adoption of the Harkin Amendment (Section 116) to the foreign assistance law, which was much stronger. It prohibited "development assistance" to "any country which engages in a consistent pattern of gross violations of internationally recognized human rights including torture or cruel, inhumane, or degrading treatment or punishment, prolonged detention without charges, or flagrant denial of the right to life, liberty, or the security of the person, unless such assistance will directly benefit the needy people in such country"—with such exceptions requiring a specific justification by the president. A similar provision governing the vote of U.S. representatives to the Interamerican Development Bank and the African Development Fund was adopted in the spring of 1976. Also in June 1976, that is, before the nomination and election of Jimmy Carter as president, the Congress established the Office of Coordinator for Human Rights and Humanitarian Affairs in the Department of State and required the submission by the State Department of annual reports on "human rights practices" in all countries receiving U.S. aid. As finally adopted, the law provided that an adverse report could result in a reduction or cutoff of military assistance by a resolution of Congress.[22]

Kennedy in the Senate and Harrington and Fraser in the House continued to press for specific human rights restrictions on Chile. The congressmen argued that the Ford administration had circumvented the 1974 $25 million limit on economic aid by excluding from the definition of aid assistance such as Food for Peace (of which Chile was one of the largest recipients in Latin America, receiving 48 percent of all food aid in the 1975 fiscal year), housing guarantees, and the investment insurance programs of the Overseas Private Investment Corporation, as well as by utilizing a very broad interpretation of "pipeline" aid that had been authorized but not delivered. The liberals were unsuccessful in cutting aid to Chile in 1975, although food and housing guarantees were specifically included in the

$90 million economic aid finally adopted. The story was very different, however, in 1976.

During 1975 it became clear that repression in Chile was not likely to end in the near future. In April, Jorge Cauas had taken over the Finance Ministry determined to administer a "shock treatment" to an economy that was reeling from the "scissors effect" of declining international prices for copper and sharply increased costs for imported petroleum. With Pinochet's support and over the objections of the civilian technocrats of Christian Democratic orientation such as Raúl Saez, who quit in protest, Cauas raised the value-added tax, sharply devalued the currency, cut government expenditures by 15 to 25 percent, and engaged in wholesale firing of civil servants. Although Cauas was not a "Chicago boy" himself, his plan marked the final victory of the Chicago approach, as those who disagreed with a drastic market-oriented program left the government. The Chilean economy contracted by 13 percent, unemployment rose to 20 percent, ninety-six thousand government workers were fired, and the only reason that there were not wholesale protests (as there were in 1983 under similar economic circumstances) was that the government continued the arrests and disappearances of earlier years, maintaining a climate of fear which prevented any public expression of opposition. The Catholic church opened more soup kitchens, the government began a WPA-like Minimum Employment Program (PEM), but most important the DINA operated with increased efficiency to intimidate and terrify the population.

Proposals for an on-the-spot investigation by the Interamerican Commission on Human Rights of the Organization of American States were sidetracked in May 1975 because the Pinochet government had promised to allow a visit by the U.N. Human Rights Commission. In July, Pinochet refused to allow the U.N. commission to come to Chile, and relations deteriorated with the United States, which had supported the OAS postponement because of the impending U.N. visit. They were sharply worsened in October when the Chileans voted for a resolution in the United Nations equating Zionism with racism, presumably in the hope of receiving Arab support in opposition to a further U.N. investigation. Pinochet repudiated the vote, and the Chileans abstained in the next vote on the subject, but the damage had been done. There were signals that the Ford administration, faced with congressional pressure and Chilean intransigence, had grown tired of continually defending Pinochet. The Ford foreign aid proposals for Chile for 1976 did not include a military aid request, presumably recognizing that Congress would be most resistant to continuing to subsidize repression. The Chileans, who had invited the OAS to meet in Santiago in 1976, were informed that the United States would not vote for Santiago unless they allowed international investigations of human rights. An American priest and three nuns were expelled for sheltering leftist guerrillas, and it was reported that there were still five thousand political prisoners in Chile (*New York Times,* Nov. 2, 1975). In November and December 1975—for the first time—the U.S. government voted in favor of U.N. resolutions accusing Chile of torture and violations of human rights. The time was clearly ripe for a new effort by congressional liberals on a cutoff of military aid to Chile.

In February 1976, Senator Kennedy introduced legislation that not only prohibited military aid, credits, and training but also cut off all cash sales in the United States, whether governmental or private, of military equipment to Chile. The Kennedy proposal also prohibited "pipeline" sales and deliveries, but this was eliminated by the House-Senate Conference Committee. As finally adopted by Congress, all military assistance and sales after June 30, 1976, to Chile were prohibited unless and until the president certified that there had been a substantial improvement in Chile's human rights record. A $27.5 million ceiling was also placed on economic aid pending improvements in the human rights situation.

The Kennedy Amendment prohibition on military aid—and especially on military sales—was a turning point in U.S. relations with Chile. More sharply than any other action, it indicated the displeasure of the American people with the continuing violations of human rights in Chile. Congressman Fraser had again held hearings in April 1976 which dramatized the police state atmosphere in Chile, and his subcommittee specifically attacked the ways in which the Ford administration had attempted to elude the congressional prohibitions and conditions on Chilean aid. When Secretary of the Treasury William Simon visited Chile in May, the Chilean press reported his favorable statements about recent improvements in the procedures for treating prisoners, but not the link that he drew between economic aid and improvement in human rights. In early June Henry Kissinger attended the OAS meeting in Santiago, which received a report by its Human Rights Commission giving details of arbitrary imprisonment, torture, and persecution in Chile. (It only learned later that shortly before the meeting twenty-nine members of the Central Committee of the Communist Party had been murdered by the DINA.) Contradicting his customary position about the place of ideals in the conduct of international relations, Kissinger asserted that human rights violations had impaired U.S.-Chilean relations and had caused widespread concern in the United States resulting in the "extraordinary step" of specific statutory limits on aid to Chile. In a ninety-minute private meeting with President Pinochet he also raised the human rights issue.

Pinochet's reaction to the criticisms from the United States and the international community was to expel Jaime Castillo, the leader of the human rights community in Chile. His government's relations with the United States deteriorated much further in September 1976 when Allende's former ambassador to the United States, Orlando Letelier, was killed by a car bomb in downtown Washington, along with an American woman, Ronni Moffitt. From the outset, the bombing was believed to be the work of the Chilean intelligence service, DINA, which had carried out other assassination attempts in Buenos Aires and Rome in previous years. The fact that such an outrageous act could be perpetrated in the heart of the U.S. capital, not a hundred yards from the official residence of the Chilean ambassador, was an indication of the arrogance of the Chilean regime at this point.

The Letelier murder once more put Chile on the front pages in the United States. The 1976 presidential campaign was in progress, and the Democratic candidate, Jimmy Carter, had already made the promotion of human rights one of the central planks of his program—and the Democratic platform criticized Republican support for the dictatorship in Chile. On October 6, during one of the presidential debates, he attacked President Ford specifically on the Chilean issue, observing, "I notice that Mr. Ford did not comment on the prisons in Chile. This is a typical example, maybe of others, that this administration overthrew an elected government and helped establish a military dictatorship" (*New York Times*, Oct. 20, 1976).

Conclusions

1. The election of Jimmy Carter fundamentally altered the relations between the United States and Chile. However, the foundation for that altered relationship had already been laid in the years since the 1973 coup. The Congress and the people had insisted on the incorporation of a concern for human rights in the conduct of U.S. foreign policy and on restraints on the covert action by U.S. intelligence agencies. That insistence had been given institutional form in ways that were to affect U.S. policy for the foreseeable future, as the State Department established the Bureau of Human Rights (upgraded under Carter to an assistant secretaryship), which began to issue annual reports on human rights for each country receiving U.S. aid (later for every country in the world), and the Congress

adopted general and specific legislation to cut off military and economic aid to countries engaged in gross violations of human rights.

2. Important limits had been placed on the clandestine operations of the Central Intelligence Agency. As a result of revelations of its role in Chile— and other abuses uncovered by investigating committees—real congressional oversight had replaced a merely nominal review, and significant disincentives had been placed on the initiation of controversial or dubious projects. Morale in the CIA was harmed, and some of its major operatives were retired (including William Colby as its director, who was succeeded by George Bush in January 1976), but it had become more responsive to democratic controls and less likely to engage in activities that violated U.S. ethical principles.

3. U.S. relations with Chile had received more attention in the period since the 1973 coup than at any earlier time. U.S. policy had been evaluated, criticized, and exposed. Economic aid programs had been seriously reduced, and military aid—and, more important, all military sales, whether government or commercial—had been cut off. Chile's links with the U.S. government in the area of military aid were broken.

4. The success of the human rights lobby, against State Department and White House resistance, was attributable partly to the post-Watergate climate in the Congress and the nation, but it was also assisted by the flood of negative information about the U.S. role in Chile. That information, partly the result of effective investigative reporting, persistent questioning by irate congressmen, and a rare willingness to cooperate with the critics of the CIA on the part of its director from 1974 until 1976, William Colby, was publicized and often exaggerated by the media and by the left worldwide. It left the erroneous impression that continues to this day, that the United States engineered the Chilean coup and had one of its citizens murdered "because he knew too much" about the U.S. role and that the Pinochet government was an American creation. The vain efforts of the Nixon and Ford administrations to defend the new regime against its congressional and international critics only reinforced that impression.[23]

5. The aid cutoffs did not hurt Chile that much, since it could still secure loans from private banks, awash since 1973 with OPEC dollars, and from the international financial institutions such as the World Bank and the Interamerican Development Bank. The administration here as elsewhere

was reluctant to interfere with private lending, as a matter of principle, and it argued that political criteria should not be used by the international financial institutions. The Ford administration's reluctance to move in these areas was criticized by congressional liberals, and in early 1976, over administration opposition, legislation was adopted which directed U.S. representatives in international financial institutions to oppose loans to countries that were gross violators of human rights, unless those loans directly benefited the needy. Attempts were also made to cut off private bank loans, but they did not succeed, and until the debt crisis of the 1980s undercut this source, Chile did not feel a real pinch as a result of the aid cutoffs. The ban on U.S. credits and sales to the Chilean military was a stronger sanction, but the Chileans were able to turn to other arms suppliers in Europe and South Africa, and eventually they built up a domestic arms industry as well.

6. The Nixon and Ford administrations seemed excessively concerned with defending the Pinochet administration against its congressional critics, thus reinforcing those who argued that a double standard was being employed—strong efforts against Allende for actions that affected the economic interest of American corporations, and little or no criticism of much more serious abuses of human rights thereafter. More fundamentally, the critics noted that the administration argued that the CIA covert aid to opposition media and parties in the Allende period was aimed at preserving democracy, but it took no action against the destruction of democracy by the Chilean military after the coup. In the last year of the Ford administration, the State Department and the president began to take a more vigorous role in criticizing the violation of human rights. There was still no mention of the restoration of democracy, a cause that seemed a vain one as one after another Latin American regime came under military rule (by 1976 only Colombia, Venezuela, Costa Rica, and Mexico had elected governments), but the very excesses of the military governments—Chile not least among them—made the promotion of human rights so popular a cause that it became an issue in the 1976 presidential election.

First Chile had been a showcase that demonstrated the successes and failures of the Alliance for Progress. Then it became a morality play for liberals and conservatives demonstrating either the evils of Communist expansionism or the dangers of mindless Cold War anti-Communism. Now it was to be cited again by both right and left in the debate over the role of the promotion of human rights—and, when the circumstances permitted it, of democracy—in the conduct of U.S. foreign policy.

5

Pinochet, Carter, and Human Rights

THE PINOCHET government reacted to the election of Jimmy Carter by announcing the release of 304 political prisoners and the closing of two notorious detention centers. From the outset—in his inaugural address, which stated, "Our commitment to human rights must be absolute"—it was clear that the Carter administration was going to take a very active role in promoting the observance of human rights internationally. The Ninety-fifth Congress was supportive. Aware that countries that had lost U.S. aid could still go to international financial institutions, the Congress brought U.S. policy in these institutions in line with overall U.S. lending policy. It passed a law requiring U.S. representatives to international financial institutions such as the World Bank to oppose loans to countries engaged in a "consistent pattern of violation of human rights," unless such aid would serve basic human needs. The Export-Import Bank and the Overseas Private Investment Corporation (OPIC) were also instructed to take human rights considerations into account in their loans and guarantees.

The Ninety-fifth Congress also upgraded the coordinator of human rights and humanitarian affairs to the position of assistant secretary of state. The combative new assistant secretary, Pat Derian, successfully asserted the right to review and "sign off" on aid proposals and entered into contentious relations with the regional bureaus, which tended to be more sympathetic to the countries in their areas. In the embassies themselves, the new legislation resulted in the appointment of (part-time) human rights officers who were charged with preparing drafts of the required annual reports. In that role they developed close relationships, sometimes for the first time, between the U.S. embassy and opposition groups.

The increasing body of human rights legislation required coordination and joint decision making by the executive agencies involved on whether or not to apply aid cutoffs to a given country. This function was assigned by the National Security Council to the Interagency Group on Human Rights and Foreign Assistance, which was to include, in addition to the

State Department representative as chairman (Deputy Secretary of State Warren Christopher), representatives of the Treasury Department, Defense, the National Security Council staff, and the Agency for International Development (AID). Other interested bodies—for example, the U.S. representatives on the boards of the international financial institutions—could also participate. The Christopher Group attempted to decide when violations of human rights were sufficiently serious to meet the statutory definition ("torture or cruel, inhumane or degrading treatment or punishment; prolonged detention without charges; or other flagrant denials of the right to life, liberty, and the security of the person") and whether the basic human needs escape clause should be invoked.

With the drop in official aid and with the encouragement of the private banks, the Chilean government turned increasingly to private loans. Over the five years from 1976 to 1981, the composition of Chilean international debt shifted dramatically, and private debt moved from 27.9 percent of Chilean indebtedness in 1976 to 83.8 percent in 1981.[1] Typically bank interest rates were linked to the London Interbank Offering Rate (LIBOR), which was variable rather than fixed and considerably higher than concessional official loans.

The net result of the human rights conditions and other legislation was a dramatic drop in U.S. official aid to Chile. Except for "pipeline" aid already committed (some of it hastily signed just before the congressional deadline), no military aid, including military sales, went to Chile after the beginning of the 1977 fiscal year. Aside from the Peace Corps, which continued to operate (it was phased out in the 1980s), economic aid dropped dramatically as well. AID loans, which had totaled $31.3 million in the 1975 fiscal year and $20.6 million in 1976, dropped to $600,000 in 1977. In 1978 they declined further to $200,000 and $300,000, and even Food for Peace, which could be defended on basic human needs grounds, dropped from $56 million in 1976 to $31 million in 1977 and $5.6 million in fiscal 1978. World Bank loans, where U.S. opposition could not block aid, rose from $33 million to $60 million. Export-Import Bank loans ceased except for a loan of $46 million in 1978 (before the sanctions related to the Letelier case were imposed in 1979).[2]

In Chile there was a sharp decline in cases of disappearances as documented by the church-sponsored Vicariate of Solidarity, but the same body continued to record cases of torture and physical abuse as well as a new form of repression, group or mass detentions. The intensity of the feeling against Chile in the Human Rights Bureau of the State Department led to a dispute with AID over whether three agricultural loans to that country met basic human needs. The decision of the Christopher committee to defer consideration of the loans for thirty to sixty days led Pinochet to reject the projected 1977 U.S. assistance program of $27.5 million in economic aid (*New York Times,* June 24 and 29, July 1, 1977).

The differences within the new administration were most dramatically revealed at the meeting of the U.N. Human Rights Commission in Geneva in March 1977. One of the newly appointed U.S. representatives, Brady Tyson, a Methodist minister, a professor at American University in Washington, and a longtime human rights activist, took the floor to express the United States' "profoundest regrets" over its role in the overthrow of the Allende government and the resulting "suffering and terror that the Chilean people . . . experienced." He was immediately called home, and at his press conference the next day President Carter observed that the U.S. congressional investigations had found no evidence that the United States was involved in Allende's overthrow—a statement that differed from his position in the preelection debate the preceding October, but one that technically was correct. At the Geneva meeting, the United States supported a strongly critical resolution denouncing human rights violations in Chile, as did twenty-six other countries with only five abstentions and Chile's negative vote.

The Chacarillas Plan and the Dissolution of the DINA

In May 1977, Carter administration officials met with Chilean opposition leaders—not only former president Eduardo Frei but also the Socialist leader, Clodomiro Almeyda—and in June, Secretary of State Cyrus Vance met Admiral Patricio Carvajal at the OAS Assembly in Grenada and urged the lifting of the state of siege which had been in place since the 1973 coup, the dissolution of the DINA (the Chilean intelligence agency), and the return of the rule of law. Partly in response to U.S. pressures, Pinochet made a speech at Chacarillas in July 1977 announcing a plan for a gradual return to democracy. It called for a three-stage process with the first stage, "recovery," lasting until 1980, at which time a new constitution would be adopted by plebiscite; a second stage, "transition," in which an appointed Congress would begin to function; and a third stage, "normalization," from 1985 to 1990, with the election of two-thirds of the Congress and one-third appointed. That Congress in turn was to elect the president.

A more direct response to U.S. pressure took place in August, at the time of the visit to Santiago of Assistant Secretary of State Terence Todman. Pinochet announced that the dreaded DINA (Directorate of National

Intelligence) was to be dissolved, and in its place an innocuous-sounding National Information Center (CNI) was to be established. Todman commented favorably on the dissolution of the DINA, although most observers argued that with the same personnel and with authorizing legislation that did not differ substantially from that of the DINA, the changes seemed to be merely cosmetic.[3]

It was significant, however, that after the dissolution of the DINA, records of the church-sponsored Vicariate of Solidarity show that disappearances, which had totaled 691 between 1973 and 1976, ceased entirely. Even more important was the removal of Manuel Contreras, the director of the CNI (ex-DINA), in early November and his replacement by retired General Odlanier Mena. That action was widely approved by the armed forces, since Contreras had used the DINA to establish a state within a state which was known to have files on prominent citizens, including the military and members of the government, and his organization outdistanced in size and activities the rival intelligence agencies of the armed forces and the national police.

How much did U.S. pressure have to do with these changes? There was already strong opposition to the DINA in the Chilean army, but the timing of the DINA dissolution was clearly linked to the Todman visit. It was also related to the forthcoming visit in September by Pinochet to Washington for the signing of the Panama Canal Treaty, to which all Latin American presidents (except Fidel Castro) had been invited. An additional factor may have been Pinochet's awareness that the continuing U.S. investigation of the Letelier murder was now discovering increasing evidence of links to the DINA.

The Letelier Case

The assassination of Orlando Letelier, carried out by a bomb placed under his steering wheel that was exploded by remote control just as he entered Sheridan Circle in Washington, had set off a massive hunt by the U.S. attorney's office and the FBI for his murderers. Although conservatives such as Senator Jesse Helms argued initially that it was the work of internecine groups on the left—citing Letelier's notebook, found in the car, which revealed extensive contacts with the Cuban government—within a month the investigation had revealed that Cuban exiles in Miami and New Jersey were deeply involved. The FBI's Cuban sources described contacts between the Cubans and a tall, blond Chilean in Union City, New Jersey, which is heavily populated by Cubans. However, it took a year of investigation (including the FBI administration of a lie detector test to the Chilean naval attaché concerning Chilean embassy contacts with the Cubans) to identify the Chilean as Michael Townley, an American who had lived most of his life in Chile and had joined the DINA after the 1973 coup. The identification was only made possible by the chance fact that Townley's picture on his application for a visa under a false name in Asunción, Paraguay, had been photographed on orders of the ambassador, who was suspicious of the application.[4]

In August 1977, in response to requests from the U.S. attorney and the FBI representative in Buenos Aires for information on possible Chilean connections with the Cubans who had been indicted for the Letelier murder, the Chilean government formally denied that it possessed any evidence of "any Chilean citizen or foreign national, civilian or military, who might have any connection" with the murder, and it refused to cooperate further except through a formal international law judicial procedure known as Letters Rogatory. Before General Pinochet's September 1977 visit to Washington to witness the signing of the Panama Canal Treaty, the U.S. attorney sent a memo to Zbigniew Brzezinski, President Carter's national security adviser, describing the evidence he had of DINA involvement and the likelihood that Pinochet had known of and approved the murder. He accused the Chileans of "stonewalling" the investigation and urged that Carter bring up the issue with Pinochet. At a press conference in Washington and in conversations with reporters, Pinochet repeatedly denied that anyone in the Chilean government had anything to do with the case. He also assured President Carter of his cooperation during his personal interview with him.[5] However, the investigators finally decided that the only way to secure a Chilean response was to issue Letters Rogatory that focused on the false visa applications in Paraguay. When this was done, in February 1978, the Letters included copies of the photographs of the two applicants, and when the story of the visa applications was published in the press, a *Washington Star* reporter used his contacts to secure the photographs. When the pictures of the two DINA agents were published in the Chilean press, one of the two was quickly identified as Michael Vernon Townley. The other, Armando Fernández Larios, turned out to have an equally lurid history of undercover involvement (see below). The identifications came from Santiago (including the Intelligence Service of the Chilean air force) as well as from a former marine guard at the U.S. embassy in Santiago. The reason it had taken well over a year to make the connection was that Townley's picture had been removed from the U.S. embassy files in Santiago, the State Department desk officer had failed to notify the FBI of the visa application in his files, and Townley's false entry forms in Miami had failed to be entered into the Immigration and Naturalization Service computer.

The Chilean connection was made at a bad time for General Pinochet. The Bolivians were agitating once again for access to the Pacific through the return of territory that had been taken from them by Chile a century ago. In March 1978 they broke relations with Chile, and in 1979 they got a 21–1 vote in the Organization of American States in favor of their claims. The Peruvians were receiving Soviet tanks and opposing any compromise with the Bolivians which did not involve their consent. Most important, in January 1978 the Argentine military government had denounced the decision of a British arbitrator to award to Chile three disputed islands in the Beagle Channel in the extreme south of both countries. Pinochet also faced increasing opposition from the air force member of the junta, General Gustavo Leigh, who had begun to criticize the delay in returning to constitutional government as a way to demonstrate his resentment at Pinochet's increasing centralization of power.

After the U.N. General Assembly (with U.S. support) voted a strong condemnation of Chilean abuses of human rights in December 1977, Pinochet called a snap "consultation" for January 4, 1978. Chileans were asked to vote "yes" or "no" on the statement "In the face of the international aggression unleashed against the government of the country, I support President Pinochet in his defense of the dignity of Chile, and I reaffirm the legitimacy of the Government of the Republic to carry out in a sovereign way the process of institutionalization of the country." Since illiterates were permitted to vote, the "yes" was identified by the Chilean flag and the "no" by a black flag. The government had earlier explained the slow pace of institutionalization as necessary because of the destruction of the electoral rolls after the coup, but now it was only necessary to show one's national identity card to participate. In voting that was not preceded by any debate and in which there was clear evidence of fraud, Pinochet secured 75 percent approval.[6] The State Department issued a statement criticizing the vote for lacking "minimum guarantees of freedom of expression."

Pinochet's difficulties with Leigh continued, and they were only resolved by a legally dubious measure that he took in July 1978 removing Leigh with the consent of the other junta members for "total disability" to perform his duties (citing the 1975 Statute of the Governing Junta). Eight air force generals were forced into retirement when they were passed over to name Leigh's successor, and eleven other air force generals resigned in sympathy. Pinochet's control of the junta was now secure.[7]

This was not the only measure that Pinochet took to shore up his position. In March 1978 he declared the end of the "state of siege" which had been imposed at the time of the 1973 coup, replacing it with "a state of emergency"—the principal effect of which was to transfer most cases involving national security from the military to the civilian courts. In April, Pinochet also lifted the curfew that had been in effect since the coup. He reorganized his cabinet, giving it a strongly civilian cast—thirteen civilians to five military men, including for the first time nonmilitary men as interior minister (Sergio Fernández) and minister of foreign affairs (Hernán Cubillos). He also permitted Jaime Castillo, the Christian Democratic human rights activist who had been expelled in August 1976, to return to Chile. Also in April the government issued an amnesty pardoning all crimes between the 1973 coup and the end of the state of siege, an action that was to have important consequences for the resolution of human rights problems after Chile returned to civilian rule.

Under pressure from the United States, the Letelier case was specifically exempted from the amnesty. Presented with the overwhelming evidence of Michael Townley's involvement in the crime, the Chilean government finally agreed to surrender him as an American citizen to U.S. authorities for prosecution. Townley was arrested and handed over to the United States on April 9, 1978, and flown under heavy security to military installations near Washington. This only occurred following the conclusion of a carefully worded agreement signed in Washington between the U.S. attorney, Carl Gilbert, and the Chilean vice minister of the interior, Enrique Montero, which specified that information received from Townley could only be used for specific criminal prosecutions in the United States and that Chilean government representatives were to have continuing access to Townley in the United States.

The agreement turned out to be important to Chile in limiting discussion of a number of non–U.S.-related acts of international terrorism by the DINA in which Townley had been involved. After Townley arrived in the United States, he agreed to cooperate fully in return for a plea-bargaining agreement that reduced his possible sentence to ten years' imprisonment. Townley first received permission from his immediate superior, General Hector Orozco, to whom he gave a full account of his crimes. (This was important in later litigation in Chile because it antedated the plea bargaining, which Chilean courts later maintained made his testimony inadmissible under Chilean law.) Then he described in detail to the U.S. investigators his direct involvement in the murder by purchasing explosives, designing and putting the bomb in place under Letelier's car in Bethesda,

Maryland, and recruiting and advising the Cuban exiles who actually pushed the button on the remote control device that exploded the bomb (by which time Townley was in Florida).

Under various pseudonyms Townley had worked on assassinations for the DINA since 1974. He had aided in the bombing that killed General Carlos Prats, Allende's self-exiled army commander, in Buenos Aires in September 1974. He had first established links with the Cuban exiles in the United States in connection with a projected bombing of a meeting of Chilean exiles in Mexico City in early 1975, and in the same year he and another Cuban had worked with an Italian terrorist group to bomb the car of Bernardo Leighton, a former interior minister under the Christian Democrats and a figure who could bring together the left and center against Pinochet. Townley's letters to Chilean officials, obtained by the *Washington Post* (Feb. 23, 1982), reveal that the chief of the Italian terrorist group, Stefano delle Chiaie, had a private meeting with Pinochet when Pinochet attended Francisco Franco's funeral in December 1975, so that he must have been aware of the attempt on Leighton. It was also later revealed that Townley had with him a powerful nerve gas to use as a backup assassination method against Letelier and that later in 1976 he had also gone to Spain to murder the Socialist leader Carlos Altamirano. (At one point, he bumped into him while observing his movements at the Madrid airport.)[8]

There had been fierce disagreements within the Pinochet administration on the surrender of Townley. They revealed a division between hard-liners and soft-liners (*duros/blandos*) which was to continue to be evident in Chilean politics. However, since Manuel Contreras was out of the picture and his successor, General Odlanier Mena, was critical of his actions as DINA head, and because more pragmatic civilians were gaining more influence in the regime, the extradition took place. (Legally it was a response to a U.S. warrant for use of a false passport under an alias.)

The publication of the picture of Armando Fernández Larios, then a lieutenant in the Chilean army, as the other applicant for a fraudulent visa in Paraguay led to the discovery of his involvement as well, including his negotiations with the Cuban exiles and his investigation of details about Letelier's habits which were transmitted to Townley. (Fernández had also entered the presidential palace with General Palacios on September 11, 1973, and had accompanied General Arellano on the "Caravan of Death" to the north in October.) In both cases, there was written evidence that the two agents were acting under orders from their DINA superiors, Pedro Espinoza and Manuel Contreras. On August 1, 1978, Townley, Fernández, Espinoza, and Contreras were indicted by a U.S. federal grand jury on charges of the murder of Orlando Letelier and Ronni Moffitt and of conspiracy to murder a foreign official. Four Cuban exile activists (two of whom had gone into hiding) were also accused of the crimes, and a fifth was charged with making false declarations to a grand jury.

Pinochet ordered the house arrest of Contreras, Espinoza, and Fernández in response to a request by the U.S. ambassador pending preparation of the extradition papers. In the trial of Townley and the Cubans the jury found all the defendants guilty, and in March 1979 the judge sentenced two of the Cubans, Guillermo Novo and Alvin Ross, to life sentences. (Two others were still in hiding.) As a result of plea bargaining, Townley received ten years in jail.

Townley was released in 1983 after serving 62 months of his sentence, counting his pretrial detention, and he assumed a new identity under the Federal Witness Protection Program. The two Cubans received a new trial in 1981 because the court held that evidence from prison informants used to convict them was inadmissible. In the retrial, the two Cubans were acquitted on the basis of defense attacks on Townley's testimony, but Novo was convicted of perjury and given a retroactive eighteen-month sentence, which was longer than he had already been in prison (*Washington Post,* May 31, 1981; *El Mercurio,* April 19, 1990). One of the two fugitive Cubans, José Dionisio Suárez, gave himself up in 1990 and received a twelve-year sentence for conspiring to murder Letelier (Suárez drove the car containing the remote-control detonator, which Townley had fashioned from a radio paging device.) The other fugitive Cuban, Virgilio Paz, who had actually pushed the button, was arrested in April 1991 as a result of a story about him on the television program *America's Most Wanted.* In September 1991, he too was sentenced to twelve years in prison.

The extradition order was served in September 1978, but the Chileans did not act on it until the following May, when Judge Israel Borquez denied the extradition, arguing that the Townley evidence on which it had been based was inadmissible under Chilean law because it was part of a plea-bargain to obtain a reduced sentence. In an interview in a Chilean news magazine, Judge Borquez declared that the judge and jury chosen for the trial were "only little brown people, maybe so that they could not show their blushing when they heard the evidence." Townley showed no remorse about killing Letelier, declaring, "He was a soldier and so was I."[9] In November 1979 the Supreme Court of Chile affirmed Judge Borquez's decision, dismissing the FBI evidence as the result of plea bargaining and the confession to General Orozco as invalid in Chile. Only the Chilean judicial proceedings concerned with passport fraud were allowed to go forward.

In response, President Carter recalled for consultations the U.S. ambassador George Landau (who as ambassador to Paraguay had ordered the photographing of the visa application which broke the case) and announced that the U.S. military mission in Chile would be cut, pending Export-Import Bank loans to Chile would be canceled, and no insurance would be granted to Chile by the Overseas Private Investment Corporation (OPIC). In June 1980, Chile was also excluded from the annual Unitas joint naval maneuvers with the United States. Additional proposals to invoke trade sanctions or restrictions on private bank lending were rejected, although such measures had recently been invoked against Iran, and they had been threatened in U.S. conversations with the Chileans.

The Chilean Supreme Court decision prompted a *New York Times* editorial (Nov. 5, 1979) which criticized the "judicial pyrotechnics" exercised by the Chilean court, and described as "most promising" a proposal by congressional liberals to cut off all private lending to Chile (estimated at $2 billion in recent months). The proposal to ban private lending to Chile was attacked in an op-ed piece by Rosemary Werrett, business editor of *Business Latin America,* for "using business connections as a weapon for foreign policy purposes" (*New York Times,* Nov. 24, 1979). The Werrett letter also cited recent improvements in human rights in Chile, in turn provoking an angry letter to the editor which denounced the "moral blindness of the two past administrations and the business community" and defended the Carter pressures as responsible for what little improvement there had been in human rights in Chile. Senator Edward Kennedy, a candidate for the Democratic presidential nomination in 1980, called for stronger measures, including recalling the ambassador, closing the military mission, and cutting off all military supplies still in the pipeline, but he did not specifically mention a ban on private lending (*New York Times,* Dec. 1 and 7, 1979).

The Letelier case would continue to be a problem for U.S.-Chilean relations until the early 1990s. Even when the Reagan administration took power in 1981 and attempted to deemphasize the human rights issue, its character as an act of international terrorism perpetrated in the nation's capital meant that the United States continued to press Chile on the case. In addition, in July 1978, Letelier's widow and Michael Moffitt initiated a suit in a U.S. federal court seeking damages from the Chilean government for the "wrongful death" of Orlando Letelier and Ronni Moffitt, citing evidence of direct involvement of agents of that government including

DINA director Manuel Contreras. After the return of democracy to Chile, the case was submitted to international arbitration, and in January 1992 the plaintiffs were awarded $2.6 million in damages.

There continued to be discussion in and outside Chile of the degree of President Pinochet's knowledge of the case. It was assumed that he had been informed of the plot against General Prats in 1974, and probably in general terms about an international effort against enemies of his government. However, he repeatedly claimed that Contreras had denied any DINA involvement in the Letelier case, and at one point he asked Contreras in front of his whole cabinet whether the DINA or anyone in the government had had anything to do with the assassination and who he believed had carried it out. Contreras replied that he thought the CIA had done it and answered on DINA or Chilean involvement, "I must respond *negativo*." José Miguel Barros, a former Chilean ambassador to the United States, responded to U.S. Letters Rogatory in 1988 that he was told that Pinochet had asked Contreras repeatedly about DINA involvement and that Contreras had always denied it. When Townley revealed the DINA involvement in April 1978, he stated that he was certain that Pinochet knew about the assassination plan and when Armando Fernández Larios gave himself up to the U.S. government in 1987, he said that Contreras had told him that the assassinations had been ordered by "the Chief" (*New York Times,* Feb. 4, 1987). However, no "smoking gun" has been produced, although the fact that Contreras continued to live and function freely in Santiago after the extradition request was rejected was attributed by journalists to a rumor that he had shipped 23 suitcases of incriminating evidence to a secret depository in Europe.[10]

The Beagle Channel Crisis

Throughout 1978, the dispute with Argentina continued to heat up—to the point, near the end of the year, that the United States began to take a very active interest. It centered around three small islands, Picton, Lenox, and Nueva, in the middle of the Beagle Channel, south of the Straits of Magellan. In 1881, when the boundaries were drawn, the Beagle Channel line was left open to arbitration. In 1967 the Chileans invited the British government to arbitrate the dispute in accordance with a 1902 treaty, and in 1971 the two countries named members to an arbitration board to be chaired by a British judge. In April 1977, Queen Elizabeth announced an Arbitral Award granting the three islands to Chile and generally denying Argentine claims that all territories to the east of the longitude of Cape

Horn belonged to Argentina. After desultory negotiations and a meeting with Pinochet at the Argentine border city of Mendoza, the head of the Argentine military junta, General Ernesto Videla, announced on January 28, 1978, that the Arbitral Award was "incurably void," and tension began to rise between the two countries. Argentines spoke of Chilean "pretensions" to vast territories in the South Atlantic based on the projection of territorial waters from the three islands, and it was rumored that there were petroleum deposits in the area. By the end of the year it looked as if the countries were going to war, as the Argentines held blackouts and moved military equipment to the south. There were also reports that Peru was preparing to move into northern Chile if the Argentines attacked.

In December the United States sent a formal note to the chairman of the Permanent Council of the Organization of American States calling on him to take action. Earlier the Chilean foreign minister had also asked the Vatican to take an interest. The papal nuncio in Buenos Aires suggested papal mediation, and on December 22, as the Argentines were preparing the attack, the Vatican announced that it was sending Cardinal Antonio Samoré to consult with the two governments on the possibility of mediation. After two visits by Samoré, the two governments agreed to the mediation of the Holy See on January 8, 1979, and pledged not to resort to force while the mediation was taking place. Samoré later proposed awarding the islands to Chile but granted Argentina territorial waters to the east beyond a twelve-mile zone around the islands. It took nearly six years and the return of civilian government to Argentina for an agreement to be signed, in November 1984. After approval in a referendum in Argentina and formal ratification by the Argentine Senate, it was finally signed at the Vatican in May 1985.[11]

Besides the U.S. efforts to involve the Organization of American States and behind-the-scenes lobbying with the Vatican, it was also reported in the Chilean press that the United States had emphasized the urgency of the need for papal mediation by passing to the Vatican intelligence information confirming the fact that the Argentines planned to attack the islands imminently. Clearly war was only hours away when the papal intervention took place.

The "Boom" and the Seven Modernizations

The cabinet changes of April 1978 had placed the ministries of Interior and Foreign Affairs in civilian hands, although a new post of vice-minister of foreign affairs was created to maintain military influence. Economic policy had been run entirely by civilians since late 1974, mostly the "Chicago boys." They had opened the economy to the world, slashing import duties, freeing the exchange rate, removing subsidies and price controls, inviting foreign investment, and encouraging nontraditional exports such as fruit, fishmeal, and lumber. In 1975, when lower copper prices and the OPEC-induced increase in the cost of oil caused a financial crisis, Cauas had carried out a brutal shock treatment to bring the economy into line. It involved a massive reduction in government expenditure, a tax reform that was successful in considerably increasing government revenues, and a further move to a realistic exchange rate. It produced a drop in gross domestic product of 12.9 percent in 1975, and unemployment soared to 21.5 percent in 1976 (including government public employment programs).[12]

However, by the time Sergio de Castro, the leading representative of the Chicago school, took over the Finance Ministry from Cauas at the end of 1976, the economy was showing clear signs of recovery. Over the next five years, the Chilean economy grew at an average of 8.5 percent a year, and the world press began to talk of the Chilean "economic miracle." Nontraditional exports soared, reducing the share of copper from 85 to 45 percent of exports. Part of the prosperity was fueled by foreign borrowing, and Chilean indebtedness rose from $9 billion to $16 billion between 1975 and 1981, but there was no question that "the boom" was transforming Chile. It increased support for the regime, at least in the middle and upper classes, which benefited most from de Castro's policies. One policy in particular, a non–Chicago school pegging of the exchange rate between 1979 and 1982, produced an overvalued Chilean peso that made Japanese cars cheaper than in Japan and Scotch whisky cheaper than in Edinburgh. (It also made other imports so cheap that Chilean producers found it difficult to compete, and bankruptcies, particularly in manufacturing, began to increase.) The *Wall Street Journal* suggested (Jan. 18, 1980) that Chile might send some of its experts to advise the Carter administration on the reduction of inflation and unemployment. (U.S. inflation figures were nearing 20 percent, while the Chicago policies brought down Chilean inflation from 700 percent in 1973 to 9.9 percent in 1981. They were less successful with unemployment, which still hovered in the low to middle teens in 1980 and 1981.)

Besides opening the economy and attempting to reduce the inflation rate, the civilians of the Chicago school had more ambitious plans for reforming Chilean public policy. They reorganized school lunch and other feeding programs, pensions and family allowances for the poor, and low-income housing to target the lowest socioeconomic strata and to involve the private sector, promoting competition and efficiency.

In 1979 "the seven modernizations," Mao Tse-tung style, were announced, involving drastic restructuring of labor law, social security, health, education, agriculture, the judiciary, and public administration. The most important single actor in designing and carrying out many of these reforms, as well as in rewriting the Mining Code to encourage foreign investment, was not a Chicago boy but a recently returned doctoral student in economics at Harvard, José Piñera.

Piñera was first appointed minister of labor in December 1978 with specific instructions to take measures to head off a boycott of Chilean goods called for by the AFL-CIO to protest the repression of labor in Chile. (In volume 2 of his memoirs Pinochet describes the boycott as "a new Marxist aggression," 201). Acting quickly to respond to the American complaints, Piñera and his advisers (one of whom was Hernán Büchi, a Chicago boy who in the mid-1980s was a highly successful finance minister and in 1989 ran for president) studied American labor legislation with a view to developing a law that would both satisfy the Americans and prevent the politicization of the labor movement. After the 1973 coup the national labor organization, the Unified Workers Central (CUT), dominated by the Communists and Socialists, had been dissolved by the junta, and more than 220 trade union leaders had been fired and 110 killed. Trade union elections had been outlawed, and a 1978 law permitted employers to fire any employee without severance pay for "illicit acts." In mid-1979, in response to the AFL-CIO pressure, Piñera announced the Plan Laboral, which would permit the organization of trade unions with elections by secret ballot—but only on the plant level, thus outlawing federations and confederations on an industry or national level. (Several illegal union groups, mostly Christian Democratic in orientation, had already been established.) Workers could strike, but after two months the employer could hire replacements and fire the striking employees. Salary negotiations were to be carried out on the plant level, but increases would begin with a full readjustment for the inflation of the preceding year. The new system, although biased toward the employer, permitted the reappearance of a (much-weakened) trade union movement, and the American unions called off their boycott threat. In the 1980s an illegal but active National Worker Command (CNT) had an important role in the antigovernment protests that began in 1983.[13]

Piñera then moved on to rewrite the Mining Code in a way that trod a fine line between the military's concern that national resources, especially the copper mines, remain ultimately under national control, and the foreign investors' desire for guarantees against confiscation of their investments. Once a formula was found, foreign investors began to move into mining, especially copper, although, at military insistence, no effort was made to privatize the large mines that had been nationalized in 1971.[14] Other members of the Chicago team reorganized the antiquated national health care system to encourage the formation of private health care plans, abandoning the previous government monopoly on the income from the compulsory medical contribution levied on all salaries. The government also began a program to permit the creation of private universities and to transfer control of primary education to the local municipalities. The power to regulate professional standards and charges was taken away from the professional organizations (*colegios*), which had been the official representatives of doctors, lawyers, engineers, architects, and the like. Most important, Piñera himself engineered a complete overhaul of the social security system which resulted in the transfer of the compulsory social security contributions to private pension fund administrators (AFP) organized by banks and financial groups, including foreign investors. Instead of a standard pension distributed to all (and often sharply reduced by inflation), the AFP pensions depended on the individual contributions and on the investments made by the pension agency (although the latter were subject to public regulation as to their safety). The contributors could transfer their pension savings from one agency to another at will, thus introducing an element of competition, although contributions were compulsory and pension fund investments were regulated by the government. A government program remained only for the very poor and for those nearing retirement who opted not to join the private system. (The cost of pensions for the latter group artificially boosted the social expenditures of the Pinochet government in the 1980s.)

The resemblance of the AFP system to the American individual retirement account (IRA) was obvious, although the difference was that it completely replaced the public social security program. *Forbes* magazine (Oct. 28, 1991) argued that the Chilean system, which had produced annual returns of 13 percent, 30 percent of which were being invested in Chilean stocks, was preferable to the U.S. Social Security Program, which was invested entirely in government bonds. *Forbes* noted that the idea of a private system was not Chilean but American, principally a product of the Chicago free-market school. In an interview with Piñera on his television program, *Firing Line,* William Buckley advocated a similar wholesale conversion of the American system, citing the success of the Chilean program. The decentralization and privatization of education also was influenced by the American model, and the private health care Institutos de Salud Previsional (ISAPRES), which by the end of the decade enrolled 2.5 million Chileans, bore a distinct resemblance to Blue Cross/Blue Shield programs in the United States. The programs were criticized because they benefited mainly the middle and upper classes, who could pay more for education and health and could contribute more to their retirement, but defenders of the modernizations argued that they produced more efficiency and competitiveness in what had been notoriously inefficient and bureaucratic public services.

The 1980 Constitution

For students of the politics of the Pinochet government, the new civilian ministers and the structural reforms that were being carried out marked the triumph of the *blandos,* those who wished to liberalize and constitutionalize the regime, over the hard-line *duros,* who favored an authoritarian corporatist mobilization regime based on a nationalist civic-military movement. A similar struggle had been taking place within the Committee for the Study of a New Constitution, which had been formed shortly after the coup. At the outset, corporatist-nationalist hard-liners seemed to dominate it, especially with the resignation of the members that had sympathies with the Christian Democratic or Radical parties such as Alejandro Silva Bascuñán, Enrique Evans, and Jorge Ovalle. The committee moved at a snail's pace, partly because of internal conflicts and partly because Pinochet was in no hurry to move in this area until he had consolidated his control. However, with the announcement at Chacarillas of Pinochet's quasi timetable in mid-1977 calling for a constitutional plebiscite in 1980, the committee began to move more rapidly. On November 10, 1977, the committee received a message from the president outlining the general principles that he wished the new constitution to embody. It directed the members to prepare an entirely new document, rather than amending the 1925 constitution. It also called for the institutionalization of a special role for the armed forces in protecting "the basic principles of institutionality" and recommended the outlawing of "doctrines, groups, and persons of totalitarian inspiration," the direct appointment of a number of senators by either the president or functional groups, and the guarantee of a free-enterprise economy as a bulwark against an "enslaving and omnipotent state." Reflecting the views of Jaime Guzmán, a member of the committee who was reported to have assisted the minister of justice in writing the message, it also spoke of the need to involve consultative groups representing the organized community which could act as intermediate organizations between the individual and the state, in accordance with the principle of subsidiarity.[15]

In July 1978 the committee presented a 301-page essay on constitutional law as its report, and in October this was followed by a draft constitution that closely followed the 1977 instructions—but, significantly, lacked any transitional provisions concerning the method and timing of the adoption of the constitution.

In September 1975, Pinochet had created an advisory Council of State made up of "representatives" of various social, educational, and functional groups as well as all former presidents. (Eduardo Frei announced that he would not participate, but his predecessor, Jorge Alessandri, who had been president from 1958 until 1964, agreed to serve and was chosen as its chairman.) In fact, the council did very little in its first years, but it acquired importance at this point because Pinochet asked it to review the committee draft. The committee also asked for advice from (mostly conservative) groups in the community. The Christian Democrats had taken the lead in organizing a group of constitutional experts which included future president Patricio Aylwin and Professor Silva Bascuñán, who had resigned from the committee. Referred to as the "Group of 24," it issued its own report, indicating its disagreement with the draft and calling for a constitutional assembly to draw up a draft that was representative of all currents (see *Hoy,* Oct. 17–23, 1979).

Former president Alessandri had his own ideas about what should be in the new constitution. (He had originally favored amending the 1925 document, which had been written under the auspices of his father, Arturo Alessandri.) When the Council of State's draft was given to Pinochet in mid-1980, it differed in significant respects from the committee's proposal. It reduced the length of the presidential term from eight years to six, strengthened the power of the president over the armed forces, and proposed that civilians be added to the National Security Council, at the time made up of the military commanders, so as to give it a civilian majority. It also added transitional provisions calling for a Congress appointed in 1980 by the president for a five-year period, with full congressional and presidential elections in 1985.

When the Alessandri draft was presented to Pinochet (officially it was forwarded to the junta on July 21, 1980, but Pinochet received it on June 26), he turned it over for massive revision to a seven-person working group, composed of Sergio Fernández, the minister of the interior; Monica Madariaga, the minister of justice (and Pinochet's daughter-in-law); representatives of the legal departments of the four armed services; and General Santiago Sinclair, the head of Pinochet's general staff. They worked feverishly to return it to its original form. They reinstated the eight-year presidential term and the military majority on the National Security Council (leaving five cabinet ministers as members without the right to vote), made constitutional amendments more difficult, and put two representatives of the National Security Council on the Constitutional Tribunal. In less than two weeks they made a total of 175 changes in the Alessandri text.

At the end of July, Pinochet also presented Interior Minister Fernández with a new draft set of provisions governing the transitional period which he said had already been approved by the junta. It replaced the five-year transition of the Alessandri draft with one of sixteen years, extending Pinochet's mandate until 1997. When the chairman of the constitutional committee saw the draft, he argued that sixteen years without presidential elections was too long and would be used by the opposition to defeat the constitution in the upcoming plebiscite. When his arguments were presented to the full junta, Pinochet agreed to divide the sixteen-year period in half, with a plebiscite on his continuation in power after eight years. To distinguish between the two terms, he also agreed to have congressional elections in 1990. The members of the junta also insisted that a provision should guarantee that, like Pinochet, they would be exempt from the four-year limit on the terms of the military commanders contained in the main body of the constitution.

The final and considerably altered version of the constitution was announced to the Chilean public on August 10, and a plebiscite on both the constitution and the election of Pinochet for an eight-year term beginning March 11, 1981, was scheduled for the seventh anniversary of the coup, September 11, 1980. The main body of the constitution included Article 8 banning "any person or group that aims to propagate doctrines against the family [or] propounds violence or a conception of society of a totalitarian character or based on the class struggle" as illicit and unconstitutional. Those judged by the Constitutional Tribunal to fit this definition would lose their rights to hold political office or positions in education, the media, or professional and trade union groups for ten years. It also provided for the election in 1989 of a lower house of 120 deputies and a senate with 26 senators, 2 from each of the thirteen regions of Chile, plus 9 appointed senators, most of them named by the president or the armed services. Presidential elections were to occur in two rounds, with a runoff between the two front runners if no one received a majority in the first round, and the legislative powers of the Congress were restricted, especially in financial matters. Reflecting perhaps the influence of U.S. constitutional practice, the Constitutional Tribunal was to have broad powers, including (as does not take place in the United States) the ability to review legislation before it is promulgated. The draft also included a type of separation of powers for the 1981–89 period, since the junta would act as legislature during the first presidential term but Pinochet would be replaced by the army general next in seniority, with the understanding that he could be removed at any time by the president in favor of the next-ranking general. Article 24 of the transitional provisions gave the president power to declare all states of emergency, arrest and detain citizens for limited periods, limit freedom of the media and assembly, expel or prohibit the entry of subversives, and send anyone into internal exile for a period of up to three months ("relegation"—a practice that was already being used). Parties and party activity were outlawed until a new party statute was adopted. The last transitional article provided that if the president lost the 1989 plebiscite, he would continue in office for an additional year and presidential elections would coincide with the congressional elections already contemplated in the main body of the text.[16]

In the month before the plebiscite, the opposition operated under considerable limitations. While the Christian Democrats had had a weekly magazine, *Hoy,* since 1977, they had no daily newspaper, and although they owned one radio station and had access to another owned by the Catholic church, they were denied access to television. (The Catholic University channel offered them time for a message by former president Frei, but the price was $170,000.) One mass meeting opposing the constitution, at which Frei spoke, was held in Santiago, but it was marred by pro-Allende chanting (some said organized by the CNI) which was audible over the radio transmission. All other rallies were forbidden. The Catholic bishops issued a statement describing the conditions for a free vote. They insisted that a plebiscite should not mix different questions with a single response (as the plebiscite on the constitution and Pinochet's election did), that there should be equitable access to the media for all currents of opinion, and that there should be guarantees of the accuracy and fairness of the vote. None of these conditions was met by the plebiscite procedures.

The plebiscite was carried out, as in the 1978 "consultation," on the basis of identification cards rather than an electoral list, and the chairmen of the voting places were selected by the government-appointed mayors, so that in many lower-class areas known to be antigovernment the elections were carried out under the direction of chairmen from outside the district. The press was barred from the count, and the opposition claimed that in some areas there were more voters than the entire population recorded in the census. Abstentions were counted as Yes votes. The result was a considerable victory for Pinochet, with 67 percent voting Yes (including 1.3 percent abstaining, who were counted as favorable) and 30 percent voting No.

Immediately following the vote, Jorge Alessandri resigned from the Council of State but did not publish his letter of resignation, which complained of the rejection of his constitutional proposals. A well-known television announcer, Patricio Bañados, was fired for refusing to read an attack on Frei. (He was later to reappear on the opposition television programs before the 1988 plebiscite.) Retired General Leigh is supposed to have told a leading Christian Democrat before the vote that government circles had told him that they had established 60 to 65 percent Yes and 30 to 40 percent No as the most credible result to be achieved in the plebiscite.

At the time of the 1980 plebiscite, the Communist Party in exile initiated a dramatic change of policy. Before 1973 the party had supported the peaceful road (*vía pacífica*) to socialism, and since 1973 it had been urging the establishment of a common "Anti-fascist Front" against Pinochet. Now the Communists began making speeches and issuing communiqués that referred to "all forms of combat, including acute violence" and "popular rebellion."[17] There was considerable speculation as to the reason for the change. Some observers related it to the recent Sandinista victory in Nicaragua, which had been the result of an armed uprising. Others saw it as a response to grass-roots pressure from young activists in the shantytowns. A third reason that has been cited was the party's increasingly close relations with the Movement of the Revolutionary Left (MIR) and the division in 1979 of the Chilean Socialist Party, the Communists' former ally, into a moderate social democratic wing that included—surprisingly—Carlos Altamirano, and a group headed by Clodomiro Alymeyda which still identified itself as Marxist-Leninist. The Communist shift meant that it would become increasingly isolated from the other parties, which embraced nonviolence. From the point of view of the strongly anti-Communist orientation of U.S. policymakers in the 1980s, the isolation of the Communist Party made it easier to support the anti-Pinochet opposition, since it rejected the Communists' endorsement of violence as the way to end the Pinochet dictatorship.

In Pinochet's press conference after his victory in the plebiscite, he singled out the United States for special criticism, urging it to leave Chile alone. He noted that it did not cost the United States a dollar to get rid of the Communists in 1973, adding, "But when we need the United States, instead of helping us, they beat on us" (*New York Times,* Sept. 13, 1980). Riding on the crest of political and economic success, he was now more willing to take on the United States by name. A year earlier he had criticized countries that, "although inspired by noble principles of freedom and human dignity," were not aware of "the risks of exporting systems . . . alien to the reality of other nations" and applied "a new doctrine with a selective and discriminatory character which deprives it of all moral force."[18]

Chile was being increasingly cited in the U.S. debate concerning the Carter human rights policy which had followed the publication of Jeane Kirkpatrick's article "Dictatorships and Double Standards" in the November 1979 *Commentary* magazine. The Letelier sanctions led the Chilean foreign minister, Hernán Cubillos, to accuse the United States of "old-fashioned imperialism" because of its pressure on the Chilean government to overrule the Chilean Supreme Court's decision rejecting the plea-bargaining evidence of Michael Townley. Cubillos's complaint was echoed in a letter to the *New York Times* (Dec. 22, 1979) from the director of foreign policy of a conservative think tank, the Heritage Foundation, attacking the pressures on Chile as "diplomatic blackmail" and based on a double standard. As the 1980 campaign heated up, the Reagan camp picked up the complaint, citing Iran and Nicaragua as examples in which right-wing authoritarian regimes had been undermined by the Carter administration and replaced by totalitarian governments.

Nevertheless, the human rights issue would not go away, and the Letelier case hit the news again in November 1980 as a federal court awarded the Letelier and Moffitt families $5 million in damages for "wrongful death." In Chile, too, the judicial investigation of fifteen skeletons found in a lime kiln at Lonquén, outside Santiago, in December 1978 indicated that the victims had been killed in early October 1973. The April 1978 amnesty blocked further judicial action, but a book entitled *Lonquén* managed to avoid censorship and was published in 1980 by Máximo Pacheco, one of the organizers of the Chilean Human Rights Commission.[19] Conservatives in the United States continued to look for improvement in the human rights situation in Chile, but the United Nations, the OAS, and private human rights organizations kept finding evidence of further repression. It was clear that the institutionalization that had taken place between 1978 and 1980 had not resulted in the establishment of the rule of law, but only a flawed constitutionalism that was undermined by the "transitional" powers of the president in Article 24, the ideological proscriptions of

Article 8, and the impunity with which the CNI could carry out arbitrary detentions, torture, and occasional assassinations.

Conclusions

What general conclusions may one draw from this account of the politics of the Carter administration?

1. U.S. pressure was a major factor in the reorganization of the instruments of repression in Chile. The CNI was an improvement over the DINA, in that it did not resort to disappearance as an instrument of policy. Torture and detentions were still used, but some legal limits—not always observed—were placed on CNI activities, especially after the adoption of the 1980 constitution, which in its transitional provisions limited the right of detention without trial to five to fifteen days (Article 24).

2. The release of most political prisoners in 1976 and 1977 was also related to the Carter human rights policy. They were forced to go into exile, but this was preferable to the harsh and sometimes murderous conditions in which they had been detained. The congressionally mandated annual human rights reports gave international publicity to regime abuses and put the U.S. embassy in touch with opposition groups through its human rights officer.

3. The Letelier case added to the pressure on the regime and led to a considerable worsening of U.S.-Chilean relations—although it also produced a major concession by Chile, the release of Michael Townley, which provided major information about the conduct of the DINA and the assassination itself. It would continue as an irritant in U.S.-Chilean relations until early 1991. A tantalizing question that remains is how much Pinochet knew and approved of the assassination effort.

4. The cutoff in military aid through the 1976 Kennedy Amendment embittered the Chilean army, even though the Pentagon continued to promote friendly relations. Although adopted before the Carter administration came to power, it was intensified under Carter as a symbol of the new U.S. emphasis on human rights. It led Chile to buy arms in other countries, especially Israel, France, and South Africa, and to develop what was to become a significant domestic arms industry.

5. The cutoffs and negative votes on economic aid were largely symbolic in their impact, since they did not prevent Chile from securing loans from international financial institutions and ample resources from private banks, although at a higher cost. For good reasons (rejected by some liberals in the United States), the administration was hesitant to prohibit private lending. Those reasons included doubt that such cutoffs would lead to democracy, unwillingness to interfere in the U.S. private sector, and questions as to the negative impact of such cutoffs on the poor and needy in Chile. While the economic pressures do not seem to have ended human rights abuses, they disassociated the United States from the worst abuses, and they expressed a new U.S. commitment—not always consistently applied—to the protection of human rights. Critics, however, have argued that punitive sanctions are often counterproductive and that except in extreme cases, publicizing abuses through the annual State Department report and giving moral, and possibly financial, support to dissidents is more effective.[20]

6. The most effective single instrument of outside pressure did not involve U.S. government action at all. The threat of a boycott by the American unions concerned over the repression of labor produced an immediate policy response from the Chilean government to satisfy their criticisms. The American unions were probably satisfied more easily than they should have been, but the reemergence of the unions in Chile was to have an effect in 1983 when the copper workers initiated what became a nationwide protest against the Pinochet government.

7. The experience and example of the United States was an important factor in Chilean economic policy and in the reforms of social and educational programs, which began to be introduced in the late 1970s. They would have a significant impact on the thinking and habits of Chileans. The government may not have been successful in changing the politics of Chile, but it did encourage by its policies more experimentation, entrepreneurship, self-reliance, and private-sector activity than had existed previously. This was accompanied by what turned out to be an excessive optimism in pro-government rhetoric about the transformation of Chile into another Taiwan or even Belgium, but it did mean a profound alteration of Chilean society.

8. Initially the economic opening had a negative impact on the lower classes, through increases in unemployment and cutbacks in health, educa-

tion, and housing. These were documented most persuasively by opposition think tanks such as CIEPLAN (Corporación de Investigaciones Económicas para Latinoamerica) and FLACSO (Facultad Latinoamericana de Ciencias Sociales), which received funding from U.S., Canadian, and European foundations. However, by 1980 there was evidence that the "boom" had reached the lower classes as well, as per capita income levels finally reached, and in 1981 exceeded, those achieved during the Allende period. The Chicago boys' policy seemed to have worked—and as Chile engaged in an orgy of consumerism, no one asked how long it would last.

9. While the human rights problem overshadowed all the other aspects of U.S.-Chilean relations during the Carter administration, significant elements in U.S. society and government approved of the economic changes that the civilian technocrats introduced during this period. Although critics argued that such changes were only possible under an authoritarian regime (an argument that was to be disproved in the 1980s), the privatization of government enterprises and social services, the reduction in the size of the government bureaucracy, the opening of domestic industry and agriculture, and the rationalization of tariffs and exchange rates were measures that many economists and public administrators endorsed. Internationally there was discussion of the "Chilean model" and debate on whether it required a dictatorship and authoritarian control of labor to be implemented. Many Americans who abhorred the repression in Chile were favorably impressed by the changes in economic and social policies which the regime had introduced. Thus there was a certain ambivalent attitude toward Chile, which became even more evident following the election of Ronald Reagan in 1980.

6

Reagan I: The Rise and Fall
of Quiet Diplomacy

RONALD REAGAN entered the White House on January 20, 1981, determined to alter the Carter foreign policy in many ways. One of those was in the area of human rights policy. Reagan and his foreign policy advisers accepted the argument of Jeane Kirkpatrick, whom Reagan appointed to head the U.S. delegation to the U.N., that public U.S. pressure on authoritarian regimes friendly to the United States which engaged in human rights violations "violated the strategic and economic interests of the United States" ("Dictatorships and Double Standards," *Commentary*, November 1979). As Reagan was taking office, Kirkpatrick published another, stronger article, "U.S. Security and Latin America" (*Commentary*, January 1981), which accused the Carter administration of bringing down the government of Anastasio Somoza because of the human rights pressures it exerted, only to see it replaced by a Marxist-Leninist Sandinista dictatorship.

The change in U.S. policy toward right-wing regimes did not go uncontested, however. Despite Reagan's substantial electoral victory, the House of Representatives was still controlled by the Democrats, and this was to be an important deterrent to carrying out the policy reversal with respect to Chile. Moreover, the administration placed special emphasis on the struggle against worldwide terrorism. Most terrorist groups were leftist in orientation, but in the still-pending Letelier assassination case in Chile, the terrorism came from the right. In addition, the first priority of the administration's Latin American policy was the effort to oppose the spread of the left in Central America, where it now controlled the government of Nicaragua and through a strong guerrilla movement threatened the government of El Salvador. Part of that opposition—and part of the administration's overall Cold War strategy—was to stress the ideological differences between Communist totalitarianism and Western democracy. As that stress became more pronounced, it was to affect the new policy toward the Pinochet regime—and at the beginning of the second Reagan administration, to reverse it—so that by 1985 the U.S. government was engaged in public criticism of, and economic pressure upon, the Chilean government, and by early 1986, it was taking the lead in introducing resolutions critical of Chile in the U.N. Human Rights Commission.

How and why did this change take place? This chapter attempts to describe and evaluate the change from little U.S. concern with the human rights conduct of a friendly authoritarian regime—or alternatively, a policy of "quiet diplomacy" which, it was argued, was more effective than public criticism in improving human rights—to a highly visible campaign in support of human rights and a return to democracy in Chile.

Besides the increased emphasis on the worldwide conflict between democracy and dictatorship, a number of other reasons have been cited for the policy shift. One that links that shift to Cold War considerations emphasizes the administration's fear of a polarization in Chile which could lead to an uprising not unlike the one that had taken place in Nicaragua, in which the Communists could take the lead. A second explanation emphasizes personal factors—personnel changes in the State Department—at the beginning of the second Reagan administration. A third looks to the internal situation in Chile, especially the continued intransigence of Pinochet and the emergence of a viable non-Communist opposition coalition. A fourth explanation links the shift to a continent-wide, indeed worldwide, movement from authoritarianism to democracy in the mid-1980s. A fifth explanation emphasizes the institutionalized concern with human rights in Congress and in the Human Rights Bureau of the State Department, as well as the legislative requirements of annual State Department reports on human rights and evaluations of foreign governments in connection with legislation regarding bilateral and multilateral aid. Finally, one must also consider the attitudes of informed American public opinion as expressed in editorials of major newspapers that kept the spotlight on Chile—and continued to urge greater U.S. activism in the area of human rights and the promotion of democracy.

None of these explanations by itself is persuasive, but it may be useful to review the course of U.S. relations with Chile between 1981 and 1985 to attempt to assess the persuasiveness and impact of each. This examination is also of broader interest for the evaluation of U.S. policy, since it provides a case study of the interaction of the goals of the promotion of U.S. ideals in the contemporary world and a more narrowly focused "Kissingerian" concern with security interests, especially the East-West struggle.

"Normalization" of U.S.-Chilean Relations

The first effects on Chilean policy of the change from Carter to Reagan were felt in February when the new administration announced that the sanctions imposed on Chile by the Carter administration as a result of its conduct in the Letelier investigation—exclusion from Export-Import Bank loans and from participation in the U.S. Navy Unitas annual maneuvers— were to be lifted. The explanatory statement on the Export-Import Bank noted that the exclusion had also hurt U.S. business and that the actions had not been intended to be permanent. Chilean participation in the navy maneuvers was defended because of its contribution to hemispheric defense and to the control of southern sea lanes of communication.

The Chilean section of the State Department's February 1981 annual report on human rights argued that "the human rights situation in Chile has improved significantly since 1977" and noted correctly that social spending was more focused on the poorer sections of the population. It did not note that overall social spending had been sharply reduced or that according to the 1981 U.N. Human Rights Commission Report on Chile, the number of arbitrary arrests and detentions had increased dramatically. At the end of February, the U.S. representatives to the U.N. Human Rights Commission voted against a resolution deploring the continuing systematic use of torture, arguing that Chile was being singled out for special attention when its record was no worse than that of many other countries (*New York Times,* Feb. 27, 1981). The United States was joined in its negative vote by Argentina, Brazil, and Uruguay, all governments under military control. On similar grounds, the administration also opposed the extension of the mandate of the special rapporteur on Chile, who had submitted annual human rights reports on Chile to the U.N. General Assembly each year.

In March, the United States invited Fernando Matthei, the air force member of the ruling junta, to visit the United States. Also in March, retired General Vernon Walters testified to the Subcommittee on Interamerican Affairs of the House Foreign Affairs Committee that it was necessary to improve relations with the Chilean navy because of the danger of "the projection of Soviet power" on a global scale. Walters also argued that training programs should be initiated with the Latin American military because it was "drifting away" from the United States.[1] The Walters testimony was delivered at a hearing (*U.S. Economic Sanctions against Chile*) which also gave extensive attention to the unresolved problems in U.S.-Chilean relations created by the refusal of the Chileans to extradite or prosecute the murderers of Orlando Letelier. The hearings were held because the administration was beginning to press for a repeal of the Kennedy Amendment of June 1976, which had cut off all military aid and sales to Chile. The terrorism issue was raised when Congressman Don Bonker accused the Reagan administration of aligning the United States with a regime that "practices, aids, and abets state terrorism" (4).

The hearings were held one day before the inauguration of Augusto Pinochet as "constitutional" president of Chile. Pinochet took advantage of the event to take possession of La Moneda, the presidential palace, which had been bombed on the day of the coup. He formally entered a tastefully reconstructed and remodeled palace that also included a garage under the adjoining Constitution Square, which had been designed to provide him and his family with protection in case of an assault on the palace. (The opposition called it "the bunker," recalling Anastasio Somoza's refuge in Managua.) Despite the criticisms of the September 1980 plebiscite, Pinochet now had an additional source of legitimacy besides his opposition to Communism and his promise of prosperity—an operative constitution designed to appeal to Chilean legalism. He also pointed to the fact that both the United States and Great Britain now had strongly anti-Communist and free-market–oriented governments. ("Seven years ago we were almost alone. Today we are part of a clear worldwide tendency. And I say to you, ladies and gentlemen, it is not Chile that has changed its point of view," *El Mercurio*, Mar. 12, 1981.)

The Reagan administration did not press the repeal of the ban on military aid to Chile, because its first priority was now to secure congressional approval of a substantial military aid package for El Salvador, and it needed the support of the chairman of the House Subcommittee on Interamerican Affairs, Michael Barnes, who opposed repeal. Reagan sent General Vernon Walters to Chile for conversations with Pinochet and received the new Chilean foreign minister, René Rojas. Rojas also had conversations with Alexander Haig, the secretary of state, and with Jeane Kirkpatrick, who had already given an interview to the press praising the adoption of the 1980 constitution in Chile as a return to "government by law" (see *U.S. News and World Report*, Mar. 2, 1981, 50).

In May, the resistance to the change in the administration's policy on human rights was extended to the Senate when the Foreign Relations Committee held hearings on the nomination of Ernest Lefever, the head of a conservative Washington think tank, to the post of assistant secretary of state for human rights. The hearings revealed an attitude toward human rights which was the mirror image of the supposed inconsistency that the Reaganites had criticized in the Carter regime. Lefever expressed a vigorous opposition to Communist violations of human rights but was hesitant to condemn the human rights record of conservative regimes allied with the United States. Lefever's testimony was made all the more dramatic by the presence in the audience of Jacobo Timerman, an Argentine journalist who had just published a searing eye-witness account of torture, cruelty, and murder in the prisons of the Argentine military regime, *Prisoner without a Name, Cell without a Number*. When the committee voted 13–4 against Lefever, he withdrew his nomination at the administration's request. The post was left vacant until the end of October, when it was filled by the appointment of Elliott Abrams, who was determined from the outset to follow a different policy—with important consequences for Chile.

The differences between the administration and the Congress on policy toward Chile surfaced again in July when administration representatives to international financial institutions such as the World Bank and the Interamerican Development Bank were directed to vote in favor of loans to Chile, reversing the Carter administration policy of abstention or negative votes. Congressman Tom Harkin, who had been responsible for the 1977 law that required U.S. representatives to vote against loans to governments that "engage in a consistent pattern of gross violations of internationally recognized human rights," denounced the action, citing the large increase in the number of arrests and arbitrary detentions in Chile in recent months. A subcommittee of the House Banking Committee held a hearing (*Human Rights and U.S. Policy in the Multilateral Development Banks*) on July 21 and 23, focusing on Argentina, Paraguay, Uruguay, and Chile—in the Chilean case discussing a $161 million loan for highway construction which had been approved on July 8. The members of the subcommittee complained that there had been no consultation with the Banking Committee, which had jurisdiction over Treasury actions, and they heard testimony on human rights violations in all four countries but took no further action. Defending the administration's approach, State Department representatives submitted testimony by Undersecretary of State Walter Stoessel which argued that while support for human rights was "an indispensable element of the American approach," it should not "be isolated and pursued as if it were the only goal in [U.S.] relations with other countries." Stoessel described U.S. policy as "one of effective pragmatism . . . directed toward attaining real results."[2]

A month later, in late August, Jeane Kirkpatrick visited Chile. She had what she described as a "most pleasant" conversation with Pinochet, expressing the desire of the Reagan administration "to fully normalize . . . relations with Chile." Citing lack of time, she did not attend a scheduled meeting with Jaime Castillo, the chairman of the Chilean Human Rights Commission. Two days after her visit Castillo and three other leading Chilean politicians were expelled by Pinochet—in Castillo's case for the second time—for signing a letter protesting the arrest of two labor leaders. Kirkpatrick met Castillo a month later, but the signal that had been delivered in Chile was clear. Pinochet did not have to fear U.S. reprisals for human rights violations. The case was cited in September by the *New York Times* when it published its fourth editorial of the year denouncing the change in policy toward Chile (Sept. 26, 1981).

Shortly after Kirkpatrick's visit, it was announced that the new ambassador to Chile, replacing George Landau, a professional foreign service officer, would be James Theberge, a colleague of Kirkpatrick's at Georgetown University who had previously served as ambassador to Anastasio Somoza in Nicaragua. (His principal scholarly credentials were books and articles on Soviet influence in Latin America.) When asked about Castillo's expulsion, Theberge was quoted as saying that it was "absolutely legal, and does not have anything to do with the policy of human rights in Chile."[3]

Just before his appointment as assistant secretary of state for human rights and humanitarian affairs, Elliott Abrams, then assistant secretary of state for international organization affairs, drafted an "eyes-only" memorandum for the secretary of state which stated that "human rights is at the core of our foreign policy."[4] As was evident in his introduction to the February 1982 edition of the State Department Country Reports on Human Rights, Abrams was determined to follow a more consistent human rights policy that would be vigorous in denouncing human rights violations by both right and left.

Prodded by the Chileans and by conservative Senator Jesse Helms, with whom the Chileans were in active contact, the administration made an attempt in the fall of 1981 to lift the Kennedy Amendment sanctions. Obsessed with Central America, the administration began to encourage the Chileans to work with the Salvadoran army, which had been given professional training by Chile when it was first established early in the century. In December the *New York Times* reported that former U.S. Green Berets had been approached by representatives of the Chilean government who wished to hire them to work on counterterrorism in El Salvador (*New York Times,* Dec. 9, 1981).

Senator Edward Kennedy worked against the effort to repeal his amendment, citing the latest report by the U.N. special rapporteur on Chile, which quoted figures from the Jesuit magazine *Mensaje* showing a substantial increase in human rights violations.[5] The foreign aid bill as finally adopted in December went through the motions of repealing the 1976 sanctions, but what it gave with one hand, it took away with the other. It tied the resumption of military aid to presidential certification that (1) Chile had made "significant progress" in complying with international human rights standards, (2) military aid would be in the national interest of the United States, and (3) Chile had taken "appropriate steps to cooperate in bringing to justice" those indicted for the murders of Orlando Letelier and Ronni Moffitt (Section 726b of 1981 Foreign Assistance Act). The last condition was to be the most difficult to fulfill, as the Chilean courts took no further action against retired General Manuel Contreras, Colonel Pedro Espinoza, and Captain Armando Fernández Larios, the three Chileans whom the United States had attempted to extradite—although a case involving the 1976 falsification of Chilean passports was reopened by the Chilean Supreme Court and the Letelier family continued to seek the compensation from the Chilean government which had been awarded by the U.S. appeals court in November 1980.

Improvement in human rights would also be difficult to certify, since the Chileans refused to cooperate in this area. In January 1982, Howard Baker, the Republican Senate majority leader, visited Chile and told a press conference, "There are still problems that complicate our relations." He added that he preferred not to go into detail about his discussions with President Pinochet and observed that the success or failure of the policy of "quiet diplomacy depends in great measure on how other countries, including Chile, respond to it" (*El Mercurio,* Jan. 11, 1982). In February the president of the Public Employees Union, Tucapel Jiménez, was found on the side of a highway with his throat cut, and in March the assistant secretary of state for Latin America, Thomas Enders, visited Santiago and noted that a decision on the Letelier case was a prerequisite to the renewal of military aid (*El Mercurio,* International Edition, Mar. 11–17, 1982). Both the Letelier case and the murder of Jiménez were cited by the *New York Times* in an editorial entitled "Quiet Diplomacy, Deaf Chile" on April 5, 1982.

Later in the same month, Argentina seized the British-owned Falkland (Malvinas) Islands, which it had claimed ever since the British expelled a small group of Argentines in the early nineteenth century. The Beagle Channel controversy with Chile was well on the way to a solution, but there were reports that the military government of Argentina, in its search for a dramatic gesture to rally popular support in the midst of an economic collapse, had considered an attack in that area before deciding on the Falklands adventure. Chile went through the motions of support for Argentina at the outset, but, along with the English-speaking members of the

Organization of American States, it abstained on OAS votes endorsing the Argentine claims (Apr. 26, 1982) and condemning the British attack (May 29, 1982). There were also unconfirmed reports that the British had been able to use Chilean airfields during the conflict. (Relations with Great Britain, broken by the Labour government in the late 1970s as a result of Chilean mistreatment of Sheila Cassidy, a British citizen, had been reestablished by the Conservative government of Margaret Thatcher.)

Collapse of "The Boom"

The attention of Chileans was not focused on the Falklands but on the domestic economy. Beginning with the failure of a major sugar company in 1981, Chile had been shaken by a series of bankruptcies and now by rumors of impending bank failures due to bad loans, often to firms that, along with the banks, were owned by the conglomerates that had emerged as a result of the sell-off of state enterprises after the 1973 coup. The "boom" was over, and the foreign banks that had showered loans on Chile began to be dubious. Yet Sergio de Castro, finance minister since 1976, insisted on maintaining a fixed exchange rate of 39 pesos to the dollar as he had done for three years—while the peso became more and more overvalued. He also refused to do anything about the large number of dollar loans (83 percent of Chile's foreign debt was now private) taken out internationally by individual Chileans. He insisted that a process of "automatic adjustment" would sort things out and that in accordance with free-market principles the private loans were at the risk of the borrowers. By early 1982, as the economy contracted, bankruptcies increased (there were 810 bankruptcies in 1982), and a run on the country's foreign reserves occurred in anticipation of a devaluation, Pinochet finally decided to fire de Castro and, just after denying that he would do so, devalue the peso.[6]

By mid-1982 it was clear that the Chilean economy was in deep depression. The gross national product had dropped by nearly 14 percent, industrial production was down 20 percent, and unemployment had risen to 30 percent of the work force, if those enrolled in the government "make-work" Minimum Employment Program (PEM) were included. The government had to take over a number of leading banks to prevent them from failing (leading wags to speak of the "Chicago way to socialism"). Many textile companies went bankrupt, reducing the number of such firms from 190 to 41 and costing 40,000 jobs. In the metal industry a third of the workers were laid off, and sales dropped by 47 percent (*Wall Street Journal*, July 14 and 27, 1982).

The government blamed rising international interest rates produced by the anti-inflationary policy of the Reagan administration, as well as the worldwide recession, which had reduced the price of copper from $1.33 a pound in 1980 to a forty-year low (in real terms) of 59 cents a pound in early 1982. However, critics pointed out that the fixed exchange rate had made Chilean exports uncompetitive and encouraged Chileans to take out dollar loans to buy foreign consumer goods like the Japanese cars that had flooded the market. They also noted that the reduction of tariff protection from an average of 100 percent in 1973 to a uniform (except for some automobiles) 10 percent rate had destroyed much of Chilean industry. Chilean indebtedness, most of it private borrowing, had soared, and the government was now forced to guarantee repayment if it did not wish Chilean creditworthiness to suffer. To top it all off, the Mexican government announced in August that it could not continue to pay interest on its international debt, and the worldwide debt crisis, much of it involving Latin American countries, made it very difficult to secure new international loans.

For the first time in a number of years Chile went to the International Monetary Fund for loans, and in August the Chilean peso was allowed to float against the dollar. Half of the outstanding loans were in actual or threatened default, and to avoid a collapse of the banking system the Central Bank announced that it would take over these debts, placing the banks in receivership and giving them ten years to pay off the resulting indebtedness to the government. Critics observed that the Pinochet government believed in "the privatization of profit, and the socialization of debt."

Middle-class borrowers suddenly saw their debt repayments of loans denominated in dollars increase dramatically as a result of devaluation, although the government made dollars available at a special exchange rate. As the depression began to affect professionals such as engineers (40 percent unemployed) and architects (60 percent unemployed), the upper classes and the economic right (which had never been happy with the opening to foreign competition) began to complain about the lack of progress on the promised transition to civilian rule, especially in the drafting of the promised Statute of Political Parties. Pinochet's response was to attack the *fronda aristocrática* ("aristocratic clique," a reference to a 1928 book by Alberto Edwards which described the opposition of the Chilean oligarchy in the nineteenth century to the growth of the central government), and he threatened to take action "against speculators and oligarchs." In January 1983 he jailed the head of the powerful Vial group, as well as his former finance minister Rolf Lüders. The government increased spending on public works, limited wage increases (which had been indexed to inflation), provided loans to businesses in trouble, and raised tariffs on a temporary basis, but the crisis continued.

With so much economic suffering, why was there still no public protest? The most important and respected opposition leader, former president Eduardo Frei, died in January 1982, just before the crisis hit, and the new head of the Christian Democratic Party, Gabriel Valdés, did not initially have the same broad appeal. Human rights, student, and labor leaders were subject to warnings, temporary detention—sometimes accompanied by torture—and legal action involving expulsion from the country or three-month sentences to internal exile ("relegation"). The leaders of the left parties were dead or out of the country. And as thousands were losing their jobs each day, there did not seem to be much of a basis for an opposition mass movement against Pinochet.

U.S. Support for the "Democratic Revolution"

On the U.S. side, it was increasingly clear that quiet diplomacy was not succeeding as a way to deal with human rights violations in Chile. In addition, for reasons that had nothing to do with Chile, administration policy was shifting in the direction of more public U.S. support for democracy. In June 1982, President Reagan made a speech before the British Parliament in which he urged the West to support the "democratic revolution" in the contemporary world and committed the United States to fostering "the infrastructure of democracy, the system of a free press, unions, political parties, universities which allows a people to choose their own way . . . to reconcile their differences through peaceful means." According to U.S. policymakers, the speech was made in an effort to change the "warmonger" image of the president which had developed in Europe in response to Reagan pressures for modernization of nuclear missilery in the NATO alliance. It was also the product of planning for an ideological offensive which had been going on in the United States Information Agency (USIA). The bureaucratic initiatives that resulted from the speech quickly became linked to an earlier effort to establish a publicly funded Democracy Program as a bipartisan organization under private auspices to disburse funds to promote democracy overseas, in particular to political parties, unions, and business groups. The result was the establishment by Congress in 1983 of the National Endowment for Democracy to fund projects to promote democracy around the world.

Another result of the June speech was greater visibility for the promotion of democracy in U.S. international relations. Statements by President Reagan and Secretary of State George Shultz (who had succeeded Haig in July 1982) began to link democracy and human rights more explicitly. When President Reagan took a trip to Costa Rica, Venezuela, and Brazil in December 1982, he answered a question about U.S. support for democracy by stating:

> The United States places great importance on the development of stable democratic institutions. . . . I believe that U.S. promotion of human rights and support for democracy in the Western hemisphere reinforce each other. History shows that the most effective guarantee of human rights lies in the creation and strengthening of open democratic institutions of government. . . . But we in the United States can only influence; we cannot determine.[7]

In January 1983, Congressman Michael Barnes headed a delegation to Latin American which reviewed the effects of the transition to civilian rule in Argentina on U.S. policy. He reported that the United States was likely to lift the ban on military sales to Argentina but that the situation in Chile did not justify a similar action for that country. Indeed, as head of the Western Hemisphere Affairs Subcommittee of the House Foreign Affairs Committee, Barnes attempted to add a further requirement for the initiation of military aid—that Chile return to civilian rule. Barnes' proposal was adopted by the committee but eliminated at a later stage (*New York Times,* Jan. 23 and Apr. 14, 1983). However, combined with a promise that Senator Charles Percy had made to Senator Kennedy that hearings would be held by the Senate Foreign Relations Committee if the administration attempted to certify Chile, Barnes' continuing opposition made it unlikely that the administration would make such an attempt. Within the administration itself, Elliott Abrams, assistant secretary of state for human rights, was also strongly opposed, even threatening to resign if such an effort were made, as had been repeatedly urged by Ambassador Theberge.

Protests and the Formation of the Democratic Alliance

The beginnings of a shift in U.S. policy toward Chile were the result of the initiation of mass protests against Pinochet in May 1983 and the emergence of a unified centrist-dominated opposition coalition. In early 1983 a group of politicians from the centrist parties established PRODEN, the Project for National Development, to offer an alternative to the Pinochet government. Then, on March 15, a Democratic Manifesto was signed by Gabriel Valdés, head of the Christian Democratic Party, and by members of the Radical, Socialist, Social Democratic, and former Liberal and Conservative parties. It became the basis for the establishment in August of the Democratic Alliance, a coalition of (banned or suspended) political parties that ranged from moderate socialist to ex-conservatives.

It was not the political parties, however, but the powerful copper workers' union that took the lead in organizing the first nationwide mass protests against the regime. The protest was organized by a 29-year-old union leader, Rodolfo Seguel, who had recently been elected president of the copper workers' confederation. In early May, Seguel announced a national strike, but after negotiations with Manifesto leaders, he called instead for a peaceful "protest" that would begin at two in the afternoon and would involve schoolchildren, shopkeepers, bus drivers, and the banging of empty pots (as in December 1971) in darkened houses, as well as the sounding of auto horns at 8 P.M. The government shut down the Christian Democratic radio station that was coordinating the protest, but it was a huge success, although two people were killed by stray bullets in lower-class areas and the police detained six hundred others. The copper mines were occupied by troops, and Seguel was indicted and in June jailed, but another and still larger protest was called by the political parties on June 14. The international press began to compare Seguel to the Polish labor leader Lech Wałesa. Following the June protest, labor, student, and professional groups—including the truckers who had helped to bring down the Allende government—called for a general strike. The strike was only partially successful, and the government made considerable concessions to the economic demands of the truckers, but another day of protest was scheduled for mid-July.

Newspaper reports in the United States (*Washington Post*, July 15, 1983; *Miami Herald*, Aug. 15, 1983) indicated that the protests had led to a reassessment of policy toward Chile within the Reagan administration, one of the results of which was a series of public statements by the State Department against the repression in Chile. After criticizing the arrest of Seguel in June, a much stronger State Department protest was issued in July when three opposition leaders, including Gabriel Valdés, were arrested for printing circulars to publicize the July 12 demonstrations. Valdés was well known in the United States, having been Latin American director of the U.N. Development Program for many years and a prominent participant in the Interamerican Dialogue, a forum organized by Sol Linowitz, former U.S. ambassador to the Organization of American States. Only a month before, Valdés had been received at the State Department. Despite Ambassador Theberge's known sympathies for the Pinochet government, since 1982 the U.S. embassy had been in frequent contact with the opposition leaders (other than the Communists) and in 1983 leading Socialists were invited for the first time to the embassy Independence Day party. In Washington the State Department found the detention and solitary confinements of prominent democratic leaders such as Mr. Valdés "regrettable" and expressed its belief in "the need for moderate leaders on all sides to find ways to establish the basic consensus needed for the transition to democracy sought by the vast majority of Chileans."[8]

American commentators noticed the new critical tone of State Department communiqués and contrasted them with the statements by the newly appointed assistant secretary of state for Latin America, A. Langhorne Motley, at his June 1983 confirmation hearings, in which he had said that elections would be held in Chile "in the next decade" and asserted that the United States could not dictate the timing of elections in that country. When Ambassador Theberge began to meet more intensively with labor and political leaders, there was speculation that the United States was attempting to promote a center-right alliance and advance the date for possible civilian elections. This was reinforced when Theberge gave an interview to the Chilean magazine *Cosas,* reiterating U.S. support for the restoration of full and stable democracy in Chile, "as in other countries of the Southern Cone," a reference to the scheduled elections in Argentina.

Public attention in the United States was drawn to Chile as a result of the protests and of the conviction of a Maryland aviation firm for supplying sonar equipment to Chile in violation of the ban on arms from the United States. Valdés's imprisonment also produced a protest from David Rockefeller, former secretary of state Cyrus Vance, and Sol Linowitz. Congressman Barnes also sent a public letter signed by seventy-one members of Congress to Secretary of State Shultz calling for a public commitment by the United States to "a rapid and peaceful restoration of democracy in Chile."

The pressure on Pinochet seemed to be intensifying, as the opposition called for another protest in August. In response to the manifestations of popular discontent, he had made minor concessions such as allowing the return of a number of exiled Chileans and lifting the censorship of books, but he insisted that he intended to follow the constitutional timetable. Pinochet also used force, calling out eighteen thousand troops to control the capital at the time of the August 11 demonstrations, which resulted in the death of twenty-four people. However, his most important response was to appoint a prominent rightist politician, Sergio Onofre Jarpa, as interior minister, with a mandate to open negotiations with the opposition.

Jarpa had earlier submitted a plan to Pinochet which included a plebiscite on the political parties law and advancing the date for congressional elections, scheduled for 1990.[9] The opposition, now formally constituted as the Democratic Alliance and headed by a rotating chairman but dominated by Gabriel Valdés and the Christian Democrats, was calling for Pinochet's resignation, the convocation of a constitutional convention, and the establishment of a provisional government ("Democracy Now").

As the violence increased with each demonstration, particularly in lower-class areas, the government began to use the specter of a revolution from the shantytowns as a way to recapture some of the support it had lost in the middle and upper classes, where for the first time anti-Pinochet jokes were circulating. On the tenth anniversary of the September 11, 1973, coup—in a ceremony that was attended by Ambassador Theberge but boycotted by the ambassadors from the European Community—Pinochet denounced the "agents of violence." The assassination of the governor of Santiago by members of the Manuel Rodríguez Patriotic Front, a newly formed guerrilla group loosely linked to the Communist Party, was also exploited in the progovernment media. Riot police and water cannon broke up the September protest, but the October gathering was held in a large public park and authorized by the government.

The intensity of the protests was also blunted by the willingness of Jarpa to carry out a public dialogue with the opposition as suggested by the new archbishop of Santiago, Juan Francisco Fresno. (Fresno, regarded as a conservative, had been appointed to succeed retiring Cardinal Raúl Silva Henríquez, a strong opponent of the government. Pinochet's wife is supposed to have exclaimed, "God has answered our prayers," but under Fresno's leadership there continued to be serious tension between the government and the church.) The talks soon revealed, however, that despite Jarpa's own desire for elections, Pinochet was intransigent about maintaining the timetable set out in the 1980 constitution.

On the U.S. side, there was an awareness of the limited effectiveness of U.S. pressures, which had now moved from behind-the-scenes discussions on the need for respect for human rights to public statements against repression and in favor of a peaceful transition to democracy. In early November the Chilean foreign minister complained that the fourteen statements critical of Chile issued by the State Department in 1983 were "excessive" and constituted "interference in Chile's internal affairs."

In October, the Western Hemisphere Subcommittee and the Human Rights and International Organizations subcommittees of the House Foreign Affairs Committee held a joint hearing on human rights in the countries of the Southern Cone. Human rights activists and academics (including this writer) testified concerning the new developments in Chile and urged more vigorous U.S. action in support of the movement toward democracy. Elliott Abrams and James Michel, the deputy assistant secretary of state for Latin America, testified that under Jarpa's tenure as minister of the interior the state of emergency had been lifted for the first time since the coup (it was reimposed in March 1984) and that the Chilean government was now willing to authorize peaceful demonstrations. They also noted that 3,500 exiles had been permitted to return. They indicated, however, that political parties were still banned and that opponents of the government were being sentenced to internal exile and expelled from the country; they further declared, "We continue to receive credible reports of violence and torture by the police and security forces."[10]

The Jarpa–Democratic Alliance talks had been terminated when it became clear that Pinochet would not accept any acceleration of the constitutional timetable. Given the deadlock, the final demonstration in mid-November, while large in numbers, lacked the intensity of earlier protests. The lifting of the U.S. ban on military aid to Argentina in December, when a civilian government took power, was not seen as so threatening to Chile as it might have been earlier, since an agreement on the Beagle Channel issue had been reached which only needed ratification by the Argentines.

By early 1984, the centrist Democratic Alliance faced alternatives on the left and right for the first time. In September 1983, the Communists, rebuffed in their attempts to join the alliance because of their endorsement of violence, formed an alliance with the left wing of the Socialist Party, led by exiled former foreign minister Clodomiro Almeyda, and with the Movement of the Revolutionary Left (MIR) to establish the Democratic Popular Movement (MDP). On the right, Jarpa encouraged a young protégé, Andrés Allamand, to form the National Union Party (UN), and the Independent Democratic Union (UDI) was established by Jaime Guzmán and others who supported Pinochet. Thus the three-thirds problem—the division of Chilean politics into three opposing blocs, which had prevented stable majority rule in the past—had reappeared, although this time the center was considerably larger and included significant elements of the Socialist Party, the main body of the Radicals (who had supported Allende), and a few conservative politicians.

In January and February 1984, Jarpa made a new effort to speed up the constitutional timetable, even drafting a constitutional amendment calling for legislative elections, which he felt could be held within three years. The U.S. annual human rights report published in February 1984 noted that respect for human rights in Chile had deteriorated during 1983 in comparison with 1982 and 1981 (i.e., before the protest movement had begun). Even Ambassador Theberge commented that the political opening had stagnated. Reports leaked out that the junta had vetoed the Jarpa plan, since it would mean surrendering its legislative powers. Despite an effort to work out a compromise involving the election only of the lower house of the Congress, it was clear by mid-March that Jarpa's project was never going to get off the ground.[11]

U.S.-Chilean relations continued to deteriorate. *Newsweek* (Mar. 19, 1984) published an interview with Pinochet in which he complained about Theberge's recent statement concerning the lack of progress in the political opening, charging that it involved interference in Chile's internal affairs. Pinochet stated, "We have always had problems with the United States. We don't like anyone, even the powerful U.S., telling us how to run our lives. We will never accept it." When asked how long he would stay in power, Pinochet answered, "I am here because my people have asked me to stay in power. . . . I did not seek this responsibility. Destiny gave it to me." The charge of interference in Chilean affairs was also made by the foreign minister at the end of the month, as he responded to another declaration by the State Department urging an agreement to return to civilian rule.

In March 1984, when the deputy assistant secretary of state for Latin America, James Michel, made a public speech in which he spoke of the danger that the "present impasse" in Chile might lead to "an increasingly destabilized political situation" in which democracy would be lost, it was clear the U.S. policy was now in favor of an acceleration of the transition and the development of a centrist political consensus, the lack of which Michel cited as the fundamental cause of the collapse of democracy in 1973. The U.S. embassy began to meet openly with the leaders of the Democratic Alliance (although those meetings were not with the ambassador). Economic relations between the two countries were increasingly delicate, both because of a request from American copper producers for protection from (lower-priced) Chilean copper inputs[12] and because Chile announced that it would not be able to pay amortization of principal on its international debts (mainly to a consortium of banks headed by Manufacturers Hanover of New York). Violence increased as the Manuel Rodríguez group blew up electric transmission towers and set off bombs in Santiago and other cities. In August, Pinochet gave an interview to the *New York Times* in which he reasserted his intention to abide by the constitutional timetable rather than hold earlier congressional elections (*New York Times*, Aug. 8,

1984). In September, mass demonstrations produced 250 arrests and 9 dead, including a French priest, André Jarlán, hit by a stray bullet as he was reading the Bible in his house in a lower-class *población*.

The State of Siege and the U.S. Reaction

At the end of October 1984, the State Department announced that it was conducting a full-scale review of its policy toward Chile, citing the increase in violence and terrorism, the lack of progress on the political parties law, and the "failure of the authorities to respond to the desires of the vast majority of Chileans for a peaceful return to democracy" (*New York Times,* Oct. 31, 1984). This was followed by strikes, bombings, and unrest that led to the death of 14 people and a government crackdown in which 140 Chileans were sent off to internal exile. In November, a curfew and the state of siege which had been lifted six years earlier were reimposed, six opposition publications were banned, three opposition leaders were arrested, and the head of the Catholic church human rights organization, a Spanish citizen, was prohibited from returning to Chile.

In reaction the State Department criticized the cycle of leftist violence and government repression, calling for a dialogue between the government and the democratic forces for an "orderly return to democracy in Chile," and the Defense Department postponed the visit to Chile of the head of the Joint Chiefs of Staff. Within the State Department there was reported to be a disagreement on whether the United States should support new loans to Chile in the Interamerican Development Bank. The decision to support the loans (over which the United States effectively had a veto) was made over the objection of Elliott Abrams, the assistant secretary for human rights, and of the Treasury Department. It was supported by the State Department Latin American Bureau and by Ambassador Theberge. Theberge's cable in support of the vote was leaked to Jack Anderson, who reported that Theberge had written "there is no possibility that the government will be overthrown in the near future." Admitting that Pinochet's intransigence had led to a policy review, Theberge reaffirmed the earlier policy of "quiet diplomacy," in accordance with which he would "quietly discuss with officials of the Chilean government the importance of political liberalization." He opposed vetoing loans to Chile from international lending institutions on the grounds that the United States had "very little influence with the Pinochet government" and said that if officials of the U.S. government put too much pressure on the government of Chile, it would be "counterproductive" and the Chilean government would no longer do "favors" for the United States (*Washington Post,* Dec. 30, 1984). Unpersuasively, the ambassador gave as examples of such favors participation in the Unitas naval exercises and support in U.N. votes. (Theberge also secured an exception to the ban on military sales for ejector-seat replacements for Chilean aircraft carrier planes.)

Despite the ambassador's recommendations, it was clear that the quiet diplomacy policy had been abandoned. When the United States voted again against the U.N. General Assembly resolution condemning Chile for human rights violations, it announced that it was doing so because Chile was being singled out on a one-sided basis, but it criticized the "harsh repression" that was being imposed on Chileans. Deputy Assistant Secretary Michel also made a trip to Chile in December 1984 in which he met government and opposition leaders and expressed U.S. interest in "the final objective of the re-establishment of democracy in Chile."[13]

A much larger impact was made in Chile by the statement of President Reagan at ceremonies in observance of Human Rights Day on December 10, in which he cited as "an affront to human consciences the lack of progress towards democracy in Chile and Paraguay."[14] Reagan's statement and the various State Department communiqués were cited by Assistant Secretary of State Abrams in a letter to the *Washington Post* (Dec. 23, 1984) criticizing an earlier op-ed piece that called on the United States to stop supporting Pinochet.

The low state of U.S. relations with Pinochet was dramatized in his comments in a meeting with three U.S. congressmen, two of them of Hispanic origin, on December 13, 1984. In response to the congressmen's questions about human rights and the lifting of the state of siege, Pinochet warned, "Don't stick your nose in affairs that don't concern you. . . . Your own democratic system is in danger. The Communists are patient and will eventually undermine your system." When asked about labor unions, he replied, "They are all corrupt and linked to the Communists. They are bought off by the Americans. I have done more for the working people than they have." He concluded, "Why should I believe anything the U.S. says or stands for? The U.S. won World War II but lost half of Europe. They lost half of Korea. You lost Vietnam. You lost Cuba. You lost Nicaragua and you will lose El Salvador if you are not careful. What kind of allies are you? You are not dependable."[15]

In January 1985, Assistant Secretary of State Motley testified to Congress that the U.S. objective was the restoration of democracy but also stated, "We have to ask ourselves whether our actions help or hinder that process." U.S. indecision seems to have been resolved, however, four days later when

Pinochet, over the reported opposition of Jarpa and other ministers (who resigned the following week), renewed the state of siege for another six months. The United States reacted by abstaining—for the first time—on a $430 million loan to Chile by the Interamerican Development Bank. A group of U.S. senators led by Jesse Helms wrote to Secretary of State Shultz to protest the decision, but it appeared to mark a shift in U.S. policy toward Chile. That impression was confirmed by an interview with Assistant Secretary of State for Human Rights Elliott Abrams by the *Baltimore Sun* (Feb. 21, 1985) in which he said that with regard to Chile, the policy of quiet diplomacy, which was "not a principle but a tactic," had been abandoned and that it was necessary to use other instruments.

A *New York Times* article (Feb. 24, 1985) quoted Assistant Secretary Motley as saying, at the end of a visit to Chile in late February, "The destiny of Chile is in the hands of Chileans and it is in good hands." The State Department, however, quickly made available the full text, in which he said, "The destiny of Chile is in very good hands, and I refer to the full national spectrum to which I have had access," and observed that in Latin America "democracy is one of the things we consider necessary to achieve our overall objectives which are peace, stability, and progress" (*El Mercurio*, Feb. 23, 1985).[16] Some interpreted a vote against a strong condemnation of Chile at the Geneva Human Rights Commission in March as a return to the earlier policy, but another abstention on a World Bank vote for a loan for Chile, followed by an explanation by Secretary Shultz that it was a reflection of U.S. "reservations" about the political situation in Chile, corrected that interpretation.

The discovery of the bodies of three well-known Communist activists on the side of a highway with their throats cut (*los degollados*) at the end of March reinforced the impression of a further deterioration in Chile (and led to a full-scale investigation by a courageous judge which pointed not to the CNI but to a special section of the national police as the perpetrators).[17] In April a resolution mandating further U.S. economic pressures on Chile, including termination of all loans and OPIC guarantees, lost by only ten votes in the House of Representatives. However, the most important development affecting U.S. policy toward Chile involved two personnel changes. At the end of April, in a change that was to have dramatic consequences for U.S. policy toward Chile, the former U.S. ambassador to India, Harry Barnes, a senior career diplomat, was appointed to replace James Theberge, and in May, Elliott Abrams succeeded Langhorne Motley as assistant secretary of state for Latin America. Barnes' appointment was part of a general effort by Secretary George Shultz at the beginning of

Ronald Reagan's second term to replace political appointees with members of the regular foreign service. President Reagan justified the actions by arguing that political appointees should only serve for a three- to four-year period. Abrams had favored an activist policy in opposition to Pinochet for some time. Some said he did so because he wished to use it to legitimize a similar activism against the Sandinistas in Nicaragua, but it also was related to fears that a similar process of polarization was beginning to take place in Chile. In addition, as a result of his position as assistant secretary of state for human rights, he had been in frequent contact with the Chilean opposition and was fully aware of the extent of the repression carried out by the Pinochet government.

Pinochet Yields to U.S. Economic Pressure

The fundamental reorientation of policy which had occurred in the first part of 1985 was dramatically demonstrated in May and June. Chile needed an infusion of nearly $2 billion in new loans from the private banks in order to finance its development plans over the next two years. The banks indicated that those loans in turn would depend on a guarantee from the World Bank. The U.S. Treasury let it be known that its support for World Bank loans and guarantees was dependent on the fulfillment of "certain conditions" that had been communicated in confidence to the Chileans. Although those conditions were not specified, it was clear that the most important was the termination of the state of siege, which had been renewed for another six months in May. On June 16 the Chilean government announced the lifting of the state of siege, and on June 17 the U.S. representatives voted for a package of loans to Chile, including the guarantee of $150 million in private bank loans for highway construction. The State Department endorsed the lifting of the state of siege but noted that although this eliminated the legal basis for press censorship and indefinite detentions, there were still considerable limits on freedom in the state of emergency which replaced it and in Article 24 of the transitional sections of the 1980 constitution.[18]

The lifting of the state of siege was directly related to U.S. pressure. It showed that in contrast to the 1970s, when private bank lending made Chile less reliant on official loans, in the post–debt-crisis period the Chilean government was much more vulnerable to U.S. government decisions to support or not support lending from the international financial institutions. It also demonstrated how far the Reagan administration had moved from the generally supportive attitude toward Pinochet which had been advocated by Jeane Kirkpatrick. (She had never had good relations with the State Department professionals, and when she left the United Nations in early 1985, there were no tears shed.)

Why the Policy Shift?

The administration's obsession with Nicaragua contributed to the policy shift. As violence and polarization seemed to be increasing in Chile, a country with a large and well-organized Communist Party, the administration became increasingly fearful of "another Nicaragua," a situation of chaos and opposition to an authoritarian ruler which could be used by the extreme left to take control of the antiauthoritarian movement.[19] It was also inconsistent for the administration to insist on genuinely free elections in Nicaragua and not do so in Chile.

Ronald Reagan's public commitment to democracy in 1982 increased the U.S. emphasis on free elections. That emphasis seemed to have paid off in 1984 as a civilian Christian Democratic president, Napoleon Duarte, was elected in El Salvador, bringing to an end congressional opposition to supporting a ruthless military regime against the guerrilla movement in that country. And as country after country in Latin America moved to elected civilian government, the administration attempted to take credit for this development. It welcomed the "new wave of democracy" in Latin America, as President Reagan did in May, when he described as the only remaining exceptions the "Communist tyrannies" in Cuba and Nicaragua and the "entrenched military regimes" in Paraguay and Chile.

U.S. public opinion was also a factor. I have described the frequent editorials on Chile in the *New York Times* and other influential newspapers, as well as the intense interest in Chile on the part of members of Congress. Individuals like Senator Edward Kennedy and Congressman Michael Barnes, the chairman of the Western Hemisphere Affairs Subcommittee of the House Foreign Affairs Committee, were particularly active in pressuring the administration toward more activism against the Pinochet regime. Within the bureaucracy, even in a conservative administration, there was an institutionalized pressure group for a more vigorous policy of support for democracy—the State Department Bureau of Human Rights and Humanitarian Affairs. His lengthy period in the Human Rights Bureau had sensitized Elliott Abrams to the seriousness of the Chilean problem and had introduced him to the leaders of the democratic opposition in Chile. George Shultz himself was responsive, because of both the longstanding connection with Chile of the University of Chicago, where he had taught, and a visit when he was chairman of the Bechtel Corporation. On the Chilean side, Pinochet's intransigence, arrogance, and anti-Americanism made it easy to argue that quiet diplomacy did not work. While there was some flexibility when Sergio Onofre Jarpa was minister of the interior, it became clear on repeated occasions that Jarpa's program to accelerate the transition was doomed because of the opposition of Pinochet, who fully intended not only to serve out his term until 1989 but also to seek reelection for another eight years through the constitutionally mandated plebiscite. In the Chilean case, there was also no evident security interest to argue against sanctions and pressures as there had been in the shah's Iran and, as it was argued until late 1985, there still was in the Philippines. Copper and fruit could be secured elsewhere; the Chileans were a kind of pariah at the United Nations; and except possibly in the Falklands War, there was no need for their assistance. It is true that there was an interest in continued good relations with the members of Chilean military, which were prejudiced to some degree by the arms embargo, but there was still a steady stream of high-level visitors to Chile from the U.S. military, and even as delicate an issue as the renewal of the NASA emergency landing strip on Easter Island was negotiated in mid-1985 successfully (although there was some resistance within and outside the Chilean government).

In summary, by 1985 there was a broad U.S. consensus from left to right in favor of action to move Chile more quickly toward a political opening. Whether for Cold War or for idealistic reasons or because of a mixture of the two, by mid-1985 everyone from Kennedy to Abrams favored the new policy, with the single exception of Senator Jesse Helms on the extreme right. In Chile, too, there was a broadened consensus on the desirability of an accelerated transition which included the left, the center, and significant elements of the right—some of them in the Democratic Alliance and others, like Jarpa, attempting to achieve that goal from within the Pinochet government. And partly owing to their own intransigence, the Communists were largely excluded from that effort.

The question that remained was what instruments did the United States have which could and should be used to exert pressure. Public statements by the State Department were now issued frequently. The June 1985 loans from the World Bank provided an opportunity to compel the Chileans to liberalize to some degree, since the lifting of the state of siege was a condition of U.S. support. U.S. "carrots and sticks" were limited, but there were additional possible measures. The stage was set for a more visible and public program of support for human rights and democracy during the second Reagan administration.

7

Reagan II: The United States versus Pinochet

THE CHANGE that had taken place in U.S. policy was dramatically demonstrated to Chileans on June 21, 1985, when Ambassador Theberge, long regarded as a strong supporter of Pinochet, made pointed remarks at the dedication of a monument to Abraham Lincoln in Santiago. Speaking out against the concentration of power "in the government, or in a single man," he stated that tyranny is never justified, "even by constitutions, electoral majorities, and complex legal arguments which try to make what is unjust appear to be just."[1]

The question of the validity of the 1980 constitution was being actively debated by the opposition Democratic Alliance, which was meeting to draft a common set of principles, under the auspices of a committee of three prominent Chileans who had been invited to do so by Archbishop (as of May 1985, Cardinal) Juan Francisco Fresno. The consultations had begun in late 1984 at a time when the church was having particularly difficult relations with the Pinochet government. The government had prohibited the head of the Vicariate of Solidarity from reentering the country and had used the state of siege to ban the publication of the archbishop's pastoral letter criticizing the "climate of subversive violence and repressive violence" in Chile and calling for a day of prayer and fasting for the poor and for the victims of violence.[2] The three members of the committee—José Zabala, head of the Christian Employers' Union; Sergio Molina, finance minister under the Christian Democratic government of Eduardo Frei; and Fernando Léniz, former editor of *El Mercurio* and economics minister after the 1973 coup—met with a wide range of political leaders from the Socialist Carlos Briones, Allende's last minister of the interior, to Andrés Allamand, the young leader of the new National Union Party, which had been founded at the suggestion of Sergio Onofre Jarpa. Particularly influential were future president Patricio Aylwin and Gabriel Valdés, initiator of the Democratic Alliance and president of the (illegal but active) Christian Democratic Party. Contacts between the party leaders had been more frequent since 1983, especially at forums under the auspices of the various foreign-financed opposition think tanks such as the conservative Centro de Estudios Públicos and the social democratic–oriented Latin American Faculty of Social Sciences (FLACSO). A similar range from conservative to "renovated" Socialist was represented in a delegation that participated in a seminar in Venezuela cosponsored by the newly created Institutes for International Affairs of the Democratic and Republican parties, which were the party instruments for National Endowment for Democracy (NED) funding.

The National Accord

On August 25, 1985, eleven Chilean parties, ranging from the Socialists and the Christian Left to the National Party and the National Union, signed a National Accord for the Transition to Full Democracy. The only groups that were not included were Jaime Guzmán's Independent Democratic Union (UDI) on the right and on the left the Communists and the Movement of the Revolutionary Left (MIR).[3]

The accord called for (1) the reestablishment of civil and political liberties, (2) the election of a Congress and president, (3) the legalization of political parties, (4) constitutional guarantees of the right of private property, and (5) efforts to overcome poverty by increasing growth and employment in a way that shared the burdens involved among all income groups. The accord seemed to accept the 1980 constitution, even the controversial section that outlawed groups whose "objectives, acts, or conduct" were opposed to the principles of democracy. The acceptance of the property guarantee and the possibility of outlawing revolutionary parties showed how far the democratic center and left were willing to go in supporting a broad anti-Pinochet alliance; the fact that it was signed by two parties that had supported Pinochet (the National Party and the National Union) indicated the impatience of a considerable part of the right with Pinochet's delay in opening the political system.

The Pinochet government rejected the accord, arguing that its call for elections was contrary to the 1980 constitution. However, Cardinal Fresno sent a letter to Pinochet endorsing it, and he seated the signers of the accord in a special section near Pinochet at the September 18 National Holiday (*Fiestas Patrias*) Te Deum religious ceremony. In the United States, the State Department issued a statement supporting the accord as the basis for a broad consensus among all who sought a peaceful solution and praising Cardinal Fresno for his moral support. Representatives of six of the signatory parties met with Assistant Secretary Abrams to discuss the accord in September. (They had been invited to Washington to a conference on political parties in the Southern Cone, organized by the Woodrow Wilson International Center for Scholars.) The House Foreign Affairs Committee and the Senate Foreign Relations Committee both voted resolutions welcoming the National Accord and supporting a peaceful transition to democracy in Chile. The one dissenting note was a statement, following a meeting with Pinochet, by Lieutenant General Robert Schweitzer, chairman of the Interamerican Defense Board, indicating sympathy with the difficulties of the Chilean government in moving toward democracy "under the double scourge of terrorism and subversion." Schweitzer's statement led to a press release by the U.S. embassy declaring that the general did not speak for the U.S. government.[4]

The Chilean press had already given considerable attention to the testimony of Mark Falcoff to the House Subcommittee on Western Hemisphere Affairs in which he criticized the 1980 constitution for establishing a semiautonomous position in the political system for the Chilean military. He had warned, "If the way to democracy is closed and the democratic forces destroyed, there is no doubt that before the end of this century, Chile will be a Marxist-Leninist state, allied to the Soviet Union." Falcoff's testimony was noticed because he was associated with the American Enterprise Institute, a Washington think tank supported by business interests. When Falcoff made a similar argument in the fall 1985 issue of *Policy Studies,* the journal of the conservative Heritage Foundation (in an article entitled "The Coming Crisis in Chile: Pinochet Is Playing into the Communists' Hands"), it became clear to the Chileans that the consensus against Pinochet in the United States now included significant sectors of the American right.

The arrival of Ambassador Barnes, delayed by the need for congressional confirmation (over the predictable opposition of Senator Jesse Helms), was anticipated as further evidence of U.S. support for a more rapid transition. (Barnes had also used his stay in Washington to assure bipartisan congressional support for a more forceful policy toward Pinochet.) Barnes' presentation of his credentials to Pinochet was a media event. Pinochet warned the ambassador of the danger that the Communists would use democratic mechanisms to destroy democratic institutions. In reply Barnes made a statement that was widely quoted in later years. "The evils of democracy can best be cured with more democracy."[5] Thereafter the Chilean press noted that Barnes had broadened the range of embassy contacts to include Socialist groups that had not been invited to the embassy since the 1973 coup. Barnes' contacts with human rights groups such as the Vicariate of Solidarity were especially visible.

The U.S. concern about lack of progress toward democracy did not diminish its interest in improving relations with the Chilean military, especially the branches other than the army. Both the air force and navy representatives on the junta were invited to the United States in 1985, and efforts were made to secure U.S. congressional authorization of a small ($100,000) military training program for Chile. Yet it continued to be clear that the United States was committed to an acceleration of the transition to democracy in Chile. In December, in testimony to the House Finance Committee, Elliott Abrams said that the U.S. support for democracy was "direct and unequivocal" and was seen as the "most effective way" to achieve other U.S. interests, including regional security, control of the drug traffic, and promotion of trade and international cooperation.[6]

The Kennedy Visit

The decision of Senator Edward Kennedy to visit Chile during a trip to Latin America in early January 1986 provoked a further deterioration in U.S.-Chilean relations. Initially President Pinochet wanted to deny Kennedy a visa, but his ambassador to the United States, at the urging of General Vernon Walters, strongly urged its issuance to avoid a propaganda triumph for Kennedy. The Pinochet government refused to see Kennedy and took steps to make sure that his reception in Chile would not be a cordial one. Militants of progovernment parties with the assistance of the Youth Secretariat (which provided walkie-talkies) blocked the senator's exit from the Santiago airport and attacked the cars of the opposition political leaders who had come to meet him. Finally it was necessary to fly Kennedy into the city by helicopter, where he met leaders of the opposition and representatives of human rights and church groups (the cardinal had withdrawn permission to use the Vicariate of Solidarity for his meetings). He then went to a luncheon at the ambassador's residence and (after a delay reportedly caused by a plea of the national police that no helicopter was available owing to lack of U.S. spare parts, prohibited by the Kennedy Amendment) was flown back to the airport.[7]

In February the State Department annual country report on human rights was much stronger in criticizing Chile's lack of progress toward a transition to democracy and the increase in detentions, torture, and politically related deaths (a total of seventy-two in 1985, including four persons who died as a result of mistreatment by the authorities). The most dramatic demonstration of U.S. concern was the introduction at the annual meeting of the U.N. Human Rights Commission in March 1986 of a U.S. resolution expressing "profound concern" over the human rights situation in Chile and calling on the Chilean government to "proceed vigorously" in the investigation of "torture, deaths, kidnappings, and other violations of human rights." The resolution was adopted unanimously. It was followed by a strange comment by Donald Regan, White House chief of staff, indicating that "for the moment" the United States did not plan to destabilize the Pinochet government, a statement that was denounced as "insolent" by Admiral Merino, the navy representative on the junta. Pinochet himself observed that Chile was different from the United States: "Our present constitution was approved by the Chilean people, while the American constitution was imposed in 1787."[8]

The U.S role in the recent overthrow of President Marcos in the Philippines and Duvalier in Haiti now led the Reagan administration to claim credit for a worldwide wave of redemocratization. Elliott Abrams declared that the United States supported the National Accord, "which we stimulated," as the best way to achieve unity of the democratic parties and a full return to democracy. The *Wall Street Journal* expressed the views of business sectors in a March 17, 1986, editorial in which it called for "clean elections" in Chile, possibly beginning at the municipal level. In May, *U.S. News and World Report* also warned of the danger that the intransigence of Pinochet would result in the ultimate triumph of a Marxist government.

The shift in conservative opinion was further documented with the publication of "Chile: The Dilemma for U.S. Policy" by Mark Falcoff in the spring 1986 issue of *Foreign Affairs*. Falcoff described three phases in the development of conservative thinking about Chile, from support for the overthrow of Allende (1973–77), to endorsement of Chile's free-market economic policy (1977–81), to concern that the intransigence of the Pinochet regime might produce an outcome similar to the triumph of the Sandinistas in Nicaragua. He concluded "The notion that the United States regards the Pinochet dictatorship as a privileged ally . . . is very wide of the mark." Falcoff suggested that the National Accord be taken as the basis for an acceptable framework for democratization, urged the United States to pressure for liberalization of the 1980 constitution's amendment procedures and the promulgation of a law on political parties, and called for direct U.S. assistance to democratic non-Communist political parties. Falcoff concluded that without a renewal of open political life and the emergence of a clear democratic alternative, "the country will gradually descend into a tracery of political upheaval, terror and counterterror, from which the Chilean president claims to have rescued his country a dozen years ago" (848).

Economic Recovery

While the U.S. government was increasingly critical of Pinochet, U.S. bankers were strongly favorable to his government's economic policies. The economy had rebounded after the 1982–83 depression with a growth rate in 1984 of 6 percent. Increased exports, especially of fruit, and prudent budget management had produced a trade surplus that was used to pay interest (but not amortization) on the $20 billion international debt. Debt restructuring, stretched-out payment terms, and lower interest rates reduced the pressure on the Chilean economy. In early 1985, with the appointment of Hernán Büchi, the Chicago boys reestablished control over economic policy (Büchi has a master's degree from Columbia). In addition, American financial institutions were making increasing use of debt-equity swaps to exchange discounted Chilean debt instruments for investments in Chile, and a number of U.S. banks and insurance companies bought shares in Chilean pension funds and financial institutions. The discovery of a high-grade copper field at La Escondida in the north of Chile also sparked foreign interest. The National Accord and their own conversations with the opposition had persuaded the foreign companies that their investments would not be threatened by a peaceful transition to democracy. The problem was that Pinochet seemed to be blocking any movement in that direction. The other military services favored a political opening and even competitive presidential elections in 1989, but Pinochet with his iron control of the army made it clear in a speech in July 1986 that he intended to be the single candidate in the 1988 plebiscite and to remain in power until 1997.

The Rojas Case

The opposition tried new ways to pressure the government for an opening. It organized a Civic Assembly (*Asamblea de la Civilidad*) made up of representatives of social and civic groups which prepared *The Demand of Chile,* listing changes needed to bring about democracy. The assembly threatened that if no actions were taken on its demands, it would call a general strike, which took place at the beginning of July. During the strike a military patrol detained two teenagers, Carmen Gloria Quintana and

Rodrígo Rojas, and, as later investigation revealed, poured gasoline over them and set them on fire. Quintana survived and was flown to Canada by human rights groups for treatment, but Rojas died of burns. At first the army denied that its patrols had been in the area, and government sources even hinted that the United States might have been involved in a destabilization effort, citing the attendance of Ambassador Barnes at Rojas's funeral.

Rojas was a native of Chile but a permanent resident in the United States. If for no other reason, this meant that his death received great attention in the U.S. press. The day of the Rojas funeral Senator Jesse Helms, at that time chairman of the Senate Foreign Relations Committee, arrived in Chile. Helms congratulated Pinochet for saving Chile from Communism and expressed his disagreement with the politics of the Reagan administration, which he attributed to the influence of the "bureaucrats in the State Department." He criticized Barnes' attendance at the Rojas funeral, which he described as a Communist activity. In reply, the White House and leading members of Congress insisted that Barnes, not Helms, represented U.S. policy, and the State Department sent Robert Gelbard, deputy assistant secretary of state for Latin America, to Chile to request a full investigation of the Rojas case and to continue U.S. pressure for a democratic transition. The controversy did not end after Helms returned to Washington. Commenting on Helms' praise for the Pinochet government, Elliott Abrams declared that those who supported an indefinite extension of military governments were "playing the game of the Communists."[9]

Later in the month, Helms accused the two burned teenagers of being Communist terrorists. It was also reported that the FBI was investigating Ambassador Barnes' report that the Chilean government had been informed by Senator Helms that the United States had a copy of the classified Chilean army report of the Rojas case. Helms had been told about the report by his assistant, Christopher Manion, who knew about it from attending a closed session of a Senate Foreign Relations subcommittee at which it was discussed. Helms, in turn, accused the CIA of spying on him while he was in Chile and demanded a Senate investigation of the accusations against him.

At the end of July, Elliott Abrams testified to a House subcommittee in opposition to a bill mandating a negative vote on all loans to Chile by U.S. representatives to international financial institutions. Observing that the United States had "few carrots or sticks" available to induce changes in Chilean behavior, Abrams asserted that U.S. votes would depend in great part on the human rights situation in Chile at the time. Significantly,

Abrams added that if he had to vote on such loans "today," he would vote no.[10]

In mid-August, General John Galvin, the commander of the U.S. Southern Command, visited Chile. Praising the professionalism of the Chilean army, which would be helpful in a transition to democracy, he called for closer relations between the two militaries, although he was careful to say that this would have to be carried out within the framework of existing law, including the Kennedy Amendment. The Chilean press speculated, however, that the real motive for Galvin's visit was to explore with the military the possibility of a graceful exit for Pinochet. U.S.-Chilean relations were at such a low point that, fearing that a U.S. negative vote would help to defeat a proposed World Bank Structural Adjustment Loan of $250 million (the United States has 20 percent of the weighted votes in the World Bank), Chile asked for postponement of its consideration until November.

Arms Caches and Failed Assassination

U.S. policy toward Chile was dramatically affected by two linked events in August and September 1986. On August 6, the Chilean government announced the discovery of what turned out to be fifty tons of arms buried in caves and abandoned mine shafts in the north of Chile. Initially there was skepticism on the part of the opposition, but as more details came out in the course of the investigation, a vast arms-smuggling operation was revealed. Cuban ships had brought the arms off the coast, and Chilean fishing boats and rubber dinghies were used to transport them ashore. U.S. experts brought in from the Pentagon subsequently identified the contents of the caches as American weaponry left behind in Vietnam and Soviet arms manufactured in 1983 and 1984, and it was reported that satellite intelligence confirmed the presence in Chilean waters of Cuban "fishing boats." From the caves they were distributed elsewhere in Chile and had been used in a wave of bombings and attacks on military and police installations in Santiago during the previous four months. The Chileans discovered a total of 3,115 M-16 rifles, 114 Soviet and 157 U.S. rocket launchers, 2 million cartridges, 2,000 hand grenades, machine guns, bombs, and many other types of explosives. U.S. Secretary of State Shultz declared that so large a quantity of arms must have been intended for use primarily against a civilian government that would succeed the present military regime (*Washington Post*, Oct. 22, 1986).

The high-powered weapons were used in a carefully planned assassination attempt by the Manuel Rodríguez Patriotic Front against President Pinochet on September 7, as he was returning from his weekend retreat. Five members of the escort party were killed and twelve seriously injured in the attack, but, almost miraculously, Pinochet escaped. Two of the rockets aimed at his car did not explode, the special armor on the car protected him from others, and his chauffeur broke through the car blockade on the highway and escaped. Subsequent investigation revealed that among the main organizers of the attack was César Bunster, son of Allende's ambassador to Great Britain, who had spent large amounts of money to rent houses and cars in connection with the assassination attempt.

Both the assassination attempt and the arms discoveries reinforced the argument of Pinochet that Communism remained a threat in Chile. The junta imposed a state of siege, banned six magazines, and reinstated newspaper censorship. Four leftist leaders, including an editor of *Análisis,* a well-known magazine published by FLACSO, were assassinated by right-wing terrorists in retaliation. A fifth target, a lawyer for the Vicariate of Solidarity, avoided death by calling out the window to an army colonel, who was a neighbor, when he saw the death squad attempting to enter the house.[11] At least fifty other leaders of the left were detained and questioned, including Ricardo Lagos, later a senatorial candidate and minister of education. Lagos' detention provoked a State Department protest.

The State Department also spoke out against the reimposition of the state of siege, which gave the government unlimited powers to detain and exile Chileans and to censor the Chilean media. The events led Elliott Abrams to urge the Chilean opposition to distance itself from the Communist Party, and this was indeed one of the results of the assassination attempt and the discovery of the arms arsenals. There had been frequent informal contacts between the members of the Democratic Alliance and the Communists, especially in attempting to control the violence that had accompanied many of the protests. However, the Communists had not been asked to join the alliance, because of their refusal to abjure violence, and in fact, during 1986 there had been public discussion by the Communists of the need for a violent solution in Chile (1986 was described as the "year of decision" by the Communist Party and the "year of titanic combats" by Volodia Teitelboim, exiled party leader and former senator, broadcasting over Radio Moscow). The alliance members had been careful to avoid giving ammunition to government charges that it was influenced by the Communists, but from September 1986, the Communists and the rest of the opposition were permanently estranged. A transition to democracy without Communist participation had been one of the U.S. objectives since 1986, and now, thanks to the actions of a *violentista* group, that objective seemed to have been achieved.

The new state of siege provisions were gradually lifted between September and the end of 1986, and the Chilean government began to work more seriously on the draft laws on political parties and elections. Talks on the proposed laws between the minister of the interior and the opposition parties took place for the first time since the Jarpa–Democratic Alliance negotiations were discontinued three years before.

When loans to Chile from the World Bank and the Interamerican Development Bank came to a vote in November, the United States abstained. Other European countries also voted against or abstained, and the World Bank Structural Adjustment Loan barely passed with 51 percent of the weighted votes. The U.S. abstention was viewed as a compromise between U.S. support for Chile's free-market economic policies and its strong disapproval of its human rights violations. The liberals who argued for a negative vote believed that the abstention was a response to the arms discoveries earlier in the year. When the United States was one of five countries to vote against the U.N. General Assembly resolutions criticizing human rights violations in Chile, this was also taken as a change of policy from the vote of the previous March in the Human Rights Commission. In fact, however, the vote was the result of a White House decision between the embassy and the Human Rights Bureau on the one side and the U.N. delegation headed by Vernon Walters on the other, with Walters arguing that in the General Assembly votes the United States had consistently opposed singling out Chile for a special resolution.[12]

In 1986, the AFL-CIO had begun to pressure the U.S. government to apply to Chile the punitive sanctions against governments that violate labor rights contained in the laws on Overseas Private Investment Corporation (OPIC) investment insurance and the special tariff exemptions for Third World countries under the Generalized System of Preferences (GSP). In December 1986, Chile was notified that the United States was looking into the question of the status of labor in Chile, which could lead to the withdrawal of tariff exemptions for important Chilean exports. Also in December, Elliott Abrams added to the U.S. complaints against Chile the lack of a full investigation of the death of Rodrígo Rojas. (The case had gone to a military court after the army admitted that its personnel had been involved. The court sentenced one officer to six months in jail for "unnecessary violence resulting in death" but released him on bail pending a new trial on a reduced charge.) Abrams concluded that "it has been a bad year" for U.S.-Chilean relations because so little had been done to move toward democracy (*Washington Post,* Dec. 16, 1986).

In early 1987 there was finally some movement in the direction of a political opening. Pinochet announced that the state of siege would not be renewed, and the curfew that had been in force since late 1984 was lifted. In addition, the political parties law, which had been drafted within the government and approved by the junta, was published with twenty-four changes made by the Constitutional Tribunal, which according to the 1980 constitution was obliged to review all laws before they were promulgated. Among the changes (which could not be appealed) was the elimination of a clause allowing the tribunal to veto the registration of a party if it suspected that it violated Article 8 outlawing unconstitutional parties. The assertion of its authority by the Constitutional Tribunal was to be of crucial importance a year later when it amended the draft election law to guarantee equal access to radio and television for the opposition in the October 1988 plebiscite.

The Statute of Political Parties required that to be legally recognized, a party had to enroll at least 0.5 percent of the voters in eight of the thirteen regions, have free internal elections, and publish a list of party members. The parties were also forbidden to accept funds from abroad and had to open their books to public audit. The Electoral Registration Law had already been approved in late 1986, and electoral rolls were opened in February. Initial registrants were mainly progovernment elements and members of the armed services, and the opposition parties continued to debate whether to ask their members to register, or even to comply with the political parties law.

The Letelier Case Again

In February 1987, another lurid chapter in the Letelier case was written as Armando Fernández Larios, one of the Chileans whom the United States had tried to extradite in connection with the Letelier assassination, left the country and gave himself up to U.S. agents in Brazil. He stated that his own guilt feelings and his father's deathbed wishes had led him to surrender, but there were those in Chile who argued that he was doing so in order to take advantage of a U.S. plea-bargaining arrangement, as had been done with Michael Townley. He also was known to have been involved in the post-coup killings carried out in the north of Chile by General Sergio Arellano (see Chapter Four). In May, Fernández was sentenced to twenty-seven to eighty-four months in federal prison on the charge of being an accessory to the murder of Letelier. A more serious charge of direct involvement in the murder was dropped. In his confession of his role in preparing the way for Townley to plant the bomb, Fernández said that he had been instructed by the head of DINA, Manuel Contreras, to deny his involvement and that Contreras had told him that he was carrying out the assassination on orders from "the Chief." Fernández's lawyer also made public Fernández's letter to the vice-commander of the Chilean army resigning his commission, in which he stated that at the time of Michael Townley's extradition in April 1987, he had written a full account of his actions in the case and given it to General Hector Orozco, head of army intelligence, but that Orozco had told him "on more than five occasions" to lie about his involvement and had burned his declaration in his presence (*Hoy*, no. 501, Feb. 16–22, 1987). Fernández also testified that during his only meeting with him, Pinochet had sought to dissuade him from going to the United States and had urged him to be "a good soldier" and remain in Chile (*El Mercurio*, Feb. 22, 1987). On September 10, the judge freed him from prison on the grounds that he had already spent fourteen months of detention in a Chilean military facility and seven months in a U.S. jail. Fernández did not make use of the Witness Protection Program and settled in Miami.

Using Fernández's testimony, the United States again requested the extradition of Contreras and Espinoza, but Chile again rejected the request on the grounds that it was based on a plea bargaining (*New York Times*, June 3, 1987). Chile also rejected a U.S. court award of damages to the mother of Rodrígo Rojas by a federal court in the District of Columbia, his U.S. residence.

In 1988, on the basis of sworn statements from Fernández, the United States sent Letters Rogatory to General Orozco, but the Chilean courts instructed him to answer only twelve of the two hundred questions in the document—those that related directly to his own actions. In December 1988, new Letters Rogatory with specific questions on the case were sent to a long list of Chilean officials involved in the case. One of them, José Miguel Barros, who had been ambassador to the United States in the late 1970s and now was active with the opposition, quoted in his response the deputy minister of the interior at the time, Enrique Montero Marx, as saying in 1978 "that intelligence genius [Contreras] mounted an operation to assassinate Letelier."[13]

In March 1987, Senators Kennedy and Harkin, longtime critics of the Chilean government, were joined by two members of the House of Representatives in introducing a bill that would impose the strongest set of sanctions ever suggested against Chile. Besides ending tariff preferences under the Generalized System of Preferences and investment insurance by the Overseas Private Investment Corporation, it mandated negative votes on Chilean loans in the international financial institutions, denied landing rights to the Chilean national airline, and forbade the importation of copper from Chile. The certification requirements were also more stringent, requiring "significant advances" toward free elections, an end to human rights abuses and exile, restoration of trade union rights, and cooperation on both the Letelier and Rojas cases. Assistant Secretary Abrams opposed the proposal as counterproductive, since it would produce a nationalist reaction and, by crippling the Chilean economy, would punish the Chileans "because they have a bad government."[14] However, the United States supported a resolution criticizing Chile at the meeting of the U.N. Human Rights Commission in Geneva. The resolution was adopted unanimously, with the United States withdrawing its resolution in favor of a compromise worked out with Mexico.

The U.S. newspapers gave considerable play to the visit to Chile of Pope John Paul II. The pope attempted to be evenhanded between the government and the opposition. He had a private meeting with Pinochet and was seen with him on the balcony of the presidential palace, but he also publicly embraced Carmen Gloria Quintana, who had been nearly burned to death by the army unit the preceding July; he used the Bible that Father André Jarlán was reading when he was killed in September; and he received the representatives of the Chilean political parties, including the Communists, in a private audience. The visit to Santiago concluded with an outdoor mass in a park before 600,000 people which was marred by the use of tear gas to keep a leftist group from assaulting the platform.[15]

Bad feeling between Pinochet and the United States was exacerbated by an interview published in the *Los Angeles Times* (Apr. 30, 1987) in which he accused the CIA of involvement in the failed assassination attempt of September 1986. This produced a reply from the State Department which noted that a Communist terrorist group had publicly claimed responsibility and termed the Pinochet statement "false and offensive." Deputy Assistant Secretary for Latin American Affairs Robert Gelbard, was not wide of the mark when he noted that U.S.-Chilean relations were at a critical and difficult moment (June 18, 1987), a view that was echoed by Ambassador Barnes in a statement that placed particular emphasis on Chilean lack of cooperation in the Letelier case (July 2, 1987). (The falsification of passports case was still on the docket in the Chilean courts, but no action was being taken, and Chile refused all extradition requests.)

Meanwhile, in Chile attention was focused on the forthcoming 1988

plebiscite. In July, the other members of the junta made statements supporting the nomination of a civilian consensus candidate, but it was clear that
Pinochet intended to be the candidate. Sergio Fernández, who had been
interior minister at the time of the 1980 plebiscite, was again named minister
of the interior, and he began to coordinate plans for the plebiscite in the
new cabinet, which was focused on a plebiscite victory in order to "project"
Pinochet for another eight years. The Christian Democrats, after a bitter
internal election that chose Patricio Aylwin as their president, decided to
register as a political party in accordance with the political parties law, as
did two new parties, the Humanists and the National Renovation Party
(RN) of Sergio Onofre Jarpa and Andrés Allamand. Jaime Guzmán's UDI
also registered after ideological and personal differences in early 1988 had
led to a split with Renovación Nacional.

U.S. Involvement Increases

In the United States there was considerable concern that the opposition
would not have the resources necessary to combat the propaganda and
spending of the government. At this point, the think tanks that had been
supported by American, Canadian, and European money played a crucial
role. With support from the Ford Foundation, which had long been a
major supporter of CIEPLAN and FLACSO, and from other American
foundations and individuals, research, dialogues, polling, and focus groups
were organized in mid-1987 by Chilean social science researchers to analyze
the changes in Chilean society and to prescribe the appropriate responses.
The work was done by social scientists from the left, the center, and the
right and led to increased collaboration of social scientists of differing
political ideologies. The research revealed that the major problem to be
overcome was a generalized climate of fear; that despite what government
propaganda maintained, there was strong dissatisfaction with the economic
situation in Chile; and that the single government candidate who would
generate the most antipathy was Pinochet. The results of this research were
then used by a Technical Committee of mainly Socialist and Christian
Democratic intellectuals to develop a strategy that focused on the No vote,
rather than the demand for free elections, and a joint program that stressed
the negative aspects of the economic and social program of the government.[16]

In December, Senator Tom Harkin introduced a bill to appropriate $1
million for the promotion of democracy in Chile, which was to be allocated
by the National Endowment for Democracy. There was no objection from

the administration, which was now hardening its line on Chile still further. For the first time in Ronald Reagan's presidency, it abstained on the U.N. General Assembly vote on human rights in Chile, and it did so on three World Bank loans as well. Most striking was a joint statement of President Reagan and Secretary Shultz on December 17, 1987, which outlined the administration's view of what would constitute a free election in Chile. Closely following the statement of the Chilean bishops' conference earlier in the year, the statement noted that "a climate of freedom and fair competition" should exist for an extended period before the actual balloting, as well as "access to the mass media, especially television, early announcement of rules . . . facilitation of registration, and freedom to campaign peacefully." It also argued that "states of exception" like the state of emergency in force in Chile were "incompatible with a legitimate electoral proceeding."[17] The statement and the congressional vote were followed by two other actions that were the product of a year-long study of the repression of labor in Chile but which were understood in Chile as further evidence of increasing U.S. antipathy to the regime—the exclusion of Chile from the Generalized System of Preferences and the termination of its eligibility for insurance by OPIC.

By the end of the year, three opposition parties had complied with the provisions of the political parties law—the Christian Democrats; the new Humanist Party, composed of students and recent graduates concerned about the environment; and a Party for Democracy (PPD), which described itself as an "instrumental" party bringing together those of differing views who supported the return of democracy. In fact, the PPD was dominated by the "renovated" Socialists, but the Socialists did not want to recognize the legitimacy of the Pinochet law by registering. Since October 1987, the opposition parties (except for the Communists and the Movement of the Revolutionary Left) had been meeting to form an anti-Pinochet coalition and to establish a common program. On February 1, 1988, the Concertación de Partidos para la Democracia (CPPD)—sixteen parties, with Patricio Aylwin, president of the Christian Democrats, as their spokesman—announced the formation of the "Command for the No" and published its consensus program. Like the National Accord, it called for a return to constitutionalism and guarantees for private enterprise, but it marked something of a change in its acceptance of the 1980 constitution as a basis from which to work, by the process of amendment to return to genuine democracy. It was also striking in the breadth of the consensus—from Socialist to conservative—which had been achieved. Its proposals included reform of the judiciary; recognition of labor rights; increased expenditures for health, education, and housing; and decentralization of government.[18]

For the first time since the coup, opposition leaders began to appear on television. At the same time, the government initiated a massive propaganda campaign extolling its accomplishments ("We Are Millions"), the State Department annual human rights report still spoke of documented cases of torture by the security services, and the print media were subject to judicial action for such offenses as insulting the armed forces. In one such case, the editor of the FLACSO publication, *Análisis,* spent each night in jail under a 541-day sentence but continued to edit the magazine during the day. Public demonstrations by the opposition were still not permitted, and the state of emergency was renewed in March, eliciting a protest from Ambassador Barnes. As registrations lagged, and as the government began a massive spending program in the poorer areas under the auspices of the Pinochet-appointed mayors, many felt that Pinochet would get a "Yes" vote in the plebiscite, which according to constitution had to be held in the last part of the year.

In early 1988, however, U.S. money began to flow into Chile in ways that, although legally nonpartisan in character, substantially assisted the opposition. The Agency for International Development had a Democratic Initiatives budget item in support of the promotion of democracy. In late 1987, it allocated $1.2 million from that program to support voter registration in Chile. The grant went to the OAS Commission for the Promotion of Free Elections (COPEL) in Costa Rica, which in turn channeled it to Caritas, a small private Chilean foundation with links to the Catholic church. Under the leadership of Monica Jiménez, former dean of the School of Social Service of the Catholic University, Caritas created the Crusade for Citizen Participation, usually referred to as the Civic Crusade. Using the papal colors of gold and white and a cross with the words "My Voice, My Vote," it set up branches all over the country, often initially using the local Catholic parish building as its base. Photographers were hired to take the required picture for the new identity cards needed to register. (The cost of the photographs, around $1.50, was prohibitive for the very poor.) Rock-music stars held concerts in forty cities, admission to which was free for those showing a voter registration card—encouraging registration by 18- to 30-year-olds who had never voted. As a result of the Civic Crusade, the number of registrants rose to an astonishing 7.2 million, or 92 percent of the potential registrants of voting age.

The National Endowment for Democracy (NED) also became involved in a major way, mainly through the National Democratic Institute for International Affairs (NDIIA) of the Democratic Party. Both the Democratic and Republican institutes had cooperated in running joint seminars with Chilean leaders in 1985 and 1986. They had supported a Committee for Free Elections which had been established by Sergio Molina, former finance minister of the Frei government. With NED-NDIIA financing, the committee established "nonpartisan" local branches to encourage registration and to develop election monitoring skills, and it commissioned public opinion polls, carried out jointly by the Socialist-dominated Latin American Faculty of the Social Sciences (FLACSO) and the Center for Development Studies (CED) of Christian Democratic orientation. One of the German political foundations, the Hans Seidel Foundation, which is related to the Christian Social Union (CSU) branch of the German Christian Democratic Party, also financed polling by the conservative Center for Public Studies (CEP, which also received NED money), and European money supported polls by the Center for the Study of Chilean Reality (CERC) of the church-sponsored Academy of Christian Humanism.

Other projects supported by NED money were seminars on democracy and elections, and the freedom of the media, as well as financial aid to a new Christian Democratic newspaper, *La Época*. In addition, along with the U.S. based Soros Foundation, the NED-funded National Democratic Institute for International Affairs paid the expenses of a number of well-known U.S. political consultants (e.g., Sawyer-Miller in New York, Peter Hart in Washington) who volunteered their services to advise on polling techniques and the use of focus groups and to assist in developing foolproof methods of reporting the vote count. They included fax and computer networks, nationwide samples and telephone reporting systems, even an alternate electric generator in case of a power cutoff. One of the U.S. consultants, Glenn Cowan, advised the Command for the No on the lessons to be drawn from the tactics of the Mexican government party to prevent the opposition from obtaining an accurate vote count—emphasizing the importance of establishing a network of informants to report the results in each election district (*New York Times,* Nov. 18, 1988).

Since 1985, the Constitutional Tribunal had taken an active role in guaranteeing the fairness of the vote. In that year, by a 4–3 vote, it had insisted that the proposed Election Tribunal would have to be set up in time to supervise the plebiscite and not be delayed until the 1990 congressional elections as the government desired. As noted above, it had also modified the proposed Statute of Political Parties in 1987. However, as it turned out, its most important role was in early 1988 when it insisted that the proposed

Elections Law assure the opposition equitable access to the radio and television. (The opposition-controlled Radio Cooperativa, belonging to the Christian Democrats, and Radio Chilena, the organ of the Catholic church, were supportive, but television had been barred to the opposition except for a series of round tables which began in early 1988.) The court also insisted that the junta's choice of a candidate be promulgated at least thirty days before the vote. As a result, the final version of the law guaranteed space in the press, radio, and television for the opposition. It was in application of this law that a decree regulating electoral advertising on television was published in mid-August which gave the government and the opposition free television time for fifteen minutes a day for twenty-seven days before the plebiscite.[19]

At the end of May the government renewed the "state of emergency," eliciting a formal protest from the State Department at its daily briefing on June 7. Expressing its concern and deep disappointment, the State Department observed, "Although there has been some increase in airing different points of view on university television, there remains a lack of equitable access to the media and arrests and imprisonment of journalists continue." One indication of the broadening of access to television was a program in which Ricardo Lagos, Socialist leader of the Committee of the Left for Free Elections (CIEL), waved his finger at Pinochet and accused him of the torture and murder of thousands of Chileans (*New York Times,* June 30, 1988).

In July, it was announced that the date of the junta nomination of its candidate for the plebiscite would be August 30, and the state of emergency was lifted. Earlier in the month, the U.S. House of Representatives and the Senate adopted a joint resolution expressing their support for the restoration of full and genuine democracy in Chile and calling for the end of states of exception, equitable access to the media, and public tabulation of the vote with full access for international visitors to the vote count centers. Senators Kennedy and Lugar also announced the formation of the Committee for the Support of Free Elections in Chile, which included former presidents Ford and Carter and former cabinet ministers Robert MacNamara and Cyrus Vance. Predictably, the committee was denounced by the Chilean Foreign Ministry as "a new attempt at intervention in the internal affairs of Chile" (*El Mercurio,* Aug. 4, 1988).

The impending plebiscite did not seem to lessen the influx of foreign investment into Chile in 1988, possibly because the opposition coalition had made it clear that it would respect the economic rules of the game. By mid-1988, the Chilean debt had been reduced by more than $4 billion as a result of debt-equity swaps of discounted Chilean debt instruments which gave U.S. and European financial institutions major investment holdings in Chile. Since 1986, many state-owned enterprises were being rapidly sold off both to small investors ("people's capitalism"), the workers themselves, and—with strict limits to avoid concentration of ownership—to pension funds and foreign investors. In mid-July a multibillion-dollar investment in the new Escondida copper mine was announced by a consortium of Australian, Japanese, and European firms. The new investment symbolized the increasing presence of non-U.S. investors and the confidence in Chilean economic stability on the part of the international investment community.

The Plebiscite Campaign

On August 30, the members of the junta met and nominated Pinochet as the official candidate in the plebiscite. In accordance with the July decree, Pinochet formally proclaimed October 5, 1988, as the day on which 7.5 million Chileans would vote "yes" or "no" on his continuation in power as president until 1997. Earlier polls had shown a significant number of undecided voters, and at least one projection using a June survey called the election a tossup. The final result was a clear victory for the No—and one can only conclude that the campaign had much to do with the change.

To counteract the influence of the regime-appointed mayors, the Command for the No had organized branches in every municipality. It distributed leaflets and broadcast messages, assuring viewers that the vote was secret. There were also wall posters and small leaflets playing on the No theme in humorous ways and recalling the repression imposed by the regime ("Nothing personal, but who is responsible for the disappeared? Vote No, like me—*Vote No, como yo*"). The progovernment literature portrayed Pinochet in civilian clothes, cited the economic accomplishments of the regime, and recalled the disorder, shortages, and violence of the Allende regime. Ricardo Lagos, a leader of the Socialists and former minister of Allende, was a particular target when the Yes forces interviewed his former wife on their private life. Lagos' picture was also on a leaflet that recycled the photograph of the policeman being beaten by a helmeted guerrilla which had produced such an impact in April 1973 (see Chapter Three).

The real electoral battle, however, was waged on television. The fifteen-minute "spots" each evening were watched by most Chileans, the vast majority of whom now had access to television. (Polls showed that 90 percent of the people watched them.) The Yes programs showed rioting, property seizures, and violence and played up the economic accomplish-ments of the regime. The No used a soft sell. It adopted the rainbow as its symbol to highlight the pluralism of the coalition, played a catchy song called *Happiness Is Coming* ("Because it's the hour to win liberty, because it's time to change when there has been enough misery, we are going to say *no*"), and emphasized that the vote should be carried out "without hatred, without fear, and without violence." The human rights issue was highlighted when the government refused to allow the showing of an opposition program in which a judge testified to human rights abuses. The social cost of the government program was portrayed by an aged female pensioner who lacked the money for tea. The announcer of the No pro-grams was Patricio Bañados, who had been banned from television by Pinochet in the early 1980s.

Americans noted the similarities of the No spots to Ronald Reagan's "It's Morning in America" ads in 1984. A U.S. observer noted that Chile was one country in which Nancy Reagan's "Just Say No" approach would receive wide support. In radio spots, Jane Fonda and Christopher Reeves (*Superman*) urged Chileans (in English) to cast their votes for the No.

Polls showed that an overwhelming majority of the viewers thought that the No programs were superior to those of the Yes. They also revealed a substantial movement of residents of poorer areas, women, and the rural population to the No vote.[20] Toward the end of the campaign, the Com-mand for the No organized a March of Happiness, starting from opposite ends of the country, which included more than fifty mass meetings and culminated in a huge demonstration in Santiago. On the weekend before the vote, the Civic Crusade tied a yellow ribbon around the entire city of Santiago (population, 4 million). The government organized an automo-bile caravan in Santiago, but it could not match the organizing ability of the opposition.

How much did U.S. financial aid have to do with the success of the opposition's campaign? The government had tried to turn it around by attacking the opposition for receiving funds from U.S. sources. Genaro Arriagada, secretary of the Command for the No, replied that he was not happy doing so, but in view of the vast resources of the government, there was no alternative. The National Democratic Institute said that its money was given in order to assure a "level playing field" and was for educational rather than partisan purposes. A reported dozen U.S. political consultants came to Chile at various times. However, the opposition media team, headed by a Socialist and a Christian Democrat, could also draw on a large number of volunteers from the numerous advertising agencies in Santiago, where typically the senior members advised the government and the younger employees worked for the opposition. Three hundred and fifty Chileans, including leading actors and public figures, worked on a volunteer basis on the opposition television ads that were a central part of the campaign (*Hoy*, no. 582, Sept. 12–18, 1988). Clearly the outside support was well used by the opposition. Whether it made a crucial difference is not certain.

U.S. Warnings to Chile

The television blitz made the No vote legitimate, and since the state of emergency had been lifted, arbitrary arrests and detentions had ceased. Yet there was still uncertainty that the vote would be a free one. Rumors circulated that an effort would be made to cancel the vote, and the national police (*carabineros*) announced that a number of their buses had been stolen. (The remaining ones were marked with special fluorescent signs to distinguish them.) There were power blackouts on the weekend and the night before the vote. The U.S. embassy received reports from church-related sources of plans to sabotage the vote, and it took immediate action. Ambassador Harry Barnes cabled Washington, and the State Department summoned the Chilean ambassador to express its concern. Barnes himself spoke to the Foreign Ministry and in a newspaper interview predicted that the No would win, "if the process does not get interrupted." This led to the usual outcries against U.S. intervention, but it also alerted the army commander (the army supervises elections in Chile) and police as well as the populace. Along with similar warnings by the Federal Republic of Germany, it indicated the strength of the feeling of the international community about the fairness of the plebiscite. It is not clear whether the events were related, but the opposition learned that a special antiriot force that had been placed on alert for the election was deactivated two days before the vote.[21]

The Command for the No had been meeting daily throughout the campaign. It advised Chileans to vote early and return to their homes, avoiding any kind of mass demonstrations in the evening when the results were reported. It also had contacted the leaders of the Communist Party to make sure that there was no violence that could be used by the government to interrupt the vote count.

There was a large turnout on October 5, the day of the plebiscite, with many Chileans standing in the sun for up to two hours because it took many of the 22,000 voting places several hours to get organized. Voters had their thumbs marked with indelible ink to prevent multiple voting, and numbered tabs on the ballots were torn off and kept separately to prevent vote stuffing. At the end of the day, the elected president of each voting table (*mesa*) supervised a public vote count in a civic ceremony of a quasi-religious nature. At each voting place the voting and the count were observed by representatives of the registered parties as well as by foreign observers and reporters, whose numbers were estimated at 1,500. (The National Democratic Institute alone sent 55 observers, including Adolfo Suárez, former prime minister of Spain, who had presided over the post-Franco transition to democracy, and Bruce Babbitt, former governor of Arizona and an early contender for the 1988 Democratic nomination. Other U.S. groups that sent observers included Freedom House, the Latin American Studies Association, and a number of human rights groups.)

The Command for the No had established two lines of reporting, one that received the regional results and another that entered faxed reports from each voting place directly to various centers in Santiago. The Committee for Free Elections had also set up its own "quick count" to give an early projection of the result, based on six hundred voting tables. The government had its own press center in the Diego Portales government building to give periodic announcements of the returns.

The Defeat of Pinochet

The opposition had agreed that it would not make any announcements until it had at least 500,000 votes, but the government was under no such constraints. At 7:30 P.M., the undersecretary of the interior announced that on the basis of 79 voting *mesas* (0.36 percent of the voters), the Yes was ahead by 57 percent to 40 percent. (The announcement led to an early Associated Press report in the United States of a Pinochet victory.) The second announcement was delayed beyond the promised hour, and according to many accounts, an effort was initiated to organize a victory demonstration by the Yes partisans, which was claimed by some sources to be an effort to provoke violence that would lead to military intervention. However, inquiries as to whether the police or the army would lift the roadblocks preventing access to the center of the city received the reply that the existing prohibition on demonstrations and access to the center of the city would be maintained. At 10 P.M. the government announced that on the basis of 677 voting tables (out of 22,000), the Yes vote was still ahead by 51 percent to 46 percent. At this point the Command, which had returns from two sources, and the Committee for Free Elections, which had nearly complete returns from its quick count, released their figures, with the Committee result almost exactly the final return, 55 percent No and 44 percent Yes. The government television station suddenly began to show soap operas, and the country waited for the next step in the drama. An unsuccessful effort by the minister of the interior to construct a million-vote total favorable to the government was canceled when it was learned that the opposition now had two million votes counted and that Sergio Onofre Jarpa, the leader of the more moderate progovernment party, Renovación Nacional, was on his way to the Catholic University station to concede the victory of the No. At 11:30 P.M., on a program with Patricio Aylwin, the president of the Christian Democratic Party, Jarpa announced that on the basis of the latest figures that Aylwin had just transmitted to him, it appeared the No vote had won.

Pinochet was furious. His pollsters had told him that a Yes victory was assured. He called in his cabinet shortly after midnight and asked for their resignations. Then he summoned the air force, navy, and *carabinero* members of the junta. As General Fernando Matthei of the air force entered the presidential palace, he told the waiting journalists that it was "rather clear" that the No had won. (He later told the Chilean press that he decided to do this because the government was delaying the publication of the results and the army had not even communicated them to his office, although the results were being announced by the opposition.) Matthei reported his announcement to Pinochet when he entered, provoking the president's fury. When the minister of the interior, Sergio Fernández, told Pinochet that the 44 percent vote he had received was extraordinary and showed that he was the most important political figure in the country, Matthei commented ironically, "Fine, and where is the champagne to celebrate?" When Fernández then asked the commanders to sign a decree giving the president special powers, Matthei refused and Admiral Merino supported him, saying the constitution must be observed. An hour later, when the vice-commander of the army told Pinochet that the army was at his disposal, Pinochet repeated Merino's words. Finally, at 2 A.M. the undersecretary of the interior announced that with 71 percent of the vote reported, the No had 53.5 percent and the Yes vote totaled 44.3 percent.

The next day there were tear gas incidents in front of the presidential palace as groups of demonstrators attempted to break the police blockade, and members of the foreign press were injured. The Command postponed its victory celebration until Friday, October 7, when hundreds of thousands of Chileans gathered at the O'Higgins Park to dance, sing, and jump up and down, Latin style, to celebrate the victory. On Thursday evening, dressed in a white uniform, Pinochet formally conceded defeat and pledged to carry out the provisions of the constitution.

Those provisions provided for a fourteen-month interim period before the congressional elections, which would now be accompanied by an open presidential contest. The Command for the No continued as the Coalition (*Concertación*) of Parties for Democracy (CPPD) and announced that it planned to offer a single presidential candidate with its joint program as the basis for a future government. It spoke of the need to amend the constitution, but its leaders made special efforts to reassure business groups that except for an increase in social spending, particularly on health, housing, and education, the main lines of the existing economic policy would be maintained.

The main influence on the Concertación's economic policy was Alejandro Foxley, whose economic think tank, CIEPLAN, had long received Ford Foundation support. Like Foxley, many of the other leaders of the coalition had done graduate work at American universities. U.S. technical assistance on the vote count appears to have played more than a marginal role in the confused events of election night, particularly in heading off a possible attempt to use false announcements of a Yes victory to provoke violence that could be used as a pretext to call off the vote. Given the legalism and constitutionalism of the Chilean armed forces and the fact that Pinochet could not count on the unconditional support of the other services, it seems unlikely, however, that an effort to cancel the plebiscite would have been successful, even without the U.S. statements and actions before the vote. However, along with the European initiatives, they provided an additional deterrent.

U.S. Intervention?

Were the U.S. actions, as the Pinochet government kept asserting, a violation of the principle of nonintervention? That depends on how that term is understood. Statements, votes in international organizations, and threats to withhold aid seem to be accepted forms of the exercise of influence in international relations. Spending money on foreign elections is not as clearly legitimate, particularly if it is not spent in a nonpartisan way. In the Chilean case, all the U.S. money went to the opponents of the government, ostensibly for "educational" purposes, in order to guarantee the objectivity of the vote by making it possible to establish electoral freedom and reliable alternative vote counts. The fact that the "nonpartisan" aid only went to one side was defended as necessary to ensure a fair election and to right the balance of resources which was heavily weighted in favor of a dictatorial government.

If intervention is defined as the use of outside power to force other countries to do something they would not otherwise do, the U.S. role can be defended, since the funding of the opposition made it possible for a very broad range of Chilean public opinion to express itself freely in circumstances in which free expression was limited by an authoritarian government with considerable resources at its disposal to influence the electoral outcome. In addition, in contrast to the earlier covert aid from the CIA, all NED and AID assistance was public knowledge and subject to accountability to the U.S. Congress.

The "level playing field" argument is capable of extension, however, as a precedent in other, more doubtful areas. It was used, for instance, to support massive U.S. assistance to the anti-Sandinista coalition that won the Nicaraguan elections in February 1990. An evaluation of that case would depend on judgments on the fairness of the 1984 Nicaraguan election, which the Sandinistas won, and of the degree to which the Sandinistas would have otherwise exceeded normal use of the advantages of incumbency.

Because of the breadth of the U.S. consensus supporting assistance to the opposition, these issues were not raised in the United States. Ambassador Barnes, who retired from the Foreign Service at the end of 1988, and the State Department received praise from a broad spectrum of opinion in the media, the universities, and the Congress. U.S. opinion, so divided over Chile for so long, had come together in support of a policy that transcended partisan and ideological differences." Both left and right agreed that it was a successful policy.

The question left for the future was, What are the appropriate guidelines for U.S. economic support of a democratic opposition to a dictatorial government? There is also the question of the nature of U.S. continuing support of a newly democratic regime after it comes to power. To that question as it was posed in Chile in the early 1990s I now turn.

8

Chile Returns to Democracy

THE 1980 constitution provided for what appeared to be a very long interim period between the plebiscite and the election of a Congress and president, from October 1988 until December 1989, and it gave Pinochet three additional months before the inauguration of the new government in March 1990. The opposition had to come up with a single candidate among sixteen very different parties—and the right also had its own internal problems, since it was divided into two major groupings and a number of other minor parties. Until March 11, 1990, the junta was legally still the legislature, with the power to adopt binding laws. In addition, the constitution contained provisions that gave the military considerable power, including a military majority on the National Security Council, a broad definition of what constituted anticonstitutional parties and individuals whose political rights could be taken away, and four appointed senators from the armed forces as well as two more to be appointed by Pinochet as outgoing president.

1989 Constitutional Amendments

The leaders of the National Renovation Party, Sergio Onofre Jarpa and Andrés Allamand, showed themselves amenable to negotiation on the constitutional issue—despite the fact that the 1980 constitution appeared to be extremely difficult to amend, requiring in its transitional provisions a national referendum on amendments during the transition period. Pinochet originally insisted that he would oppose any change in the constitution, but by March 1989 he appeared to be more conciliatory. After several months of negotiations between Jarpa and his supporters and the representatives of the Concertación, there was agreement on fifty-four changes, most of them minor but some of great importance, which were to be submitted to a vote.

The important changes included:

1. adding the controller general (oddly, not the minister of defense) to the National Security Council so as to eliminate the military majority, and modifying the description of its duties to make them more advisory in character;

2. reducing the term of the first elected president from eight years to four, in recognition of the transitional character of the next government;

3. facilitating the process of constitutional amendment by reducing the required extraordinary congressional majorities for amendments and constitutional basic (organic) laws;

4. eliminating the controversial Article 8 concerning unconstitutional parties and individuals, while adding wording to another article which still allowed the Constitutional Tribunal to outlaw subversive groups; and

5. enlarging the Senate from twenty-six to thirty-eight elected members so as to reduce the influence of the nine appointed senators. (An informal agreement was made to phase them out after their current terms expire.)

On July 30, 1989, 93.5 percent of the registered voters turned out to ratify the proposed reforms by an overwhelming vote of 87 percent to 8 percent. Since the Communist Party had told its militants to boycott the vote or abstain, the high participation and approval rates were described by the government as a repudiation of Communism.

In 1988, the Communists had initially instructed their members to boycott the October plebiscite but as a result of internal pressure shifted their policy to favor a No vote. They had not been asked to join the Command for the No or the Concertación of Parties for Democracy (CPPD), but in late 1988, when a leftist "instrumental" coalition, the Broad Party of the Socialist Left (PAIS), was created, they became active members. In May 1990 the Communist Party held its first public congress since before the 1973 coup. It affirmed the 1980 policy of "mass popular rebellion" and admitted responsibility for the importation of arms in 1986. However, the congress recommended against participation in the extremist Manuel Rodríguez Popular Front (FPMR), which had itself split into two factions over the issue of relations with its parent party. The party congress also allowed party members to support the opposition presidential candidate in the forthcoming elections, and following the meeting, the party leaders officially abjured armed struggle during the election period.[1]

The U.S. role was diminished in this period. The Democratic Initiatives program of AID gave $3 million for civic and voter education projects to be carried out by Participa, the successor organization to the Civic Crusade, and the National Endowment for Democracy gave one of its two annual awards to Monica Jiménez, the Civic Crusade's organizer. The National

Democratic Institute also sent a large delegation to the December 1989 election, not to prevent irregularities but to help representatives of African, Central American, and Eastern European countries that were initiating a democratic transition to learn how to organize an effective election.

The Poisoned Grapes Case

In March 1989, a new issue emerged which would continue to disturb U.S.-Chilean relations. Between 1985 and 1989, there had been a twofold increase in the export of grapes from Chile to the United States in the Northern Hemisphere winter, mainly to the port of Philadelphia. (In the late 1980s, Chile exported 86 percent of all grapes in international trade, two-thirds of them to the United States.) On March 2, the U.S. embassy in Chile received a telephone call from a Spanish-speaking male warning that shipments of grapes to Japan and the United States had been poisoned with cyanide. The call was repeated on March 8 and March 17. As a result of the embassy warning, the Food and Drug Administration (FDA) inspectors in Philadelphia stepped up their inspection of grapes from Chile in what was the height of the season from such shipments. On March 12, an inspector found three grapes at the top of a box which contained small white rings that appeared to have been the result of an injection. The grapes were immediately sent to the FDA laboratory in Philadelphia, which determined that two of the grapes contained small amounts of cyanide. The grapes were then sent to the FDA laboratory in Cincinnati, which found no traces of cyanide in the Philadelphia sample, in the third untested grape, or in two other grapes found to have similar white rings. Because of the Philadelphia findings, however, the FDA had banned all shipments of grapes to the United States from Chile and recommended that all existing stocks of Chilean grapes be destroyed. Grapes waiting for shipment in Chile were also ordered destroyed. A total of 4 million grapes in the United States and 2 million in Chile were destroyed. Five days later, after establishing an intensive examination program, the FDA permitted shipments to be resumed, but Chilean grape growers claimed that they had lost $330 million because of the FDA ban. (The Chilean government gave partial reimbursement to the growers in Chile.) Chile's international balance of payments, which for many years had been in surplus, was only slightly reduced, but the dollar loss was considerable.

Shortly after the ban was lifted, questions began to be raised about the whole incident. Why had the FDA been able to find the needle in the haystack, two grapes in a shipment of several million grapes? How could the cyanide have survived if injected in Chile? The grapes came from a small shipment of twenty-six pallets out of four thousand on the ship which seemed to have been singled out for inspection. Ricardo Claro, a prominent exporter in Chile, argued that the whole incident had been staged by the U.S. government in order to weaken the Pinochet government and to show its determination to engineer his departure. (Claro is also a radio commentator, newspaper columnist, and, more recently, owner of a television station. He repeated his theories to Senator Richard Lugar when he visited Santiago in August.)

The 2,800-member Chilean Exporters Association then hired a laboratory at the University of California at Davis to conduct tests on grapes spiked with cyanide. They concluded that the only way that the reported amounts could have been in the grapes was for them to have been injected or contaminated with cyanide shortly before the lab tests—that is, at the port of Philadelphia or in the Philadelphia laboratory. Other critics also argue that the findings resulted from laboratory contamination from earlier tests, that the FDA chemists overstated the amount of cyanide, and that cyanide does not produce white rings in grapes.

The FDA replied that it had a study of cyanide injected into grapes which had survived the two weeks that it takes for a ship to come from Chile. It admitted that most such injected grapes shriveled up in the process, but it argued that two had survived in good shape. Senator Jesse Helms began to take an interest in the case in May, and at his request the General Accounting Office (GAO) commissioned four outside consultants to review the adequacy of FDA testing methods. The GAO report was only submitted to Senator Helms in September 1990, but it concluded that the testing methods were appropriate and that refrigerated grapes, like those in question, could retain their shape and color for up to sixteen days. It noted that simulations done by the growers in Chile had been performed on unrefrigerated grapes. The report mentioned the Davis study but did not evaluate its conclusions.

The argument was publicized in a lengthy article in the *Wall Street Journal* (Nov. 6, 1989), and the Chilean government hired Arnold and Porter, a prominent Washington law firm, to push its claim in U.S. administrative courts for $246 million in costs to the Chilean state. The Chilean grape exporters also sued for $212 million. The administrative court rejected both claims, but in February 1992 the growers initiated a suit in the federal district court in Philadelphia, where it was still being argued at the time of writing. The Chilean government chose not to pursue its claim further, pending the Philadelphia court's decision on whether the U.S. government was exempt from suit under the doctrine of sovereign immunity.[2]

The evidence seems to favor a technical error in the Philadelphia laboratory and an administrative overreaction. The resulting furor in Chile was due partly to Chilean sensitivity to the dependence on their export market, which had resulted from the reorientation of Chilean economic policy, and partly, in the Claro case, to a readiness to find American conspiratorial plots against Pinochet.

An additional irritant in U.S. relations with Chile developed in 1989 as well. Following complaints by U.S. pharmaceutical companies, the United States began to press the Pinochet government to adopt a law enforcing patent protection in the pharmaceutical area. After some resistance from Chileans who argued that this would raise the price of medicine for the poor, the junta adopted a decree law, shortly before the return of civilian government, complying with the U.S. wishes. The controller general raised questions about its validity, and a new law had to be pushed through the Chilean Congress in 1990.

Neither of the problems discussed here diminished the enthusiasm of foreign investors for Chile, especially when such investment could be carried out at what was then a 40 percent discount under the debt-equity exchange provisions of Chapter XIX of the foreign exchange regulations. (As the economy improved, the discount almost disappeared.) New foreign investment increased in 1989 to $900 million, including part of a $5 billion investment in the Escondida copper mine by a consortium of Australian, British, and Japanese companies. (Construction of the mine was completed in record time, and it began exports to Europe and Japan in late 1990.) Chile also joined the World Bank International Center for the Settlement of Investment Disputes (ICSID). Other new mines were opened, copper exports soared, and foreign investment increased by 26 percent in 1991. Chilean debt to the United States was reduced not only by debt-equity arrangements but also by direct write-offs of U.S. government indebtedness under the Brady Plan. In 1991, Chile's overall foreign debt was reduced by $1 billion to $17 billion (*Chile Economic Report,* no. 24, May 1992, 4).

Presidential and Congressional Elections

In early 1989, the other members of the Concertación complained about Christian Democratic dominance, but they had no other presidential candidate with the same kind of mass support. After the usual bruising internal struggle within the party, Patricio Aylwin, the obvious candidate, was nominated by the Christian Democrats and by CPPD. This was followed by a complex set of negotiations among the parties on the CPPD slate for the congressional elections. The leftist PAIS coalition finally ran separate candidates in four of the nineteen senatorial districts and in fifteen of the sixty districts for the Chamber of Deputies. Many Socialist—officially PPD—candidates were nominated on the CPPD ticket, as well as some Radicals and Independents, but the majority of its candidates were Christian Democrats.

The right had difficulty finding a candidate to run against Aylwin, although the two major rightist parties were easily able to form a coalition to run congressional candidates. After a long delay that involved his acceptance, rejection, and finally acceptance of the nomination, Hernán Büchi, Pinochet's finance minister who had led the successful economic recovery since 1985 (Chile's growth rate in 1988 had been 7 percent and would be over 9 percent in 1989), was nominated in August. Francisco Javier Errázuriz, a wealthy independent businessman who described himself as the candidate of the "Center-Center," also was a candidate—although, without party backing, he was not given much chance.

The Büchi campaign emphasized the economic growth that Chile had experienced under his management and gradually but perceptibly moved away from defending Pinochet, being especially sensitive on the human rights issue. Errázuriz appealed to those who were fearful of both right and left and combined this with a populist set of promises to raise the minimum wage and expand social spending. The Aylwin campaign continued the happiness theme that had been used in the plebiscite, and with another bouncy theme song and slogan, "The People Are Winning" (*Gana la Gente*),[3] it projected an image of broad support and experience that the Concertación represented. Aylwin had been president of the Christian Democratic Party six times, had been elected to the Senate in the 1960s, and was a known figure in Chilean politics who could not be accused of leftist sympathies, since he was elected to head the party as the candidate of the hard-line anti-Allende wing shortly before the 1973 coup. Yet his coalition included many Socialists, and the Büchi forces tried to focus again on Ricardo Lagos, Allende's former ambassador and minister, as typical of those who would come to power with an Aylwin victory. Nevertheless, as long as the Concertación held together, comprising as it did the center and much of the left, there was no doubt about who would win.

The trick, therefore, was to limit the new government beforehand by legal constraints as much as possible. The constitution already included many limits. The current military commanders were exempt from the limit to a four-year term in the 1980 constitution and could only be removed with the consent of the National Security Council, half of which was composed of military men. Government employees were covered by a civil service law that gave most of them tenure. The Supreme Court justices over the age of 75 were offered generous retirement benefits that led eight of the ten eligible to do so to retire, enabling Pinochet to appoint their successors. More than three hundred mayors and members of development councils were appointed directly by the president and would continue to serve unless the new Congress amended the constitution to provide for their direct election. The nine appointed senators would be named between the election and the inauguration, providing a swing vote in the upper house of the Congress. The 1978 amnesty law covered those accused of human rights abuses before April 1978, except for those involved in the Letelier assassination. And the junta was working on an armed forces law that prohibited cuts in the military budget and gave the military commanders a decisive role in appointment and retirements. The Central Bank was autonomous, and its board of directors was to be named by the Pinochet government. To some observers, it appeared that Aylwin would be tied in so many ways that he would not really be able to act, as Chilean presidents had traditionally acted, to carry out the program upon which he had been elected.

An additional unwelcome surprise for the Concertación was the complex voting law for the congressional elections. Designed by a progovernment professor of law (the numerous and able Chilean political scientists were not consulted), it was blatantly constructed to overrepresent the minority. It provided that the nineteen senatorial districts and the sixty districts for the Chamber of Deputies would each be represented by *two* senators or deputies. The party or coalition with the largest number of votes would get the first seat, but the second seat would go to the party or group of parties with the next largest number of votes unless the vote of the leading party or group was over twice that of the runner-up party or coalition. Thus the first minority grouping could theoretically get half the seats, unless the leading Concertación candidates received in excess of about 60 percent of the votes.

As before the plebiscite, the candidates had free television programs to appeal for support. The Büchi programs again referred to the threat of a recurrence of the disorders of the Allende period, the Errázuriz pitch was to his centrist and business-oriented credentials, and the Aylwin forces spoke of the need to repay the "social debt" to the poor in spending for health, education, and housing. In a campaign in which all polls gave Aylwin nearly a 2 to 1 lead over Büchi, and during which demonstrations were large and boisterous but notably free of the violence that had characterized such gatherings in earlier years, the contrast with the tension surrounding the plebiscite fourteen months earlier was striking.

The vote was held on December 14, 1989, in an atmosphere of what Chilean authorities described as "complete tranquillity." The final result in the presidential election was a sweeping victory for Aylwin with 54 percent to 29 percent for Büchi and 15 percent for Errázuriz, and 2 percent blank or invalid votes, in a total of 7,142,000 votes. Observers pointed out that by combining the votes of the two opponents of Aylwin, one could arrive at almost exactly the same result as in the 1988 plebiscite. However, polls argued that Errázuriz had in fact drawn some support from potential Aylwin voters, so that without his candidacy Aylwin's victory would have been greater.

The congressional results predictably led to an overrepresentation of the rightist coalition of Jarpa's Renovación Nacional (RN) and Guzmán's Independent Democratic Union (UDI). Although the rightist coalition carried no senatorial districts and only four of the sixty districts for members of the Chamber of Deputies, the Concertación was only able to win a large enough majority to win the second seat in two (out of nineteen) senatorial districts and six of the sixty deputies' districts. The left PAIS–Radical Social Democrat coalition won two of the runner-up deputy seats, one of them won by Orlando Letelier's son, Juan Pablo Letelier, and a few well-known leaders of the left, such as the popular Socialist Mario Palestro in the Chamber of Deputies and former Radical leader Anselmo Sule in the Senate, won seats on the Concertación ticket. However, one of the striking results of the election was that, partly as a result of the electoral system and partly as a result of their own lack of electoral appeal, no Communists were elected. Two Communist senatorial candidates, running on the PAIS ticket, Fanny Pollarolo (who later left the Party) and Jorge Insunza, came in second in the totals for individual candidates but failed to get elected because the other candidate on their ticket did badly.

The most blatant injustice that resulted from the electoral system took place in the senatorial district for western Santiago. There the Concertación had put up two strong rival candidates, Andrés Zaldívar, a leading Christian Democrat, and Ricardo Lagos, the well-known Socialist running on the PPD ticket. Zaldívar won the first seat, but the second seat went to Jaime Guzmán of the UDI with 224,302 votes even though Lagos had received 399,408 votes, because the combination of Zaldívar's and Lagos' votes was

2 percent short of the needed target of double the RN-UDI vote. For similar reasons, in Valparaiso, Christian Democrat Juan Hamilton received 112,626 votes, but the candidate of the right, with 69,708 votes, was elected to the Senate.

There were those who defended the system on the ground that it gave the right a larger stake in the system than they would have had under the proportional representation system used in the past. In reply, however, it was noted that the right already was assured of substantial representation in the Senate because of the nine appointed senators.

The appointed senators turned out to be very important in giving the right a veto over legislation. The final result in the Chamber of Deputies gave the Concertación 69 to 48 for the right, along with 2 seats for the PAIS, which would probably vote with the Concertación, as well as 1 independent. In the Senate however, a 22–16 majority for the Concertación would be reversed by the addition of the nine appointed senators.[4]

In late December and early January, the senatorial appointments were announced. Three were chosen by the Supreme Court, two of them judges and one a former controller general. The National Security Council appointed four, a former commander from each of the four armed services. And following the constitutional specifications, the (outgoing) president—Pinochet—appointed two, one a former university rector (ex–Christian Democrat William Thayer) and the other a former minister (Sergio Fernández). When the appointments were completed, it was clear that even with occasional defections such as by the controller general, the Aylwin government, despite its popular victory, was unlikely to have a majority in the Senate.

In January, Aylwin announced his cabinet appointments. (Aware of the problems that Allende had had with his Popular Unity coalition's insistence on dividing up the ministries, the Concertación had agreed very early to give him complete freedom in his appointments.) The new cabinet was predictably dominated by Christian Democrats, including Alejandro Foxley as finance minister and Edgardo Boeninger as secretary general to the president, but representatives of other parties included the head of the Radical Party, Enrique Silva Cimma, as foreign minister, and Socialists in ministries such as Education (Ricardo Lagos) and Economics (Carlos Ominami, who insisted that nationalization was not part of his program). The furthest left in terms of past affiliation was the transportation minister, Germán Correa, who had moved from the Christian Democrats to a radicalized MAPU and then to membership of the left (Almeyda) wing of the Socialists. (The longstanding split in the Socialist Party had been healed at the end of 1989 through a fusion of the two wings, with the "renovated" or moderate wing in the ascendancy.)

The Transfer of Power

As the Aylwin government prepared to take power on March 11, 1990, Pinochet was busy preparing for his role as army commander. Ownership of the presidential Mercedes limousines was transferred to the army, the luxurious new presidential residence (never occupied, since security experts said it was very vulnerable to terrorist attack) was turned into an officer's club, and, most important, the CNI building and its one thousand army members became part of army intelligence (DINE). A government-owned airport, one of the torture centers of the CNI, and a news agency were sold to friends of the president, and proposals were made to privatize the government and university television stations. The Armed Forces Law was finally adopted with some concessions (later disputed by Pinochet) to presidential power to promote and retire officers (but only on names proposed by the armed forces commanders). It prohibited any reduction in the military budget and was classified as an organic law so that a larger majority was required to amend it. The Central Bank board was named, headed by a technocrat from the U.N. Economic Commission for Latin America who had earlier been a Christian Democrat. In the summer lull in February, preparations were made for a gala inaugural (*"transmisión del mando"*) on March 11.

That ceremony was not without its problems, since many invited foreign observers as well as members of the opposition did not recognize Pinochet's legitimacy. The solution for most of the foreign presidents or their representatives (all except the United States, Argentina, Brazil, and Paraguay) was to arrive for the celebrations that followed the formal ceremony, since Pinochet insisted on a ceremonial visit by foreign representatives as long as he was still president.

The principal U.S. representatives, Vice President Dan Quayle and Senator Edward Kennedy, arrived on March 10. The arrival of Senator Kennedy was ignored by the national television. Quayle was heckled by rightists when he visited Pinochet to pay his respects. That evening Kennedy attended an emotional dinner with human rights workers which concluded with the presentation of a plaque to Jaime Castillo, the president of the Chilean Human Rights Commission, who had been twice expelled from Chile by Pinochet. Kennedy received one of the largest ovations at the moving inaugural address ceremonies, on March 12, when the foreign dignitaries were introduced.

The actual inauguration took place in the new Congress building in Valparaiso, the construction of which had been ordered by Pinochet some years earlier with the intention of weakening the governmental role of the Congress by placing it 66 miles from the capital. Pinochet was heckled as he entered, and at the appropriate time he took off the presidential sash. To symbolize the discontinuity between the two administrations, the president of the Senate, Gabriel Valdés, placed a different sash on President Aylwin. (The medallion on the original sash that had belonged to Bernardo O'Higgins, the country's founding father, had been destroyed in the bombing of the presidential palace in 1973.)

At the exact moment of the placing of the sash on Aylwin, control of the national television passed to the Aylwin forces. Salvador Allende ceased to be a "nonperson" as the TV showed Allende's widow (accompanied by Volodia Teitelboim, the head of the Communist Party) placing a rose below the window of La Moneda, the presidential palace, where her husband had been last seen alive. The television also showed a dramatic speech by a member of the new Congress, Maria Maluenda, as she took the chair as president pro tem to supervise the Chamber of Deputies elections, speaking of the murder of her son five years earlier by a death squad and paying tribute to the role of the church in the defense of human rights.

A similar tribute was paid by Aylwin during his inauguration address the next day in the National Stadium, the place where thousands had been detained, tortured, and murdered in 1973 (as portrayed in the film *Missing*). Looking at Senator Kennedy and others to whom he had given a special greeting on his arrival, he thanked those foreign visitors "who supported us [the anti-Pinochet forces] in times of suffering, and now celebrate with us in this time of joy." His speech had been preceded by a memorial ceremony for the disappeared which included a list of their names in the stadium lights, a memorial musical composition dedicated to Victor Jara, a well-known folk singer killed after the coup, and the lighting of candles by relatives of the disappeared.[5]

The Human Rights Issue

The human rights issue was one of the first problems for the new administration. Pinochet had promised that no one would touch what he called "my people," (*mi gente*), and he saw his role as army commander in chief as principally concerned with preventing human rights prosecutions. On the other hand, the country had become much more aware of the extent of the abuses that had taken place as a flood of books about the atrocities of the postcoup period appeared. Most devastating in its impact and a runaway best seller was Patricia Verdugo's *Los zarpazos del puma*, an account of the October 1973 "Caravan of Death" that had gone by Puma helicopter to the jails and detention centers in several cities in the north of Chile and had taken out seventy-two prisoners whose sentences appeared too light and shot and buried them. The paperback book, inexpensively priced, was available on every newsstand and went through many printings. Then a series of excavations, notably at Pisagua and Paine, uncovered many more bodies and focused more attention on the problem.

One of Aylwin's early official actions was to name an eight-member Commission on Truth and Reconciliation headed by Raúl Rettig, a centrist Radical lawyer and former senator, which included not only human rights activists and sympathizers but respected conservative jurists and educators as well, two of whom had been members of the Pinochet government in the 1970s. Its charge was to hear testimony in a nonjudicial setting and prepare a report on "the most serious violations of human rights committed during the last years," defined as "detentions, disappearances, executions, and torture, resulting in death, involving the moral responsibility of the state by reason of acts of its agents or persons in its service, as well as kidnappings and attempts on the life of persons committed by private individuals for political reasons" (Decree No. 355, Apr. 25, 1990). The commission was instructed to publish a fully documented report with recommendations on possible reparations to those affected and ways to prevent recurrence of such violations in the future.

This was one of the first areas affected by the existence of the appointed senators, since it was clear that a repeal of the 1978 amnesty would not pass the Senate because of the opposition of the right plus the appointed senators. The post-1978 cases, such as the murder of the labor leader Tucapel Jiménez in 1982 and the throat slittings of four Communists in 1985, were in the courts. However, for the pre-1978 cases—which included most of the deaths to be studied by the commission, since no criminal prosecution could be carried out—there was a hesitancy by the judiciary even to initiate investigations. The appointment of the Commission on Truth and Reconciliation took some of the heat off this issue, since investigation was exactly what they were doing, although they were prohibited by the terms of their creation from engaging in a judicial proceeding.

The status of political prisoners was also an issue. It was partially resolved by release of those who were not guilty of "crimes of blood," and the new minister of justice, Francisco Cumplido, put together a packet of laws transferring most of the other cases from the military to the civilian courts, but it took the Chilean Congress nearly a year to pass the laws.

Also included in the Cumplido proposals were the transfer of the Letelier case to the civilian courts and the appointment of a special investigating magistrate to deal with the matter. These were introduced as a way to comply with the requirement in the 1981 U.S. legislation that in order for military sales or aid to Chile to be resumed, the president had to certify that Chile was "cooperating in bringing to justice in Chile or the U.S. the murderers of Orlando Letelier and Ronni Moffitt." Before his departure, Ambassador Barnes had secured congressional approval for a small training program in the United States for Chilean officers, and in 1989 two shipments of helicopters to the Chilean military were permitted on the theory that their primary use was for civilian rather than military purposes. In May 1990, the Aylwin government negotiated an agreement with the State Department legal counsel to submit the issue of compensation for the Letelier and Moffitt families to arbitration by an international Bryan Commission (after William Jennings Bryan, who had signed the U.S.-Chile arbitration treaty in 1914), composed of five jurists from Chile, the United States, Venezuela, Uruguay, and Britain. The commission was to be asked to make recommendations concerning an ex gratia (of free will—not admitting guilt) payment of damages to the families which a U.S. court had earlier set at $2.9 million plus interest. In January 1992, the commission ordered the Chilean government to pay $2.6 million in damages to the relatives of Orlando Letelier and Ronni Moffitt (*New York Times,* Jan. 13, 1992).

The agreement to resort to the Bryan Commission to assess damages required the approval of the Chilean Congress, and there was some doubt as to whether it would pass the Senate. However, on July 3, 1991—in a secret vote, but evidently with the support of several of the appointed senators—the agreement received senatorial approval. Formal presidential certification on the Letelier issue, leading to a lifting of the ban on military sales to Chile, had already been issued earlier in the year, following a visit by President Bush and the introduction of the Cumplido bills.

Curiously there was also some delay in the lifting of the 1987 sanctions, imposed for labor abuses, excluding Chile from the Generalized System of Preferences (GSP) and Overseas Private Investment Corporation (OPIC) insurance. The OPIC insurance was reinstated when President Aylwin visited Bush in early October 1990, but the GSP question had become linked to the continuing problem of the Chilean treatment of "intellectual property," specifically pharmaceuticals, and it was not until Bush's December 1990 visit to Chile that the U.S. special trade representative recommended lifting the sanctions, and they were not formally lifted until February 1991. Reinstating Chile meant that 452 nontraditional exports could enter the United States duty-free, resulting in an estimated increase in exports of $300 million over the next three years (*Chile Economic Report,* Feb. 1991, 3).

There were also trade problems relating to excessively strict "marketing orders" concerning the importation of Chilean fruit that might conceivably compete with California growers. (Chilean fruit is imported when California fruit is not available, but there were still pressures concerning quality and timing that took time to resolve.) However, a proposal in the U.S. Senate to tighten the restrictions on Chilean fruit imports was not adopted.

Economic Program

Finance Minister Foxley took pains to reassure the international banks that Chile would continue to maintain an export surplus and observe its international obligations. As had happened often during the 1980s, the debt service timing was renegotiated, stretching it out and postponing some payments to relieve the burden of debt service. Following the announcement of President Bush's Enterprise Initiative for the Americas in June 1990 and the initiation of negotiations with Mexico concerning a possible free-trade agreement similar to the one that the United States had negotiated with Canada, Chile let it be known that it was strongly interested in a similar arrangement, and a framework agreement for future economic relations was signed on October 1, 1990. Follow-up meetings were held in Santiago and Washington, a bilateral Trade and Investment Council was created, and a working group was established in 1991 to do technical work preparatory to negotiating a free-trade agreement. Chile also took advantage of opportunities offered by the program to reduce its Food for Peace (P.L. 480) indebtedness by 40 percent, to finance additional structural reforms to promote investment (a $150 million loan from the Interamerican Development Bank), and to use interest payments on the debt in local currency to support programs on the environment.

In his public statements, Foxley described his policy as "fiscally conservative and socially progressive." He spoke of the danger of following what he called "the populist cycle" of heavy deficit spending at the beginning of the term of a new democratic government leading later to runaway inflation that finally discredits democracy. Since Chileans could see striking examples of this phenomenon in neighboring Peru and Argentina, Foxley was able to get cooperation in limiting wage demands and social spending, although the Concertación delivered on its promise to increase pensions, the minimum wage, and spending on education and health care. (Foxley claimed that social spending had increased by 31 percent in 1990 and 1991 and budgeted further increases in 1992.) To finance the new expenditures, a small increase in the value-added and corporation taxes was adopted by the Congress with the cooperation of the rightist Renovación Nacional. (A reduction in spending for the armed forces was not possible because of the provisions of the Armed Forces Law. Since the 1973 coup, the army had increased in size by 66 percent and the air force and navy by over 50 percent. Pensions, housing, and medical care for current and retired military are also much better than for civilians.)

The Aylwin government had hoped for U.S. aid to finance social spending at least for the transition period before the new taxes took effect. The U.S. Congress only voted a $10 million health care program, proposed by Senator Kennedy, far less than the $300 million programs also voted for Nicaragua and Panama. Its purpose was to support primary medical clinics, a priority of the new government. An existing AID program of low-income–housing guarantees was also increased to $20 million, and a World Bank loan financed job training programs for 100,000 young people between 1991 and 1995. Outside aid programs, however, were no longer central to Chilean economic health as inflation dropped to 15 percent and the unemployment in greater Santiago dipped under 5 percent. (By 1992 it was 4.4 percent, an all-time low. See *Chile Economic News,* no. 250, June 1992, 2.)

Continuing Tension with Pinochet

There still remained the problem of Pinochet's continuing role as commander in chief of the army. The navy commander, Admiral Merino, had retired at the time of the change of government, and the heads of the air force and the national police had been asked by Aylwin to stay on, but he had made it clear that he preferred that Pinochet retire as army chief. (The constitution provides that as a former president he can become a senator for life.) Citing the issue of possible army prosecutions, however, Pinochet insisted on remaining. Tension between Pinochet and the government was inevitable. Initially he refused to meet with the defense minister, arguing that he could only discuss policy matters with the president. Then he sent the second in command in the army to the formal opening of Congress and presidential address on May 18, 1990. After the Commission on Truth and Reconciliation was appointed, he had the army issue a communiqué that defended its actions as a war against subversion which had successfully prevented guerrillas and terrorists from taking over the country. It also warned that "irresponsible treatment" of these matters could lead to "reactions or regressive consequences" (Declaración del Ejercito, June 17, 1990). On the anniversary of the September 11 coup, he declared that if the circumstances in which it took place were repeated, he would not have had "a moment's doubt about taking action" (*El Mercurio,* Sept. 12, 1990). Representatives of the armed forces were significantly absent when, a week earlier, the Aylwin government took another step toward national reconciliation, the reburial of Salvador Allende in the presidential section of Santiago's cemetery. Allende's body was exhumed from its unmarked grave in the family plot in Viña del Mar, near Valparaiso, and following a funeral mass in the national cathedral was interred beneath a 30-foot monument not far from the graves of his two predecessors, Presidents Frei and Alessandri. President Aylwin made a speech in which he declared that while he would still oppose the government if circumstances similar to those of 1973 were to occur, Chileans should make sure that such circumstances are never repeated and should commit themselves "to bury violence and intolerance forever" (*New York Times,* Sept. 5, 1990).

Allende's reburial also led to an article in the leftist magazine *Análisis* reviewing the evidence on Allende's death and including an account of the opening of the casket and an interview with one of those who had performed the autopsy. It concluded that there was no longer any doubt that Allende took his own life on September 11, 1973 (*Análisis,* no. 348, Sept. 10–16, 1990).

In September, twenty-nine bodies of those killed in the postcoup period were exhumed in Patio 29 of Santiago's General Cemetery. Informed that some were discovered buried two to a coffin, Pinochet responded, "How economical."

In October, when the list of senior officers recommended for promotion was submitted to President Aylwin, he rejected two of those proposed by Pinochet, and in accordance with military custom, they were forced into retirement. The army protested that this was a violation of the Armed Forces Law, but the controller general upheld Aylwin's action as within his constitutional powers, as declared in Article 32, Section 18, to "dispose of" (*disponer*) nominations, promotions, and retirements.

Also in October, two scandals hurt Pinochet's position. The first, involving his son, Augusto, Jr., produced a congressional investigation of financial manipulation involving the purchase at an inflated price by the army of an arms manufacturing complex that his son had bought for a very low price. The army purchase had been revealed when the Congress got photocopies of three checks made out to Augusto, Jr., totaling more than $3 million dollars. The second was the revelation that numerous high-ranking officers were financially involved in an illegal mutual fund involving shares in companies with which the army did business. Pinochet took steps to remove the officers involved in the mutual fund scandal, and a congressional investigation did not find convincing evidence that he knew about his son's financial manipulations. However, his prestige suffered in both cases.

By the end of the year, there were reports that Pinochet was negotiating the conditions of his resignation with the Aylwin government, and a later *New York Times* report (Jan. 22, 1991) told of a December 18 meeting between Aylwin and Pinochet in which each hesitated to bring up that delicate subject. The day after the meeting, the army was called to quarters in a billeting operation (*acuartelamiento*) that was described as a "readiness exercise." (A Spanish newspaper described it as a "fake military uprising.")

The "exercise" only lasted seventeen hours, but no one doubted its purpose. In case there was any doubt, the army issued a public declaration on January 8, 1991, reaffirming its "unlimited loyalty to its commander in chief" and its "indestructible institutional cohesion around Captain General Augusto Pinochet Ugarte."[6] Then with the publication of the Rettig commission report in early March 1991, Pinochet seemed determined to remain in order to resist possible prosecution of army officers. Yet at 75 and no longer shielded and surrounded by a large propaganda apparatus, as more and more details of the abuses of his regime became publicized, he was in a much weakened position, while public opinion polls showed that Aylwin's approval rating had risen to over 70 percent (suggesting to some that the constitution might be amended to permit him to run again).

While the Congress could not cut the military budget as a whole, it used its power of the purse to reduce the number of ex-CNI employees in army intelligence by 350 (from 1,000 to 650), and Congressmen complained about a secret fund of $3 million available to Pinochet as army commander, as well as the secret law earmarking copper export receipts for arms purchases.

The Report of the Rettig Commission

On March 4, 1991, President Aylwin delivered an emotional address to the nation analyzing the report of the Commission on Truth and Reconciliation. He summarized its contents, which included detailed individual accounts of the death of more than two thousand persons and proposals for monetary and moral compensation to the victims, such as pensions, scholarships, and subsidies for health care and housing. He also supported its proposals for a human rights public defender and judicial reforms, and he urged investigation and determination of responsibility of the cases exempted from prosecution by the 1978 amnesty. He concluded with a solemn appeal to the armed forces and "all those who participated in the excesses committed, to acknowledge the pain they have caused and make efforts to lessen it" (*El Mercurio,* International Edition, Feb. 28–Mar. 6, 1991).

The commission report was published in three volumes, comprising more than 1,300 pages, the last volume of which was devoted to accounts of the deaths of each of the 2,279 Chileans that it had determined had died as a result of state action or political violence. The report was strongly critical of the military's claim that Chile was in a state of war after the coup, which had been the justification of the continued activity of military courts. It also criticized the military courts for imposing retroactive punishment for actions that had occurred before they were made illegal, for refusing to make the bodies of those executed available to their families, and for "infraction of fundamental legal norms and essential ethical principles." The commission was still more critical of the civilian judiciary, which, it said, "because of the constitution, the law, and the nature of its functions" was the state institution "responsible for the protection of such rights." It accused the judiciary of "worsening the process of the systematic violation of human rights, both by not offering protection to the persons whose cases were denounced to it, and by providing the agents of repression with increasing certainty that they would not be punished for their criminal acts." Examples cited by the commission included indefinite delays in responding to habeas corpus requests and inaction on persons held incommunicado for periods of up to a year.[7]

During one hundred sessions between May 1990 and February 1991, the commission had reviewed evidence concerning 3,400 cases and was able to make a definitive judgment concerning responsibility for 2,279 of them. Ninety of those cases involved political murders by private individuals of the left or right, and 164 died in political protests or confrontations, but the overwhelming majority of those killed (2,025) were victims of state action. After the report was published, approximately 700 more cases were reported to the commission.

Predictably, the army was critical of the report, arguing that it lacked historical and juridical value (despite the strongly legalistic cast of the report, and the lengthy historical sections, written by Gonzalo Vial, a former minister of education and a distinguished conservative historian). The navy disputed the report's criticisms of the judiciary and argued that Chile was in a state of war in 1973, and the national police opposed the proposed reforms that might undermine its function in keeping order (*El Mercurio,* Mar. 28– Apr. 3, 1991). General Fernando Matthei of the air force was more positive in his response, and General Gustavo Leigh, who had been removed from the air force in 1978 by Pinochet, said he took full responsibility for the events of 1973–78 (when most of the violations had taken place). The Supreme Court attacked the commission's criticisms of the judiciary as "politically biased, rash, and tendentious," accusing it of assuming judicial functions that it was not qualified to exercise (*Estudios Públicos,* no. 42, Fall 1991, 237–50).

The issue of the April 1978 amnesty divided the country, with the left arguing for repeal (unlikely, given the Senate majority composed of the right and the appointed senators), the center in favor of investigation without judicial trials, and the right favoring "turning the page" on the human rights question. The argument of the right that the new government was not sufficiently active against terrorism received a powerful confirmation in early April 1991 when Senator Jaime Guzmán was assassinated as he left the Catholic University campus where he lectured. Conspiracy theorists of the center and left attributed the action to General Contreras, former head of the DINA, since Guzmán was known to have been instrumental in his removal in 1977, but most believed that the assassination was the work of the "autonomous" faction of the Manuel Rodríguez Patriotic Front. The government increased expenditure for the investigative police and created a council to coordinate antiterrorism, but the assassins were not identified. The press noted that fifty-five Chileans had died as a result of terrorist actions in 1990 and fifteen so far in 1991, increasing the pressure for government action.

The criticisms of the judiciary in the Rettig report focused attention on the need to "modernize" Chile's antiquated judicial system, but the government's proposals to enlarge the Supreme Court and to create a Council on the Judiciary ran into the accusations of politicization of the notoriously pro-Pinochet judiciary. The small U.S. aid program began to focus in Chile, as elsewhere, on technical assistance to support judicial modernization, as well as strengthening the capacities of the legislative branch.

As democracy became institutionalized in Chile, there was discussion, partly stimulated by American political scientists such as Juan Linz and Arturo Valenzuela, of amending the constitution to change from a presidential system to some kind of parliamentary or mixed system that would introduce more flexibility by abandoning the "winner-take-all" eight-year presidency. (Under the existing constitutional provisions, a president taking office in 1994 would govern into the twenty-first century.) The proposal was made in part to prevent a repetition of the 1970–73 deadlock that produced the coup, but it also recognized the inevitability of a multiparty system in Chile. There had been some simplification of parties in Chile. The center and center-left were dominated by the Christian Democrats and the Socialists-PPD, while the right had two parties that differed ideologically, especially in their attitudes toward Pinochet. The Communist Party was demoralized and deeply split. It had "suspended" one of its leading candidates in the 1989 election and was divided over attitudes toward the present government and toward the changes in the Soviet Union and Europe. In October 1990, it formally applied for legal recognition, but it was clear that it was a shadow of its former self. A Chilean humor magazine published a cartoon portraying Volodia Teitelboim, party president, in a hospital intensive care ward vehemently denying that the party was ill (*Topaze*, Oct. 21, 1991). In late 1991, it organized the Allende Movement of the Democratic Left (MIDA) to link the left groups that objected to the coalition policy of the Socialist Party. In the municipal elections on June 28, 1992, the Communist candidates received 6.62 percent of the votes.[8] To the left of the Communists was the Manuel Rodríguez Patriotic Front (also split), with one faction announcing its intention to enter democratic politics, as well as another extremist group, the Lautaro Popular Revolutionary Front, which carried out bank robberies, bombing of police stations, and the murder of policemen.

The Triumph of Democracy

Chile's return to democracy and the normalization of its relationship with the United States and the rest of Latin America were symbolized by the highly successful Twenty-first General Assembly of the Organization of American States, held in Santiago during the first week of June 1991. Delegates recalled that the last General Assembly to be held in Santiago had taken place in 1976, at the height of the repression, when three-quarters of the population of Latin American was under military or dictatorial regimes. Now, for the first time, all the delegates represented elected governments, and a major issue was how to use the OAS to assure that that situation would not change. After the predictable disagreements between Venezuela, which favored an immediate rupture of relations with any government that took power by force (the Betancourt Doctrine), and Mexico, which favored nonintervention, the thirty-four members voted unanimously for the Declaration of Santiago—officially entitled the Santiago Commitment to Democracy and the Renewal of the Interamerican System—which committed the organization to support democracy, human rights, and liberalization of trade and investments. The assembly passed a resolution directing the Permanent Council to call a foreign ministers meeting or a special General Assembly within ten days if a legitimate democratic government is overthrown. It also called for the adoption of additional programs in support of democracy at its 1992 meeting. The Chilean ambassador to the OAS, Heraldo Muñoz, was particularly active in promoting the resolutions. Senator Máximo Pacheco, former vice-chairman of the Chilean Human Rights Commission, was elected by a very large vote to the Interamerican Court on Human Rights, and its jurisdiction was strengthened. President Bush's Enterprise Initiative for the Americas was endorsed, as well as common action against drugs and arms proliferation. The assembly was notable for the absence of the anti-Americanism that had characterized some earlier OAS meetings. Also noteworthy was a speech by Deputy Secretary of State Laurence Eagleburger acknowledging that the United States had made mistakes in viewing Latin America "through the sometimes distorting prism of the Cold War," promising "to look at the hemisphere with new eyes," and pledging continuing support for democracy and human rights.[9]

Within three months, the policy of opposition to the overthrow of elected governments was put to the test. When President Jean-Bertrand Aristide of Haiti was overthrown in September, the new mechanism went into effect. OAS members were asked to cut off economic relations with the military government, and an OAS mission attempted to negotiate Aristide's return.

The stormy history of U.S.-Chilean relations had given way to a situation in which there was substantial consensus both between the United States and Chile and within Chile itself. The alliance of the Christian Democrats and the Socialists as well as other minor parties still held together and was able to cooperate on at least some issues with a significant part of the right.

A broad consensus supported the market system, and the desirability of foreign investment was not a subject of disagreement. The United States no longer had the high visibility in Chile of earlier years, as Chile had diversified its external relationships and the opposition no longer needed outside assistance. (The right opposition became increasingly critical of U.S. policy in 1990 and 1991.)[10] Conversely, Chile was less visible to Americans. Its successful transition to democracy in late 1989 and early 1990 had been overshadowed for most Americans by the upheavals in Eastern Europe and the Soviet Union, and this had been followed by the Gulf war. Perhaps given the errors and mistakes of the past, Chileans might be justified in preferring a policy of benign neglect on the part of the United States. Yet in one area at least, that of support for democracy and human rights, the relationship between the two countries had had mutually beneficial results. The conclusion of this work evaluates those results and makes recommendations for future policy.

9

Conclusion: Chile and
the Promotion of Democracy

THE STORY OF U.S. relations with Chile is often told as a morality play. The history examined in this book has many lessons, and I have already attempted to draw out some of them. This conclusion reviews the findings of the previous chapters and looks again at the relation of the promotion of democratic values to U.S. foreign policy in Latin America, and especially in Chile, over the last three decades.

My examination of the U.S. role in Chile has suggested some modifications to the conventional views. The chapter on the Alliance for Progress and the effort of the Chilean Christian Democrats, led by Eduardo Frei, to carry out a Revolution in Liberty proposed that U.S. covert CIA intervention in Frei's 1964 election did not make any significant difference, since he already had the support of two of the "three-thirds"—the right, the center, and the left—into which the Chilean electorate was divided. While recognizing that U.S. diplomats have a responsibility to protect the lives and property of U.S. citizens, it argued that U.S. involvement in Chile was primarily motivated by Cold War concerns rather than the economic interest of U.S. corporations, citing the case of U.S. pressure on the Anaconda Corporation to accede to the 1969 Chileanization program, which forced it to give up majority control of its most lucrative mine, Chuquicamata. That pressure resulted from a desire to support a government that was seen as opposed to the extension of Cuban and Soviet influence, but at least part of the support for Chile also involved endorsement of democratic reformism by a Republican administration that has often been seen as preferring to support the military in Latin America.

The chapter analyzed U.S. relations with the Chilean military in the 1960s and noted that, despite a considerable literature arguing that the anti-Communism of the Latin American military resulted from U.S. inculcation of the Doctrine of National Security, the Chilean military had been strongly anti-Communist ever since the 1920s and did not need U.S. instructors to persuade them of the evils of Communism. It also examined what is known about U.S. involvement in the 1970 Chilean presidential election and found a divided U.S. administration that on a number of occasions was hesitant to intervene, especially when that intervention involved the use of means such as bribery to influence outcomes. Covert financing of anti-Communist propaganda in 1970 and of anti-Communist parties and candidates in 1964 and 1969 was not, however, seen as objectionable, since it was believed that the Soviet Union was also subsidizing the left FRAP coalition through the Chilean Communist Party and because there were longstanding European precedents in Italy and France for support of anti-Communist parties and labor unions.

There was one area in which the U.S. role may have had negative consequences for Chilean democracy—the priority that the Alliance for Progress gave to agrarian reform. The 1967 agrarian reform law—involving absolute limits on landed property and compensation that was only partly readjustable for inflation—clearly exacerbated the polarization of Chilean politics which contributed to the three-way division that made Allende's election possible in 1970. It is not possible to assess the degree to which U.S. influence and advice, as well as the enthusiastic support of the American ambassador, affected the adoption of the land reform law, which had long been an issue in Chilean politics, but along with the radicalization of the left in the same period, they contributed to the intense divisions that led to the debacle of the early 1970s. On the other hand, the alliance also induced reforms in the areas of taxation, educational modernization, administrative reform, and concern for the problems of housing, health, and poverty which marked positive advances in Chilean democracy. The Chilean right has argued that those reforms raised hopes that were impossible to satisfy and thus contributed to the expansion of the left, but the electoral results in 1970 in which Allende received 36 percent of the vote, versus 39 percent in 1964, do not support this interpretation.

The following chapter on U.S. policy toward the Allende administration and its relation to the September 1973 coup also provided some new information and interpretations. Contrary to a widespread belief, the activities of the International Telephone and Telegraph Company in conspiring against Allende and lobbying with the U.S. government to subvert him did not demonstrate that U.S. foreign policy is dictated by large corporations. ITT's proposals were rejected by the U.S. government, and in turn, when ITT was asked to take actions by the United States, it did not do so.

When it subsequently attempted to get the support of other corporations and the U.S. government to carry out a program of drastic economic strangulation against Allende, it did not receive it. While large U.S. corporations have access to U.S. policymakers, ITT was something of a special case, since ITT agents in Chile had ties to the Central Intelligence Agency, and one of ITT's directors, John McCone, was a former head of the CIA. The chapter also argues that the U.S. attempt to prevent Allende from becoming president in 1970 by promoting a military coup led indirectly to the murder of the Chilean army commander and, in attempting to reverse the results of a democratic election, marked a clear violation of American principles of self-government. It was carried out by the CIA at the direct behest of President Nixon without the knowledge of the ambassador, the Congress, or the rest of the government. Nixon acted after conferring with a prominent Chilean who was brought to the White House by an American businessman, but his own motives seemed to be a visceral anti-Communist and personal dislike of Allende. Kissinger's motives were also not economic but motivated by his well-known realist or balance-of-power philosophy of international relations, although he justified his opposition to Allende by arguing that his accession to power would mark the end of free elections in Chile and the subversion of its neighbors (see his Sept. 16, 1970, Chicago speech).

The unsuccessful U.S. effort to promote a coup was followed by a CIA program of support for opposition media and parties between 1971 and 1973. A small amount of this money went to extreme right groups, but most of it was spent to support opposition newspapers, radio stations, and electoral propaganda. The Senate Intelligence Committee also found evidence of one forged document being passed to the military, and the CIA was in touch with the opposition military until four months before the coup. However, "destabilization" is not an accurate term to describe these actions, and the term was not used until after the coup. Contrary to the assertions in the book and film *Missing,* there is no evidence that the United States actively promoted a military coup in September 1973, nor is there evidence to support the stories of direct involvement by the United States in the coup itself or in the murder of Charles Horman, an American citizen, shortly thereafter.

Beginning in November 1970, the United States carried out a policy of economic pressure on the Allende government. New aid was discontinued, and lending to Chile by banks and international financial institutions was discouraged, but aid in the "pipeline" was not cut off; humanitarian programs such as the Peace Corps and Food for Peace were continued; and the United States supported an Interamerican Development Bank loan to two private universities. Military aid was also continued, and several loans for aircraft and landing vessels were approved, partly out of fear that a cutoff would lead to Chilean acceptance of Soviet military assistance. It is not accurate to describe the U.S. economic pressures, as President Allende did, as "an invisible blockade," and Chile was able to secure substantial aid from many other countries in Europe and Latin America, although it only received limited assistance from the Soviet Union.

While the U.S. contacts with the Chilean military probably conveyed the message that it would not be opposed to military intervention, the coup itself took place for reasons related to policy errors by the Allende government and its opponents, especially the runaway inflation, rising violence on both sides, and the increasingly uncompromising attitude of the pro- and anti-Allende forces. By 1973 a majority of Chileans probably favored a coup—but along with most foreign observers, they expected a brief intervention by the military, which would then call elections, after outlawing the Communist Party. No one in the United States or in Chile anticipated seventeen years of military rule, and those in the United States and in Chile who opposed the Allende regime thought that they were defending democracy against a regime that was increasingly dominated by the violent left. In retrospect, this looks like destroying "democracy in order to save it," but this was not the perspective of 1973.

After examining what is known about the CIA relationship to the *White Book* issued by the junta, especially the (probably forged) Plan Z document, which intensified the military reaction against the left in the postcoup period, the chapter on U.S. policy after the coup questioned the conventional view that the U.S. government was strongly positive in its attitude toward the Pinochet government,[1] but it documented the reluctance of the executive branch to react to the convincing evidence of serious human rights violations until forced to do so by Congress. For many Americans, Chile became one of the prime examples of the wrong direction that U.S. policy was taking, and well before the administration of President Jimmy Carter, the Congress began to place human rights restrictions on U.S. military and economic aid. Beginning in 1973, increasingly successful efforts were made to limit or condition aid to Chile, culminating in the total cutoff of U.S. military sales or aid to Chile in June 1976.

In the same period, covert action in Chile became the subject of a special case study in connection with congressional efforts to place controls on CIA covert activities. The controversy generated by the revelations of CIA activity in Chile and elsewhere resulted in important legislative restraints on CIA covert action which limited its activities. (It also led to the use of alternative channels in support of the Nicaraguan contras in the 1980s.)

This was also the period in which the "Chicago boys," a group of free-market–oriented economists who had been trained at the University of Chicago, with support from U.S. foundations and AID, were given control of the Chilean economy and carried out a drastic reorientation of Chilean economic policy. The chapter notes, however, that U.S. foundation support also went to opposition think tanks that emerged as alternatives to the military-controlled universities. The Ford Foundation, for example, supported the Christian Democratic–oriented CIEPLAN and the social democratic FLACSO, enabling them to resist military government pressures and to carry out research that was critical of Pinochet government policy. The church-sponsored Academy of Christian Humanism also received limited support from U.S. foundations, although its principal funding came from European sources.

The promotion of human rights received a further boost from the election of Jimmy Carter in 1976—an event that led directly to the release of several hundred political prisoners in Chile. For the purposes of implementation of the punitive aspects of the new legislation, human rights were defined in a narrow sense as freedom from being tortured, murdered, detained without trial, and the like, but the annual reports on each country mandated by the Congress for submission by the State Department also included information on political rights. The existence of those reports meant that the embassy in Chile was now in regular touch with human rights and opposition groups rather than only with government officials.

The chapter on the Carter administration's policy also describes the investigation of the murder in Washington in September 1976 of Orlando Letelier, Allende's ambassador to the United States, which increased the U.S. sanctions against Chile—principally for noncooperation in the extradition of the Chileans involved (although one American involved was extradicted and convicted). The Letelier investigation also led to the dissolution of the major Chilean agency of repression, the DINA, and the ending of disappearances—although not of torture and occasionally murder—carried out by government-related agencies.

The various pressures placed on Chile were not notably effective in producing a response, both because the reduction in U.S. official economic assistance could be replaced by easily available loans from U.S. private banks that were awash with OPEC dollars and because Chile was able to buy arms from Brazil, France, South Africa, and Israel and to develop an arms industry of its own. (Each of the services has an armaments company, and a private company, Cardoen, founded in 1978, became a significant arms exporter.) However, the very fact that human rights conditions were now being placed on U.S. aid sent a signal to the Latin American military that the United States opposed military takeovers, a signal that was reinforced by Carter's direct involvement in heading off a military coup in the Dominican Republic at the time of its 1978 presidential election. The one U.S. action that produced an immediate Chilean response was a threatened AFL-CIO boycott of Chilean exports because of Chilean restrictions on labor freedom. The resulting labor law was part of a large number of "libertarian" reforms in such areas as health, social security, and education in 1979 and 1980 which were influenced by—but often moved well beyond—the U.S. example.

As the next chapter reveals, the Reagan administration came to power determined to change the Carter policy on human rights, on the basis of Jeane Kirkpatrick's distinction between friendly authoritarian regimes and hostile totalitarians. Chile appeared to be in the former category, but Chile's intransigence on the Letelier case and the continuing government repression, documented by human rights groups in Chile (often funded in part by U.S. foundations and individuals), made it impossible for the Reagan administration to end the sanctions. Then a drastic recession in Chile cast doubt on what had appeared to be a successful implementation of the free-market economic model. This was followed by the initiation of mass protests in 1983, as well as the formation of a broad opposition political alliance ranging from moderate Socialists to a few members of the right. Coinciding with the initiation of President Reagan's program to support democratic forces around the world, the protests and Pinochet's continuing intransigence resulted in a shift in U.S. policy to explicit promotion of a return to democracy in Chile. The shift culminated in the 1985 appointment as U.S. ambassador of Harry Barnes, a career diplomat, who from the time of his arrival gave public expression to U.S. support for democracy. Direct U.S. economic pressure also forced the lifting of the state of siege in the same year. The chapter examines the dynamics of that shift and evaluates the reasons that have been put forward for the policy reversal. In doing so, it places less emphasis than most earlier writing on the effect of Central American policy and more on the influence of individual actors and of the general reassertion of control over foreign policy by State Department moderates and professionals, as well as on the fear of political polarization resulting from Pinochet's intransigence.

The description in the ensuing chapter of the U.S. role in assisting in the transition from military rule focuses on the impact of assistance from the National Endowment for Democracy and the Agency for International Development, but it also describes the remarkable activities of Chileans themselves in defeating an entrenched dictatorship in the 1988 plebiscite and forging and electing a viable broadly based democratic alternative. U.S. assistance, as described in the chapter, was significant in four areas— support for a very successful preplebiscite voter registration drive; advice and technical assistance on the use of polling, focus groups, and the media; the organization of a large multinational election monitoring group to discourage fraud; and funding of alternative reporting systems, such as the "quick count," which acted to sidetrack several last-minute attempts to cancel or manipulate the results. The issue of the appropriateness of such U.S. intervention was raised, and the chapter concluded with an argument for such assistance in cases in which an authoritarian government possesses overwhelming control of the financial and media instruments to influence public opinion and where the opposition is broadly based and democratically organized.

The discussion in the next chapter of Chile's successful transition to democracy—led by a government that includes more holders of advanced degrees, many of them American, than any government in the contemporary world—examines the resolution of the many internal and external problems inherited by the Aylwin administration when it took power in early 1990. With the possible exception of some minor economic irritants such as discriminatory "marketing orders" regulating Chilean exports to the United States, all of the negative elements that for so long impeded normal relations between the two countries have now been resolved. There is Chilean-American agreement on democracy and on the desirability of a market-based economy. Foreign investment is welcomed, not condemned. As a result of the transformations in Eastern Europe and the Soviet Union, the Cold War is over, and the issue of national security, defined in East-West terms, no longer contaminates the relationship between the two countries. We are not at the "end of history," but U.S. policy is now firmly committed to the support of democracy and human rights in Latin

America. And it no longer is simply a means to other ends but has become an end in itself—although not the only one—of American policy. As this book has argued, the course of U.S.-Chilean relations over the last three decades had much to do with this change.

Policy Recommendations

Given the disappearance of the earlier irritants and of the traditional Cold War guidelines that have directed U.S. policy toward Chile for nearly half a century, what are the directions in which future U.S. policy should go?

1. The Chileans have already indicated their strong interest in the signing of a free-trade agreement incorporating them into the emerging North American Common Market, and they have supported the Bush Enterprise for the Americas Initiative. Chile has also signed a free-trade agreement with Mexico, and Venezuela and Colombia are also taking action to join the free-trade movement. There is for the first time a genuine possibility of a single hemispheric trading group that can compete and trade with the European Community and Japan. While maintaining its links with the other groupings, the United States should support hemispheric economic integration and should sign a free-trade agreement with Chile. If, as President Bush has said, trade and investment have replaced the East-West conflict as the central orienting principle of U.S. policy toward Latin America, a free-trade agreement can do more to promote those objectives than any other single action.

2. The Chilean model of export orientation, low tariffs, realistic exchange rates, and reduced government involvement now has wide support internationally, and Chilean experts have been called in as advisers on the privatization of industry and social services by the Eastern Europeans and Russians. In the past, the Chilean example was often dismissed because it appeared to require authoritarian government and the repression of labor for it to function. Now, however, in Chile and elsewhere, such reforms are being carried out under democratic auspices and often with the cooperation of labor. Because of its rapid growth rate under democratic auspices, Chile is a prime candidate to move from the Third to the First World[2]—although many problems, especially the poverty of the lowest 20 to 30 percent of the population, remain. The United States should continue to support the integration of Chile into the international economy and worldwide economic expansion based primarily on market incentives.

3. The important steps taken at the 1991 meeting in Santiago of the

Organization of American States to promote democracy and reduce military expenditures can be advanced by Chile and the United States together, and new ways can be found to achieve both objectives on a cooperative rather than unilateral basis.[3] While the United States no longer has the preponderant influence it once had on the Chilean military, it can support arms reductions, democracy, and human rights in training programs in which the Chilean military participates. Except for Cuba, Chile has the largest per capita military budget in Latin America, but an organic law requiring an extraordinary majority for repeal currently limits reductions in military expenditures. However, reductions in the military threat from Argentina and Peru and the eventual departure of General Pinochet as army commander should make future cuts possible.

4. Although the more grandiose ambitions of the Alliance for Progress to transform the continent in a decade were not realized, the objective of the promotion of stable and just democratic societies in the Western Hemisphere is still valid. U.S. diplomatic, technical, and educational cooperation in areas such as judicial reform, assistance to legislative bodies, and support for hemispheric action to promote and protect democracy can assist in attaining that objective. Already proposed in connection with the threat to democracy posed by the 1991 Haitian coup, an OAS Peacekeeping Force on a permanent or ad hoc basis—probably without direct U.S. participation—can now be seriously considered, overcoming earlier Latin American objections based on the principle of nonintervention. Given the consensus in the OAS, it could play a significant role in assisting or reinstating democracy in the countries of the hemisphere.

5. The Chilean case showed the need for congressional controls on covert action, and the Iran-contra scandal reinforced that lesson. In 1991 the Congress tightened the requirements for covert action. At the outset the president must make a "finding" in writing that such action is necessary and must make a report to the Intelligence Committees of Congress before it begins, or in exceptional circumstances, "within a few days." The president is forbidden to use third countries to evade legislative limitations— as happened in the Iran-contra case. These new restrictions are helpful, but we may still ask whether, now that the Cold War is over, such fundamentally antidemocratic activities as those involved in covert action are any longer necessary.

Defenders of covert action point to the case of Saddam Hussein in Iraq to justify a continuing covert capability, but so far that capability has not produced a change of government in Iraq. The abuses illustrated in the Chilean case in the 1970s and Iran-contra in the 1980s argue at least for the restriction of covert action to wartime or periods of national crisis rather than its use as a normal policy instrument.[4]

6. New areas of cooperation such as the control of drug traffic and the protection of the environment have emerged and now form part of the basis for the "renewal" of the interamerican system, called for at the 1991 Santiago meeting of the OAS. Chile has not been part of international drug smuggling in any major way—although after the 1973 coup, both sides accused each other of involvement—but drug shipments from Bolivia have increased in northern Chile (*New York Times,* Jan. 23, 1992). In the case of the environment, Chile's interest in fishing conservation and joint hemispheric action to limit the depletion of the ozone layer in the Antarctic is evident and should receive U.S. support and assistance.

Support for Democracy as an Independent Variable

Most commentators on the U.S. international promotion of democratic values seem to take pleasure in pointing out how little those values are reflected in the conduct of U.S. foreign policy toward Latin America. It is customary to describe support for democracy as either a facade to conceal "real" policy objectives in order to sell an executive policy to a gullible Congress and the public, or as a laudable objective that is consistently overridden by security and economic interests, or in the case of "realist" critics, a policy that interferes with the pursuit of the national interest. For example, the (mostly liberal) contributors to *Exporting Democracy* (edited by Abraham Lowenthal) take a consistently critical view of U.S. efforts to promote democracy in Latin America. Paul W. Drake argues that in the case of earlier U.S. efforts in this century, "the primary U.S. goals were strategic protection and economic expansion, for which engineering democracy was normally a tool or a subordinate objective" (7), while Leslie Bethell asserts that "the 'hard' or 'primary' interests of the United States in Latin America have always been geopolitical and strategic" and that "democracy was in the last analysis disposable" (48). Thomas Carothers admits that the Reagan administration shifted from "purely rhetorical" support for democracy to politics in which "democracy was a real concern" but describes the administration's conception of democracy as promoting only "very limited top-down forms of democratic change that do not risk snowballing into uncontrollable populist movements" (115, 118). Laurence Whitehead quotes approvingly G. Pope Atkins' description of U.S. promotion of democracy as "ambiguous and vacillating. When resources have been committed to the goal of democratic development, it has usually been viewed as an instrumental objective aimed at achieving one or the other of the long-range goals" of security or political stability (358). Abraham Lowenthal's concluding essay argues that "recurrent efforts to promote Latin American democracy have not been long sustained . . . and the inconstancy of U.S. policy has tended not only to erode the efficacy of U.S. policy but actually to undermine the conditions for democratic politics" (400). Heraldo Muñoz takes a more nuanced position in his essay on the Chilean case. As he describes it, U.S. policy toward Chile has exhibited "an obsessive tendency to halt the ascendancy of the left in Chile at the cost of eroding Chilean democracy . . . [although] in specific periods the United States did contribute to the promotion of democracy in Chile, guided by humanitarian motives and libertarian ideals" (172). Muñoz recognizes, as many other writers do not, that "the U.S. executive cannot totally dismiss for very long periods the humanitarian values in foreign policy without provoking adverse reactions from various important domestic governmental and nongovernmental sectors" (162).

Undeniably there are many examples in which security or economic interests have overridden U.S. commitment to democracy, but what needs to be explained—and only Muñoz attempts to do so—is the continual recurrence to, and importance of, the theme of the promotion of democracy in U.S. policy toward Latin America. It is easy to view this simply as rhetorical, hypocritical, or utopian, but it marks a significant difference between the objectives and instruments of U.S. policy and those of the other contemporary great powers—including some with a strong commitment to democratic values in their domestic political life. To paraphrase Dr. Samuel Johnson's observation, as reported by Boswell, on the case of the dog that walked on two legs, "What is surprising is not that it is done well, but that it is done at all."

Democracy has not always been promoted well by the United States over the last thirty years, but since the announcement of the Alliance for Progress it has been a significant component, with varying degrees of saliency, in U.S. policy toward Latin America—and Chile has been regarded as an important testing ground for that component. As previous chapters have shown, Americans and their representatives in Congress refuse to accept a Realpolitik approach in U.S. foreign policy and persist in believing that democracy has universal appeal and moral legitimacy as a distinctive objective of U.S. policy.

Was the promotion of democracy in Chile something more than propagandistic "window dressing" or Cold War rhetoric? One possible way to answer that question would be to ask another. Can one identify at least some instances in which support for democracy can be identified as an independent variable—as a goal pursued for its own sake which actually has overridden other goals? The Cold War anti-Soviet objectives of U.S. policy in the promotion of democracy under the Alliance for Progress, the "defense" of democracy under Allende, the human rights campaign of Carter, and the support for democratic transitions under Reagan are there for all to see. The economic interests involved in making life difficult for Allende, and in not cutting off private bank loans to Pinochet, are also clear. However, as counterexamples against a reductionism that limits U.S. policy entirely to security and economic interests,[5] this study has argued that (1) the promotion of democracy in Chile harmed at least our short-term security interests in alienating the Chilean army through the continuing arms embargo from 1976 until 1991; (2) at least in the case of the Anaconda Company in 1969, the United States did significant economic damage to an American company in compelling it to accede to the Chileanization program of the Frei government; and (3) at some point between 1975 and 1985, the institutional and ideological impetus of the promotion of democracy had become so great that it came to be a goal in itself rather than an instrument to be used for other purposes.

Concern for human rights and democracy has been institutionalized as, if not an independent, at least a separate concern in the US. policy-making process. The assistant secretary of state for human rights and humanitarian affairs, the officer in each embassy who must prepare the annual country report on human rights, the congressional limitations on bilateral and multilateral aid, the creation of the National Endowment for Democracy, the "democratic initiatives" section of the foreign aid program, the promotion of democracy and human rights in military training programs, democracy's role in the international media activities of the United States Information Agency—all are examples of the structural formalization of this concern, a concern that may be overridden but cannot be ignored. This study has told the part of this story related to Chile, but it deserves much fuller treatment.

The ending of the Cold War has not changed this, nor should it do so. Both because it now has become part of our collective responsibility to the OAS and because it is in our national interest to do so, it is important that the United States continue to make it clear that it supports free elections and democracy in the hemisphere. As the Haitian case has demonstrated, illegitimate and coercive military governments create problems of migration, instability, and violence which affect their neighbors in negative ways and justify collective action against them. Now that all the countries of

Latin America except Cuba are under elected governments, it is important that continued U.S. and hemispheric actions assure that the pendulum does not swing back to authoritarianism as it did in the late 1960s and 1970s. Given its recent past experience, Chile can be expected to continue to take an active role in support of democratic government.

Over the last thirty years, social scientists have tried to analyze Latin American politics in terms of a number of different analytic tools. Over time each of them has been recognized as oversimplified and of limited validity. Yet it is possible to combine those different approaches in concluding this study. Drawing first on the modernization theories of the early 1960s, one can say that over this period, Chile has indeed become more modern in its educational system, economy, social attitudes, and politics— and this has taken place in part because of its relationship to the United States. The old hierarchical, ascriptive, and semifeudal structures and relationships still have left their traces, but Chile is evolving into a more democratic, equalitarian, and participatory society. From the point of view of the dependency theory that emerged in the late 1960s, Chile is less dependent on a single product, copper, or a single country, the United States (in 1991, Japan replaced the United States as its largest customer), and is now more and more a part of an interdependent world characterized by integration into the world economy, communications system, and political organization. Marxists saw the U.S. intervention in Chile before and during the Allende presidency (1970–73) as a confirmation of Lenin's theory of imperialism, but Allende's economic policies (along with Cuba's increasing economic dependence on the Soviet Union) was one of the factors that led to disillusion with Marxist alternatives to market-oriented economics.[6] The political culture approach of the 1970s which emphasized Latin America's Iberian heritage and corporatist social structure needs to be modified as Chile reorients its attention and its educational system to northern Europe, the Pacific Basin, and the United States and eliminates the rigidities of the corporatist organization of the economy which gave special privileges to specific groups and impeded the operation of the competitive market in economics and politics. Chile is still, fortunately, a society in which family and group attachments are strong, but they are increasingly combined with individualist and competitive entrepreneurial values. Finally, the earlier political science approach that emphasized the importance of legal and political institutions and leadership has now been reasserted as Chile seeks to reestablish and readapt its democratic, constitutionalist, and legalist traditions.

The story I have told and the verdict one must reach on U.S.-Chilean relations is a mixed one. There are elements of which both Americans and Chileans can be proud, and there are elements of which one or both should be ashamed. But so far it is a story that, on balance, has a happy ending— one in which there is a basis for hope in a future of cooperation between two societies that are committed to freedom, democracy, human rights, and economic and social development.

Notes

Chapter 1: Introduction

1. There are probably a thousand books on the 1970–73 period—one for each day of the Allende government. Nearly all of them deal in some way with the U.S. role.

2. For an extended discussion of this question, see Sigmund, *Multinationals in Latin America*, especially chap. 3 on Chile.

Chapter 2: Chile, the United States, and the Alliance for Progress

1. Muñoz and Portales, *Elusive Friendship: A Survey of U.S.-Chilean Relations*, emphasizes the anti–United States feelings in the earlier period. For the World War II period, see Francis, *Limits of Hegemony*, and Bowers, *Chile through Embassy Windows*, as well as Humphreys, *Latin America and the Second World War*, vol. 2, chap. 4.

2. On Chilean copper policy, see Moran, *Multinational Corporations*.

3. On the Klein-Saks mission, see Hirschman, *Journeys towards Progress*, 161–223.

4. Quoted in Levinson and de Onis, *Alliance That Lost Its Way*, 52. On the Alliance for Progress see Dreier, *Alliance for Progress*; Alba, *Alliance without Allies*; Rogers, *Twilight Struggle*; Perloff, *Alliance for Progress*; Packenham, *Liberal America and the Third World*; and especially Scheman, *Alliance for Progress*.

5. U.S. Department of State, *Bulletin*, Apr. 3, 1961.

6. For the full text of the charter, see Levinson and de Onis, *Alliance That Lost Its Way*, 352–71.

7. Kaufman, *Politics of Land Reform*, 67; Swift, *Agrarian Reform*, 35. See also Garrido, *Historia de la reforma agraria*, chaps. 4 and 5.

8. See Wolpin, *Cuba and Chilean Foreign Policy*.

9. For a detailed account of the origins of the program, see Valdés, *La escuela de Chicago: Operación Chile*.

10. Cf. Childs, *Unequal Alliance*, chap. 5, which draws on declassified documents of the State and Defense departments. For an earlier account see Barber and Ronning, *Internal Security and Military Power*. For a critical view, see McClintock, *Instruments of Statecraft*.

For an example of a Canal Zone course designed to help make "the Chilean military . . . more aware of the dangers which the Communists pose to their country," see the declassified message from the commanding general of Southcom to Attorney General Robert Kennedy inviting him to speak at a two-week course aimed at giving the Chilean military "a realistic view of the current threats" and overcoming their resistance to U.S. instruction programs in counterinsurgency (Declassified Documents Reference System [DDRS], May 2, 1964, Lyndon Baines Johnson Library, declassified July 15, 1977).

11. Phillips' *Night Watch* also includes an account of his work on Chilean problems from 1973 to 1975 as head of the Western Hemisphere Division of the CIA in Washington. The CIA infiltration of Chilean student, youth, labor, and peasant groups was revealed in 1967. A sensationalized account was published in Chile by Labarca Godard, *Chile invadido*. The most detailed and useful account is Senate Select Committee on Intelligence Activities, *Covert Action in Chile, 1963–1973*, Staff Report (henceforth referred to as *Covert Action in Chile*), which is the source for details on CIA expenditures on Chilean political parties.

12. On the Christian Democratic Party, see Grayson, *El Partido Demócrata Cristiano Chileno;* Wayland-Smith, *Christian Democratic Party in Chile;* Castillo Velasco, *Las fuentes de la Democracia Cristiana;* Yocelevsky, *La Democracia Cristiana Chilena;* and Gonzalez Errazuriz, *El Partido Demócrata Cristiano*. For a hostile interpretation of the role of the Christian Democrats from a conservative point of view, see Whelan, *Out of the Ashes: The Life, Death, and Transfiguration of Democracy in Chile, 1833–1988*, chap. 4. (Despite its title, Whelan's book devotes 900 of its 1,100 pages to the Allende [1970–73] and Pinochet [1973–90] regimes.) At the other end of the political spectrum, Fleet, *Rise and Fall*, predicted—without any evidence—in the mid-1980s that "the party's recent revival is likely to be short-lived" (285) and criticized Christian Democratic thought because it "failed to give the movement an adequate ideological foundation" (226). For a thoughtful evaluation of the role of the Christian Democratic Party at the center of the Chilean political spectrum, see Scully, *Rethinking the Center*, chaps. 4–5.

13. For documentation of the internal dynamics and financial resources of the Jesuits in Chile, see Mutchler, *The Church as a Political Factor*, chaps. 12–14. For a more scholarly account, see Smith, *The Church and Politics in Chile*. For Vekemans' documented defense of his role in this period see Vekemans, *CIA-DC-DESAL*.

14. See discussion in Sigmund, *Overthrow of Allende*, 36ff.; Dooner, *Cambios sociales y conflícto político*, chap. 4; and Fleet; *Rise and Fall*, chap. 3. A hostile but detailed six-volume account of the Frei administration is Olavarría Bravo, *Chile bajo la Democracia Cristiana*.

15. For an analysis of the origin and impact of the project, especially as it relates to government control and the objectivity of social scientists, see Horowitz, *The Rise and Fall of Project Camelot*.

16. Loveman, *Chile: the Legacy of Hispanic Capitalism*, 291.

17. For the U.S. view, see the testimony of Sidney Weintraub in the *Hearings on U.S. Aid Operations under the Alliance for Progress*, Feb. 4, 1968, 340ff. For the view that the adoption of a strong constitutional amendment limiting property rights was a case of "overkill," since it antagonized all propertied groups, see Ascher, *Scheming for the Poor*, 131–34.

18. On the radicalization of the Socialist Party, see Walker, "Del populismo al Leninismo y la inevitabilidad del conflicto: El Partido Socialista de Chile (1933–1973)," *CIEPLAN, Notas técnicas*, no. 91 (December 1986), and Walker, *Socialismo y democracia*, chap. 7.

19. Senate Committee on Government Operations, Subcommittee on Foreign Aid Expenditures, *U.S. Foreign Aid in Action: A Case Study*, by Senator Ernest Gruening, 1966. The fact that this highly critical study was carried out by Ernest Gruening, usually considered to be a liberal, gave it all the more impact. For a more favorable evaluation by Sidney Weintraub, Chile mission director of the Agency for International Development, see House Committee on Foreign Affairs, *Foreign Assistance Act of 1969*, pt. 3, 774ff. Weintraub emphasizes the improvements in education, tax collection, public investment, and population control. He is more critical of the efforts to improve agricultural production.

20. Sigmund, *Overthrow of Allende*, 74–75.

21. See the evaluation of the agreement in Sigmund, *Multinationals in Latin America*, 142–45. The agreements would probably not have been concluded without strong U.S. government involvement. Anaconda's stock dropped sharply on Wall Street after the agreement.

22. Hersh, *Price of Power*, 263. Hersh claims that the Chilean withdrawal of the invitation to Nelson Rockefeller was in retaliation for a Nixon-ordered cancellation of a $20 million aid program. By 1970, economic aid to Chile had been reduced to $18 million—well before the election of Allende. (The 1970 fiscal year ended on June 30.)

23. See the comparison of the two programs in Sigmund, *Overthrow of Allende*, 302–3. For the details on the formation of the Popular Unity coalition, see Sigmund, *Overthrow of Allende*, 88–91.

24. Kissinger, *White House Years*, 663.

25. Hersh, *Price of Power*, 260. The comment was originally reported by Hersh in an article in the *New York Times* in September 1974.

26. Sigmund, *Overthrow of Allende*, 103–4. For confidential memoranda leaked from ITT files to Jack Anderson in 1972 and the records of the ensuing investigation in March and April 1973, see Senate Committee on Foreign Relations, Subcommittee on Multinational Corporations, *Multinational Corporations and United States Foreign Policy*, (subsequently referred to as *ITT Hearings*).

27. For the conservative view, see Packenham, *Liberal America and the Third World*, and Howard Wiarda, "Did the Alliance 'Lose Its Way,' or Were Its Assumptions All Wrong from the Beginning?" in Scheman, *Alliance for Progress*, 95–118. On the liberals and the radicals see Abraham F. Lowenthal, " 'Liberal,' 'Radical,' and 'Bureaucratic' Perspectives on U.S. Latin American Policy: The Alliance for Progress in Retrospect," in Cotler and Fagen, *Latin America and the United States*, 212–35.

28. Garrido, *Historia de la reforma agraria*, 176.

29. See Pipes and Garfinkle, *Friendly Tyrants*, especially the chapter by James Theberge, U.S. ambassador to Chile (1981–85).

Chapter 3: The United States and the Allende Government (1970–1973)

1. In addition to *Covert Action in Chile* and the *ITT Hearings*, already referred to, another important source is the section on Chile in Senate Select Committee on Intelligence Activities, *Alleged Assassination Plots involving Foreign Leaders, Interim*

Report, Nov. 20, 1975 (hereafter referred to as *Alleged Assassination Plots*), also published commercially with an introduction by Senator Frank Church (New York: W. W. Norton, 1976), 225–74. Also important are Kissinger, *White House Years,* chap. 17; Powers, *Man Who Kept the Secrets,* chap. 13; and Hersh, *Price of Power,* chap. 21–22. For useful summary accounts, see Sigmund, *Overthrow of Allende,* chap. 6, and Moss, *Chile's Marxist Experiment,* chap. 9. For more partisan versions, see, on the left, Petras and Morley, *United States and Chile,* chap. 2 (written before the important Senate investigation), as well as Israel, *Politics and Ideology in Allende's Chile,* and, on the right, Whelan, *Out of the Ashes,* chap. 6. For an astonishingly detailed analysis by a Danish observer, see Poul Jensen, *The Garotte: U.S. Policy towards Chile.*

2. Senate Select Committee on Intelligence Activities, *Hearings, December 4–5, 1975,* 32.

3. *Alleged Assassination Plots,* 227–29, 234. Helms later claimed that he had told President Nixon, "You are giving me an almost impossible job," and that Henry Kissinger later advised him that Nixon was merely expressing his frustration and should not have been taken literally. See Woodward, *Veil, The Secret Wars of the CIA,* 41.

4. Powers, *Man Who Kept the Secrets,* 360.

5. *ITT Hearings,* pt. 2 (ITT Papers), 626–28, 643. The Forty Committee had met again on September 29 and approved a plan to cut off credits to Chile and to ask American companies to reduce investment there (*Covert Action in Chile,* 25).

6. Hersh, *Price of Power,* 283–85, based on 1980 interviews with Edward Korry and the Forty Committee minutes made available to the Church committee. Extracts from the Viaux court-martial in September 1972 are published in *El caso Schneider* (Santiago: Editorial Quimantu, 1973). On "Reyes" see p. 91.

7. Kissinger, *White House Years,* 676. See also Hersh, *Price of Power,* 286–88, and *Alleged Assassination Plots,* 243–54.

8. National Security Decision Memorandum 93 (Nov. 9, 1970) is available on microfiche from Declassified Documents Reference System (DDRS) as the revised Options Paper on Chile (Nov. 3, 1970) circulated prior to the November 6 National Security Council meeting, which begins, "The Allende government will seek to establish in Chile as soon as possible an authoritarian system following Marxist principles," and predicts problems with the military and with the economy. Also declassified is a Nov. 18, 1970, report by the CIA on its Track II effort to prevent Allende's election, carried out independently of the Forty Committee. Describing the sending of four agents and many foreign journalists to Chile, it blamed the failure of the program on President Frei, ignoring the important role that the decision of his Christian Democratic Party—of which he was a cofounder–played in insisting on observance of constitutional processes.

9. The Chilean record of the interview appears in Uribe, *Black Book,* 74–80. Allende's inaugural address is translated from *El Mercurio,* Nov. 6, 1970.

10. *Covert Action in Chile,* 59 (chronology).

11. Nixon, *RN: The Memoirs of Richard Nixon,* 488.

12. See Debray, *The Chilean Revolution: Conversations with Allende,* 71, 91, 119. See also Arriagada, *De la vía chilena a la vía armada,* for an analysis of the Allende regime in terms of the movement in Allende's policy from the observance of legal

norms to an increasing reliance on violence. He notes that after 1971, Allende no longer referred to the *vía chilena* in his speeches (85).

13. For an account by Allende's chief adviser on copper issues, see Novoa Monreal, *La batalla por el cobre*. See also Sigmund, *Multinationals in Latin America*, chap. 5, and Ingram, *Expropriation of U.S. Property*, 268–90. On the bureaucratic politics of U.S. policy, see Einhorn, *Expropriation Politics*, 268–90.

14. Senate Select Committee on Intelligence Activities, *Intelligence Activities*, vol. 7, *Covert Action in Chile*, 128–35.

15. *ITT Hearings*, pt. 2, 943–85.

16. See Paul E. Sigmund, "The Invisible Blockade and the Overthrow of Allende," *Foreign Affairs* 52, no. 2 (January 1974), 322–40, and Jonathan Sanford, "The Multilateral Banks and the Suspension of Lending to Allende's Chile," in House Committee on Foreign Affairs, Subcommittee on Interamerican Affairs, *United States and Chile during the Allende Years, 1970–1973*, July 1, 1971–Sept. 18, 1974, 417–48.

17. Pinochet interview in *Ercilla*, no. 2015 (Mar. 12–19, 1974), 14.

18. Davis, *The Last Two Years of Salvador Allende*, 63, reproducing leaked excerpts published in Jack Anderson's column, Mar. 28, 1972. (Davis had replaced Ambassador Korry in October 1971.) The sense of the dispatch has been reversed by several writers through selective quotation to make Davis *advocate* the creation of discontent to provoke a coup. See Seymour Hersh in the *New York Times*, Nov. 3, 1974; Joseph Collins, the *National Catholic Reporter*, Oct. 12, 1973; and Petras and Morley, *United States and Chile*, 81–82. The December 1971 CIA-fabricated letter is incorrectly described as being passed to the military in mid-1973 in Constable and Valenzuela, *A Nation of Enemies*, 51.

19. For details and an insight into his political evolution see Prats' posthumously published memoirs (he was murdered by Chilean intelligence agents in Buenos Aires in 1974), *Memorias: Testimonio de un soldado*. The memoirs were completed and edited by Prats' daughters, after an unauthorized version (containing excerpts from his diary between Feb. 1, 1973, and Aug. 4, 1974) had been published in Mexico City as *Una vía por la legalidad* in 1976.

20. Davis, *Last Two Years*, 96–97.

21. Senate Committee on Foreign Relations, Subcommittee on Multinational Corporations, *Hearings, March 20–April 2, 1973*, 95, 99, and 104. For an accessible and readable account, see Sampson, *Sovereign State of ITT*, chap. 13 ("The Spymasters").

22. Davis, *Last Two Years*, 94–95; Sigmund, *Overthrow of Allende*, 209.

23. See the table of monthly prices and industrial output from October 1970 to November 1973 in Sigmund, *Overthrow of Allende*, 281.

24. See Orrego, *El paro nacional*.

25. On the divisions within the military at this time, see Rojas Sandford, *Murder of Allende*, 91–93.

26. See Sigmund, *Overthrow of Allende*, 199–201, for a more complete breakdown and analysis of the March election. A summary of the law faculty report appears as annex no. 3 in Pinochet, *Crucial Day*, 173–80. For a critical analysis, see Sigmund, *Overthrow of Allende*, 219–20.

27. Pinochet, *Crucial Day*, 80–81. See also the interview with Pinochet in *El Mercurio* (Intl. Ed.), Aug. 5–11, 1974, 7.

28. See Farrell, *National Unified School.*

29. *El Mercurio* (Int. Ed.), May 14–20, 1973, 8.

30. Phillips, *Night Watch,* 238.

31. Garcés, *El estado y los problemas tácticos del gobierno de Allende,* 38–39.

32. Allende's actual words were, "I call on the people to take over all the industries and enterprises, and to be prepared to go to the center of the city . . . to act with prudence with whatever material is at hand. . . . If the coup comes, the people will have arms, but I am confident that the armed forces are loyal to the government" (translated from the official government account in Sigmund, *Overthrow of Allende,* 214).

33. Sigmund, *Overthrow of Allende,* 215–18, 221–22.

34. Accounts of the dramatic developments in August in Sigmund, *Overthrow of Allende,* and Davis, *Last Two Years,* are less complete than the hour-by-hour account in Prats, *Memorias,* which is based on his diary. See also the slightly divergent accounts, based on a document submitted by Joan Garcés to the United Nations, which appear in Touraine, *Vie et mort du Chili populaire,* 94, and Rojas Sandford, *Murder of Allende,* 178ff. All agree, however, that Prats asked for, and was denied, an expression of support from his fellow generals.

35. Sigmund, *Overthrow of Allende,* 232–33. Prats, *Memorias,* 482–83. Prats read the congressional resolution just before General Pinochet informed him that the generals did not support him and that the two generals who were his closest supporters were resigning.

36. The *Time* and *New York Times* stories left a lasting impact on even well-informed U.S. observers. See, for example, the reference to the "assassination of Chilean president Salvador Allende" in *Newsweek,* Oct. 16, 1989, 34, and George Ball's assertion in the *New York Review of Books,* Feb. 13, 1992, "We helped finance a military coup in Chile in 1974 [*sic*] which murdered Allende and left that country to the brutal rule of General Pinochet." For persuasive evidence that Allende committed suicide, see n. 39.

37. For the text of the note, see Davis, *Last Two Years,* 222, translated from *Qué Pasa* (Santiago), Sept. 8–14, 1974.

38. *Harper's* (March 1974), 58.

39. For the transcript of the ham radio operators' recordings, see *Análisis,* Dec. 24–30, 1985. For the medical report in 1973 see *El Mercurio* (Intl. Ed.), Oct. 29–Nov. 4, 1973, and for the account of the 1990 reburial, see *Análisis,* Sept. 10–16, 1990, and the *New York Times,* Sept. 17, 1990. The interview with Miriam Contreras ("La Payita") appears in *El Mercurio,* Jan. 14, 1988. See also Boizard, *El último día de Allende,* and González Camus, *El día en que murió Allende.*

40. Davis, *Last Two Years,* 354–58; Kissinger, *Years of Upheaval,* 404. On the Unitas story, see Davis, *Last Two Years,* 350ff. Evans, *Disaster in Chile,* tells the story of the bombing by U.S. pilots (256).

41. Davis, *Last Two Years,* 352–53. A lawsuit, initiated by Davis, Frederick Purdy, the U.S. consul at the time, and Ray Davis of the U.S. Navy military mission, asked for $150 million in libel damages. After the judge ruled that the plaintiffs were "public figures" and therefore would have to prove actual malice or reckless disregard of truth by the filmmakers, the two sides agreed on a public statement by the filmmakers that they did not intend to suggest complicity by the plaintiffs in

Horman's death and would not wish viewers to draw such a conclusion from the film. No damages were awarded. See Davis' letter in *Foreign Service Journal* (June 1991), 6.

Chapter 4: Chile and U.S. Human Rights Policy

1. See *100 primeros decretos leyes* (Santiago, 1973), 6–19.

2. *Libro blanco del cambio de gobierno en Chile* (Santiago, 1973), 53–65. The pagination in the English translation differs slightly.

3. Davis, *Last Two Years,* 371; 454, fn. 65; 460, fn. 18. The Landis claims appear in "The CIA Makes Headlines: Psychological Warfare in Chile, 1970–1973," *Liberation* 19, no. 3 (March–April 1975), 29ff., and in Freed and Landis, *Death in Washington,* 103, 109. Chilean conservatives were known to have been in close touch with the Brazilian embassy.

4. See specific references to Plan Z in Verdugo, *Los zarpazos del puma,* 29, 31, 176. See also earlier stories in *Análisis,* Oct. 22–28, 1985, and May 6–12, 1986, as well as *APSI,* Apr. 27–May 3, 1986.

5. House Committee on Foreign Affairs, Subcommittee on Interamerican Affairs, *United States and Chile during the Allende Years, 1970–1973* (hereafter referred to as *United States and Chile during the Allende Years*), Kubisch testimony, Sept. 20 and 25, 1973, 95, 110–11.

6. Colby and Forbath, *Honorable Men: My Life in the CIA,* 379–80.

7. Senate Judiciary Committee, Refugee Subcommittee, *Refugee and Humanitarian Problems in Chile,* Sept. 28, 1973, app. 54, 60, 47.

8. For Fagen's charges see the *New York Times,* Nov. 19, 1973, and *United States and Chile during the Allende Years,* 258.

9. *United States and Chile during the Allende Years,* 177, 179–80.

10. Further details have been drawn from Cavallo Castro et al., *La historia oculta,* 20–21. On the rise of the Chicago school in Chile, see Valdés, *La escuela de Chicago: Operación Chile.*

11. *Declaración de principios del gobierno de Chile* (Santiago, 1974), 7–8, 13–15. In 1989 and 1990, Guzmán claimed that in the postcoup period he had argued to Pinochet for "laws that would limit the abuses and excesses of the security organs" (*Análisis,* July 1–7, 1991).

12. Cavallo Castro et al., *La historia oculta,* 9, 65–66, 589.

13. Robert Moss, "The Tribulation of Chile," *National Review* 27, no. 39 (Oct. 10, 1975), 1111.

14. House Committee on Foreign Affairs, Subcommittees on Interamerican Affairs and on International Organizations and Movements, *Human Rights in Chile,* 112–18. The Dec. 7, 1973, hearing, along with the bill to establish a Bureau of Human Rights and Humanitarian Affairs, is also printed in House Committee on Foreign Affairs, Subcommittee on International Organizations and Movements, *International Protection of Human Rights,* 531ff., 594–97.

15. The letter is printed in House Armed Services Committee, Special Subcommittee on Intelligence, *Inquiry into Matters regarding Classified Testimony,* Sept. 25, 1974, 31–34.

16. Sigmund, *Overthrow of Allende*, 259, 317.

17. House Foreign Affairs Committee, Subcommittees on Interamerican Affairs and on International Organizations and Movements, *Human Rights in Chile*, Nov. 19, 1975. Congressional subcommittees held hearings on human rights in Chile nearly every year until the 1988 plebiscite. For an example of the new information developed at such hearings, see the testimony of the former Lutheran bishop of Chile, Helmut Frenz, on his meeting with Pinochet after the coup. When he referred to "physical pressures" on detainees, Pinochet corrected him, saying, "You mean torture," and then attacked the naiveté of church groups in opposing its use to fight the Marxist conspiracy. See Senate Committee on Foreign Relations, Subcommittee on Interamerican Affairs, *Human Rights and Foreign Aid in Chile*, 175. When he returned to Chile following the transfer of power to the Aylwin government in 1990, Bishop Frenz quoted Pinochet as saying, "It is necessary to torture them or they will not 'sing.' Torture is necessary to extirpate Communism" (*Fortín Mapocho*, Mar. 16, 1990, 5).

18. Senate Committee on Foreign Relations, *CIA Foreign and Domestic Activities, Hearings, January 22, 1975*, 6.

19. Senate Select Committee on Intelligence Activities, *Supplementary Detailed Staff Reports on Foreign and Military Intelligence*, bk. 4, Apr. 23, 1976, 124–25, 162–65. The supplementary report also highlighted the discrepancy between the Nixon and Kissinger claims that Track II was ended on October 15 and the CIA insistence that it continued until the death of General Schneider, concluding, "If, as CIA officials testified, the coup activity was authorized from the beginning and the White House was kept informed until the end, then the accounts of Mr. Nixon and Dr. Kissinger are called into question" (124).

20. These quotations and many of the earlier details have been taken from the account of the investigation published by an American Political Science Association Congressional Fellow who participated, Loch K. Johnson, *A Season of Inquiry: The Senate Intelligence Investigation*, esp. 103–4.

21. Johnson, *Season of Inquiry*, 258–59. The House had also established a Select Committee on Intelligence under the chairmanship of Congressman Otis Pike. When the White House said that the House committee's report compromised national security, the House voted that it not be published, but a copy was leaked and published by the *Village Voice* in February 1976. The House did not establish a permanent Intelligence Committee until July 1977, under a weaker mandate than that of the Senate. The Pike committee's case studies had involved CIA activities in Italy and Angola, and it did not concern itself with Chile. For a review and evaluation of the question of congressional controls on covert intelligence operations by one of the authors of the Church committee report on Chile, see Treverton, *Covert Action*.

22. For a review of the development of human rights legislation, see the Congressional Research Service report to the Senate Committee on Foreign Relations, *Human Rights and U.S. Foreign Assistance*, November 1979, Washington, D.C.: U.S. Government Printing Office, 1979, 16–24. For an analysis of the political forces at work within and outside government, see Schoultz, *Human Rights and United States Policy*. Schoultz notes that the Harkin Amendment, which he describes as "the cornerstone of human rights legislation related to U.S. bilateral economic

assistance," was passed in the House by a coalition of human rights liberals and anti–foreign aid conservatives and in the Senate as an amendment offered on the floor by the liberals after they had been twice defeated in committee (195–97).

23. It is an overstatement, however, to say, as Heraldo Muñoz does (in Valenzuela and Valenzuela, *Chile under Military Rule*), that U.S.-Chilean relations between 1974 and 1971 "were quite warm" (306).

Chapter 5: Pinochet, Carter, and Human Rights

1. Muñoz and Portales, *Elusive Friendship: A Survey of U.S.-Chilean Relations*, 55.

2. Agency for International Development, *Overseas Loans, Grants, and Assistance from International Organizations* (Washington, D.C.: 1977, 1981).

3. Todman consistently put a favorable interpretation on Pinochet government actions. He had supported the agricultural loans over the opposition of the State Department in June. On his next visit to Chile in October 1977, he praised Chile's "public commitment to a timetable" for elections—presumably a reference to the Chacarillas speech, which had only promised partial legislative elections in 1985. In Washington, the State Department reacted to his statement by observing that Todman had tried to emphasize the positive side in Chile but that "at no time did he allege that the human rights situation in the Southern Cone countries was satisfactory." It added, "The Department continues to be disappointed with the lack of political freedom in Chile" (quoted in Schoultz, *Human Rights and United States Policy*, 117–18). In early 1978, Todman was named U.S. ambassador to Spain.

On the role of the Council of Generals of the army in the dissolution of the DINA—a rare instance of collective deliberation which led to the forced retirement of several generals—see Arturo Valenzuela, "The Military in Power: The Consolidation of One-Man Rule," in Drake and Jaksic, *Struggle for Democracy in Chile*, 67.

4. A detailed account of the lurid spy story that is the Letelier case may be found in Branch and Propper, *Labyrinth*. Propper was the assistant U.S. attorney who prosecuted the case. For a less complete account by a friend of Letelier's at the Institute for Policy Studies in Washington, and a journalist who covered the case in Santiago, see Dinges and Landau, *Assassination on Embassy Row*. A Chilean version is Orrego and Varas, *El caso Letelier*.

5. Pinochet discusses his visit to Washington in vol. 2 of his memoirs, *Camino recurrido*, 148–50. He describes former ambassador Sol Linowitz, whom he calls "Liminowitz," as one "whose ideas reflected" his "frankly Communist tendency" (149). Pinochet continued to attribute U.S. opposition to leftist influences in the State Department and Congress. See his statements in Politzer and Subercaseaux, *Ego sum Pinochet*, 101.

6. Michael Townley told the authors of *Labyrinth* that he and his wife voted in the consultation several times under DINA aliases as well as in the names of their children and their dog Fifi (Branch and Propper, 378, fn.).

7. For an analysis of Pinochet's manipulation of promotion and retirement policies to maintain control of the army, see Arriagada, *Pinochet*, chaps. 12–14. Within a few years, all the other generals involved in the 1973 coup had been retired. A principal rival, General Oscar Bonilla, died in a mysterious helicopter accident

in 1975. On the role of the military, see Varas, *Los militares en el poder,* and "The Crisis of Legitimacy of Military Rule in the 1980s," in Drake and Jaksic, *Struggle for Democracy in Chile,* 73–97, as well as Correa et al., *Los generales del régimen.*

8. Branch and Propper, *Labyrinth,* 326. Townley was under great pressure from his DINA superior, Pedro Espinoza, who refused to accept his explanations for not carrying out the assassination of Altamirano, shouting over the telephone, "Kill him!, Kill him!" (325). Pinochet's meeting with the Italian terrorist is described on p. 314.

9. Branch and Propper, *Labyrinth,* 590. The Borquez quote appears on p. 593.

10. Cavallo Castro et al., *La historia oculta,* 152, 219.

11. On the Beagle controversy, see Marín Madrid, *El arbitraje del Beagle;* Villalobos, *El Beagle;* and especially Carrasco, *El laudo arbitral del Canal Beagle.* A bilingual set of documents on the dispute has been published by Chile with the English title *Chilean-Argentine Relations: The Beagle Channel Controversy* (Geneva: Atar, 1978). An Argentine admiral's view of the Chilean claims as aimed at the domination of the South Atlantic and the Antarctic appears in Rojas, *La Argentina en el Beagle y el Atlántico Sur.* The Argentine attack was scheduled for December 22 but postponed for a day because of bad weather (interview with Hernán Cubillos, Oct. 31, 1991). The memoirs of former Chilean diplomat Enrique Bernstein cite the Buenos Aires publication *Somos* as a source for the Argentine war plan, which included bombing Punta Arenas in the south of Chile and occupying Santiago and Valparaiso. Twenty thousand troops had been mobilized for the effort.

12. See table 7 in Foxley, *Latin American Experiments,* 46. See also Edwards and Cox Edwards, *Monetarism and Liberalization,* and Delano and Hugo Translaviña, *La herencia de los Chicago boys.*

13. See Campero and Valenzuela, *El movimiento sindical chileno.* For an evaluation of the antipoverty programs, see Vergara, *Políticas hacia la extrema pobreza en Chile.*

14. For details see José Piñera, *Legislación minera.* The military wished the main copper mines to remain nationalized because of the unpublished law (*ley reservada*) which earmarked 10 percent of foreign copper sales revenue from the Gran Minería for arms purchases. Eleven secret laws had been adopted between 1926 and 1958. Under Pinochet, 124 examples of this legislative monstrosity were added. See Friedmann, *Chile unter Pinochet,* 134.

15. For the text of the message as well as the constitutional drafts submitted by the Constitutional Committee in 1978 and the Council of State in 1980, see *Revista chilena de derecho* 8, no. 1–6 (January–December 1981), 137ff. The issue also includes Pinochet's address presenting the very different final version announced on Aug. 10, 1980, as well as the results of the plebiscite of Sept. 11, 1980. The details on the preparation of the constitution have been drawn from Cavallo Castro et al., *La historia oculta,* 310–32, and from interviews with participants.

16. *Constitución política de la República de Chile* (Santiago: Editorial Juridica, 1981), passim.

17. On the Chilean Communist Party, see Varas, *El Partido Comunista en Chile,* and Andrés Benavente, "Panorama de la izquierda chilena, 1973–1984," *Estudios Públicos,* no. 18 (Autumn 1985), 155–99. On the changes in the Socialist Party, see Walker, *El Partido Socialista de Chile,* "Un nuevo socialismo democrático en Chile," *Estudios CIEPLAN,* no. 24 (June 1988), 5–36; and *Socialismo y democracia,* chap. 7;

and Politzer, *Altamirano*. For sympathetic and critical views of the Communists in English, see Furci, *Chilean Communist Party*, and the articles under "Chile" in Staar, *Yearbook on International Communist Affairs*. On the Christian Democratic Party's policy toward Pinochet, see the documents in *Chile-America* (Rome), no. 4 (1975), 49ff.

18. Quoted in Whelan, *Out of the Ashes*, 884.

19. Máximo Pacheco, *Lonquén* (Santiago: Editorial Aconcagua, 1980). For a fictionalized version of the case, see Isabel Allende, *Of Love and Shadows*.

20. This is the argument of Muravchik, *Uncertain Crusade*. Muravchik notes that because of the seriousness of Chile's human rights violations, the Carter administration even voted against international loans to Chile which fit "the basic human needs" exception (126). He quotes the Congressional Research Service to the effect that punitive measures against Chile led to a "significant deterioration of bilateral relations" (179).

Chapter 6: Reagan I: The Rise and Fall of Quiet Diplomacy

1. House Committee on Foreign Affairs, Subcommittees on International Economic Policy and Trade and on Interamerican Affairs, *U.S. Economic Sanctions against Chile*, Mar. 10, 1981, 58.

2. House Committee on Banking, Finance, and Urban Affairs, Subcommittee on International Development Institutions and Finance, *Human Rights and U.S. Policy in the Multilateral Development Banks*, July 21 and 23, 1981, 29.

3. Peter R. Kornbluh, "Chile-U.S. Relations—Tea and Normalization," *NACLA Report on the Americas* (January–February 1982), 47.

4. *New York Times*, Nov. 5, 1981. See also Tamar Jacoby, "The Reagan Turnaround on Human Rights," *Foreign Affairs* (Summer 1976), 1070–73.

5. According to the report, arbitrary arrests had nearly doubled, political prisoners had increased from 86 to 117, and out of nearly 200 persons detained by the security services, only 8 had been brought before the courts. See U.N. General Assembly, Economic and Social Council, *Report of the Special Rapporteur on the Situation of Human Rights in Chile*, A/36/594 annex, English, November 1981, 30.

6. On the economic collapse, see Edwards and Cox Edwards, *Monetarism and Liberalization*, chap. 8, and Paul E. Sigmund, "The Rise and Fall of the Chicago Boys in Chile," *SAIS Review* (Summer 1984), 44–58. For a year-by-year count of bankruptcies, see Barrios, *Deindustrialization in Chile*, 38. The Barrios book only covers the period up to 1986. Its principal thesis—that the decline in manufacturing and industrial employment was not compensated for by expanded exports and employment in nontraditional areas (65)—was invalidated by the doubling of exports and substantial drop in unemployment between 1986 and 1990.

7. Quoted in Washington Office on Latin America, *The Southern Cone: U.S. Policy and the Transition to Democracy* (Conference Proceedings), Apr. 8, 1983, 14. On the creation of the National Endowment for Democracy, see Carothers, *In the Name of Democracy*, chap. 6 ("The Rediscovery of Political Development Assistance").

8. U.S. Department of State, *Briefing*, July 11, 1983 (mimeo).

9. For the Jarpa plan, see Cavallo Castro et al., *La historia oculta,* 405.

10. House Committee on Foreign Affairs, Subcommittees on Human Rights and International Organizations and on Western Hemisphere Affairs, *Human Rights in Argentina, Chile, Paraguay, and Uruguay,* Oct. 4 and 21, 1983, 145.

11. For details see Cavallo Castro et al., *La historia oculta,* 425–30.

12. The imposition of a tariff was recommended by a split vote of the International Trade Commission, but in September, President Reagan rejected the recommendation because of its potentially inflationary impact.

13. Alicia Frohmann, "Relaciones Chile-Estados Unidos," *Cono Sur* 4, no. 2 (April–June 1985), 18. For a view of U.S.-Chilean relations in this period which seems unaware of the shift that took place, see Brown, *With Friends like These,* chap. 3.

14. Quoted in Carlos Portales, "Democracia y relaciones EE. UU.-Chile: Discurso y realidad," *Cono Sur* 4, no. 2 (April–June 1985), 4.

15. National Democratic Institute of International Affairs, interview transcript, Washington, D.C., Dec. 13, 1984.

16. In a 1989 interview, Motley described his purpose in going to Chile as persuading Pinochet to lift the state of siege but admitted that he never asked him formally or informally to do so. He had been warned by General Vernon Walters, who had succeeded Jeane Kirkpatrick as U.S. ambassador to the United Nations and knew Pinochet, that he would find him difficult to deal with. As he told the interviewer, "Pinochet did not surprise or disappoint me. He is the toughest son-of-a-bitch on two feet," but he also observed that the Chilean opposition seemed to be "living in a fantasy world," expecting the United States to force Pinochet out of office. Quoted in Whitney Tilson, "Reagan Administration Policy toward Chile, 1981–1986: The Importance of Individuals," senior honors thesis, Harvard College, Department of Government, 1989, 60.

17. For details and documentation, see Monckeberg et al., *Crimen bajo estado de sitio.*

18. See Muñoz and Portales, *Elusive Friendship,* 68–70. For the argument that the United States should take stronger measures against Pinochet, suspending the Unitas maneuvers, opposing all multilateral international bank loans, and using its influence with the military to promote a transition, see the op-ed article by Peter Bell in the *New York Times,* July 15, 1985, and Peter D. Bell, "Democracy and Double Standards: The View from Chile," *World Policy Journal* (Fall 1985): 711–30.

19. The fear of increasing polarization in Chile was expressed in testimony by the deputy assistant secretary of state for Latin America, James Michel, and Wade Matthews, the deputy chief of mission in Santiago, in hearings before the House Committee on Foreign Affairs, subcommittees on Human Rights and on Western Hemisphere Affairs, *Human Rights in Chile,* on Mar. 21, 1985. Michel spoke of the increase in bombings carried out by the Manuel Rodríguez Patriotic Front (FPMR) from 139 in 1983 to 735 in 1984 and called on the opposition to develop a consensus on key transition issues "including the future role of non-domestic forces in the political system and respect for private property" (41). Matthews observed that the Communist Party in its January plenum had supported the FPMR in its campaign of violence and that 678 persons had been sent by the government into internal exile by the Chilean government and 8 expelled from the country.

Chapter 7: Reagan II: The United States versus Pinochet

1. Quoted in Alicia Frohmann, "Relaciones Chile–Estados Unidos," *Cono Sur* 4, no. 4 (September–October 1985), 19.

2. For the English text of the letter, see "Chile: Pastoral Letter Banned," *Freedom at Issue* (New York), no. 82 (January–February 1985), 49–51.

3. For details on the negotiations and contacts leading to the National Accord, see Cavallo Castro et al., *La historia oculta,* chap. 43. It indicates that at one point the group even considered involving Pinochet's former minister of justice, Monica Madariaga (a coauthor of the 1980 constitution). Madariaga had recently returned from a stint as ambassador to the Organization of American States in Washington and had given an interview entitled "The Girl in the Bubble" to a Chilean magazine, in which she described her growing disillusion with the Pinochet regime after she had moved outside the isolation of her cabinet position.

4. Alicia Frohmann, "Relaciones Chile–Estados Unidos," *Cono Sur* 5, no. 1 (January–March 1986), 17.

5. Quoted in Alicia Frohmann, "Relaciones Chile–Estados Unidos," *Cono Sur* 5, no. 2 (April–May 1986), 15.

6. Muñoz and Portales, *Elusive Friendship,* 71.

7. Cavallo Castro et al., *La historia oculta,* 491–93.

8. Quoted in Alicia Frohmann, "Relaciones Chile–Estados Unidos," *Cono Sur* 5, no. 3 (June–July 1986), 18–19.

9. Quoted in Alicia Frohmann, "Relaciones Chile–Estados Unidos," *Cono Sur* 5, no. 5 (October–December 1986), supplement.

10. House Banking Committee, Subcommittees on International Development Institutions and Finance, *Human Rights Abuses in Chile,* July 30, 1986, 26.

11. For details on the attempted assassination of Pinochet as well as the discovery of the arms arsenals, see Cavallo Castro et al., *La historia oculta,* chap. 47, and Verdugo and Hertz, *Operación Siglo XX.*

12. Muñoz and Portales, *Elusive Friendship,* 81.

13. Alicia Frohmann, "Relaciones Chile–Estados Unidos," *Cono Sur* 8, no. 3 (May–June 1989), supplement; *La Nación,* Sept. 14, 1991.

14. Alicia Frohmann, "Relaciones Chile–Estados Unidos," *Cono Sur* 6, no. 3 (June–July 1987), supplement.

15. A full account of the papal visit is contained in Cavallo Castro et al., *La historia oculta,* chaps. 48–50.

16. On the role of foreign support in promoting dialogue among Chilean intellectuals, supporting polling and political research, and assisting the opposition to mount a successful campaign in 1988, see Jeffrey M. Puryear, "Building Democracy: Foreign Donors and Chile," Columbia University and New York University Conference Paper #57, 1991. Puryear notes that outside support was very important in developing cooperation between the left, the center, and the right, which was central to the democratic transition. He estimates total U.S. government support to the opposition between 1984 and 1988 at $6.8 million, with additional support of $500,000 from the Ford Foundation and $30,000 from the Soros Foundation (5). See also Michael Pinto-Duschinsky, "Foreign Political Aid: The German Political

Foundations and Their U.S. Counterparts," *International Affairs* 67 (January 1991), 33–63.

17. Statement by the president of the United States and the secretary of state, "In Support of Democracy in Chile," Dec. 17, 1987, in U.S. Embassy, Santiago, Chile, *Resource Book, Chile: 1988 Plebiscite* (Santiago, 1988), 69–70.

18. Concertación de Partidos para la Democracia, "Bases programáticas político-institucionales," February 1, 1988.

19. On the role of the Constitutional Tribunal, see Cavallo Castro et al., *La historia oculta*, chap. 52.

20. Roberto Mendez et al., "Por que ganó el No," *Estudios públicos*, no. 33 (Summer 1989), 83–134. See also the printed report of the fifty-five–person National Democratic Institute for International Affairs observer delegation, *Chile's Transition to Democracy* (Washington, D.C., 1988), 61.

21. Cavallo Castro et al., *La historia oculta*, chap. 53, which is the principal source for this section. Its account has been compared with postplebiscite reports in *Qué Pasa, Análisis*, and *APSI*, as well as Abraham Santibañez, *El plebiscito de Pinochet* (Santiago: Editorial Atena, 1988), and *La campaña de no vista por sus creadores* (Santiago: Melquiades, 1988).

22. Compare, for example, the favorable reception that was accorded to the report on the Chilean plebiscite by an International Commission of the Latin American Studies Association, composed of representatives of a variety of U.S. and international opinions, with the intense polemics that followed the publication of a similar LASA report on the 1984 elections in Nicaragua. Following the Chilean plebiscite, however, the National Endowment for Democracy's extensive support for the opposition UNO coalition in Nicaragua, which won an upset victory of the Sandinistas in February 1990, produced strong criticism from pro-Sandinista groups. See, for example, the Council on Hemispheric Affairs/the Interhemispheric Resource Center, *National Endowment for Democracy (NED): A Foreign Policy Branch Gone Awry* (Albuquerque: Interhemispheric Resource Center, 1990), which attacks NED for "creating and supporting organizations which conform to a narrow interventionist U.S. political agenda" (14). NED has also been attacked by conservatives as ineffective and wasteful. See Martin Morse Wooster, "This Is No Way to Promote Democracy," *Wall Street Journal*, July 17, 1991.

Chapter 8: Chile Returns to Democracy

1. See Paul E. Sigmund, "Chile," in Staar, *Yearbook on International Communist Affairs, 1990*, 59–60.

2. Besides the *Wall Street Journal* article, sources include chronologies and summaries from the unclassified files of the U.S. embassy in Chile and U.S. General Accounting Office, Report to the Ranking Minority Member, Senate Foreign Relations Committee, *Food Tampering: FDA's Actions on Chilean Fruit Based on Sound Evidence*, HRD 90–164, September 1990.

3. The Concertación slogan was said to have used *la gente* instead of *el pueblo* for "the people" because *el pueblo* is identified with Marxism and the class struggle, while *la gente* is all-inclusive.

4. All election figures are based on final results as published in *El Mercurio* and *La Época,* Dec. 16, 1989. For further analyses of the 1989 election, see Caviédes, *Elections in Chile,* chaps. 4–5, and Friedmann, *Chile unter Pinochet,* 275–93.

5. Paul E. Sigmund, "The Eerie Presence of Allende," *Trenton Times,* Mar. 13, 1990.

6. *La Nación,* Jan. 9, 1991, quoted in Brian Loveman, "Misión Cumplida? Civil Military Relations and the Chilean Political Translation," Paper delivered at the meeting of the Latin American Studies Association, Washington, D.C., April 1991.

7. Rettig Guissen et al., *Informe de la Comisión Nacional de Verdad y Reconciliación,* 55–57, 95–104.

8. *El Mercurio* (Intl. Ed.), June 25–July 1, 1992, 7. The candidates of the coalition received 53.3 percent of the votes; the right got 29.8 percent—very similar to the Aylwin and Büchi votes in 1989.

9. Address to Twenty-first General Assembly of the Organization of American States, June 3, 1991 (mimeo). The texts of the General Assembly resolutions are published as OEA/Sev. P/AG/docs.5.2734ff. (June 3–8, 1991).

10. The problem created for the right opposition by the fiscally conservative policy of the Aylwin government was illustrated by a forum in which two principal economic policymakers of the Pinochet government, now members of the Pinochetista UDI, attacked the Foxley policies for discouraging investment because of the increase in taxes and in the minimum wage. Their critical comments were followed by an intervention by Arnold Harberger, the University of Chicago economist who had trained the "Chicago boys." Harberger criticized the overheated state of the economy under Büchi in 1989 and asserted that Chile today "continues to be the best economy in the world" (*El Mercurio,* May 26, 1991).

Chapter 9: Conclusion: Chile and the Promotion of Democracy

1. See, for example, the assertion by Abraham Lowenthal, in the concluding chapter of *Exporting Democracy,* that "the U.S. government welcomed General Pinochet's overthrow of the democratically elected government of Salvador Allende" (389).

2. Mark Falcoff argues that Chile is the most likely country in Latin America "to complete the transition to first world status." See Payne et al., *Latin America after the Cold War,* 43.

3. See, for example, the proposals made in Bloomfield and Treverton, *Alternative to Intervention,* 129ff., that Latin American security problems be dealt with collectively, primarily by Latin Americans rather than the United States.

4. As a result of the ending of the Cold War, the Congress is now seriously considering a general restructuring of U.S. intelligence. See David L. Boren, "The Intelligence Community: How Crucial?" and Ernest R. May, "Intelligence: Backing into the Future," *Foreign Affairs* 71, no. 2 (Summer 1992), 52–72.

5. It is always possible to argue that U.S. concern for democracy is "really" motivated only by power politics or the defense of capitalism. However, a more

sophisticated analysis will attempt to analyze different motives, including national ideals, which help to explain policy.

6. For an unreconstructed Marxist criticism of post-Pinochet economic policy in Chile, see James Petras, "El 'Milagro Económico' Chileno: crítica empírica," *Nueva sociedad* (Caracas), no. 113 (May–June 1991), 146–58.

Bibliography

Alba, Victor. *Alliance without Allies*. New York: Praeger, 1965.

Allende, Isabel. *Of Love and Shadows*. New York: Pantheon, 1988.

Angell, Alan. *Politics and the Labor Movement in Chile*. London: Oxford University Press, 1972.

Arriagada, Genaro. *De la vía chilena a la vía armada*. Santiago: Editorial del Pacífico, 1974.

Arriagada, Genaro. *Pinochet: The Politics of Power*. Boston: Unwin Hyman, 1988.

Ascher, William. *Scheming for the Poor: The Politics of Redistribution in Latin America*. Cambridge: Harvard University Press, 1988.

Barber, Willard, and C. Neale Ronning. *Internal Security and Military Power: Counterinsurgency and Civic Action in Latin America*. Columbus: Ohio State University Press, 1966.

Barrios, Gatíca Jaime. *Deindustrialization in Chile*. Boulder, Colo.: Westview Press, 1989.

Blakemore, Harold. *British Nitrates and Chilean Politics, 1886–1896*. London: Athlone Press, 1974.

Bloomfield, Richard J., and Gregory F. Treverton, eds. *Alternative to Intervention: A New U.S.–Latin American Security Relationship*. Boulder, Colo.: Lynn Rienner, 1990.

Boizard, Ricardo. *El último día de Allende*. Santiago: Editorial del Pacífico, 1973.

Bowers, Claude G. *Chile through Embassy Windows: 1939–1953*. New York: Simon and Schuster, 1958.

Branch, Taylor, and Eugene M. Propper. *Labyrinth*. New York: Penguin Books, 1983.

Brown, Cynthia. *With Friends like These*. New York: Pantheon, 1985.

Campero, Guillermo, and José Valenzuela. *El movimiento sindical chileno en el capitalismo autoritario (1973–1981)*. Santiago: ILET, 1981.

Carothers, Thomas. *In the Name of Democracy*. Berkeley: University of California Press, 1991.

Carrasco, Germán. *El laudo arbitral del Canal Beagle*. Santiago: Editorial Juridica, 1978.

Castillo Velasco, Jaime. *Las fuentes de la Democracia Cristiana*. Santiago: Editorial del Pacífico, 1968.

Cavallo Castro, Ascanio, et al. *La historia oculta del régimen militar*. 2d ed. Santiago: Editorial Antartica, 1989.

Caviédes, Cesar. *Elections in Chile: The Road toward Redemocratization*. Boulder, Colo.: Lynn Rienner, 1991.

Childs, John. *Unequal Alliance: The Inter-American Military System, 1938–1978.* Boulder, Colo.: Westview Press, 1980.

Colby, William, and Peter Forbath. *Honorable Men: My Life in the CIA.* New York: Simon and Schuster, 1978.

Constable, Pamela, and Arturo Valenzuela. *A Nation of Enemies.* New York: W. W. Norton, 1991.

Correa, Raquél, et al. *Los generales del régimen.* Santiago: Editorial Aconcagua, 1983.

Cotler, Julio, and Richard R. Fagen, eds. *Latin America and the United States: The Changing Political Realities.* Stanford: Stanford University Press, 1974.

Davis, Nathaniel. *The Last Two Years of Salvador Allende.* Ithaca, N.Y.: Cornell University Press, 1985.

Debray, Regis. *The Chilean Revolution: Conversations with Allende.* New York: Pantheon, 1972.

Delano, Manuel, and Hugo Traslaviña. *La herencia de los Chicago Boys.* Santiago: Ornítorrinco, 1989.

De Vylder, Stefan. *Allende's Chile: The Political Economy of the Rise and Fall of the Unidad Popular.* Cambridge: Cambridge University Press, 1976.

Dinges, John, and Saul Landau. *Assassination on Embassy Row.* New York: Pantheon, 1980.

Dooner, Patricio. *Cambios sociales y conflicto político: El conflicto político nacional durante el gobierno de Eduardo Frei (1964–1970).* Santiago: Corporación de Promoción Universitaria, 1984.

Drake, Paul W., and Ivan Jaksic. *The Struggle for Democracy in Chile, 1982–1990.* Lincoln: University of Nebraska Press, 1991.

Dreier, John C., ed. *The Alliance for Progress: Problems and Perspectives.* Baltimore: Johns Hopkins University Press, 1962.

Edwards, Sebastian, and Alejandra Cox Edwards. *Monetarism and Liberalization: Chilean Economic Policy, 1973–1986.* Cambridge, Mass.: Ballinger Books, 1987.

Einhorn, Jessica. *Expropriation Politics.* Lexington, Mass.: D.C. Health, 1974.

Evans, Les. *Disaster in Chile.* New York: Pathfinder, 1974.

Falcoff, Mark. *Modern Chile, 1970–1989: A Critical History.* New Brunswick, N.J.: Transaction Books, 1989.

Farrell, Joseph P. *The National Unified School in Allende's Chile.* Vancouver: University of British Columbia Press, 1986.

Fleet, Michael. *The Rise and Fall of Chilean Christian Democracy.* Princeton: Princeton University Press, 1985.

Fontaine Aldunate, Arturo. *Los economistas y el Presidente Pinochet.* Santiago: Zig-Zag, 1988.

Foxley, Alejandro. *Latin American Experiments in Neoconservative Economics.* Berkeley: University of California Press, 1983.

Francis, Michael. *The Limits of Hegemony: United States Relations with Argentina and Chile during World War II.* Notre Dame, Ind.: Notre Dame University Press, 1977.

Freed, Donald, and Fred S. Landis. *Death in Washington: The Murder of Orlando Letelier.* Westport, Conn.: Lawrence Hill, 1980.

Friedmann, Reinhard. *Chile unter Pinochet.* Freiburg: Arnold Bergstraesser Institut, 1990.

Furci, Carmelo. *The Chilean Communist Party and the Road to Socialism.* London: Zed, 1984.

Garcés, Joan. *El estado y los problemas tácticos del gobierno de Allende.* Madrid: Siglo XXI, 1974.

Garreton, Manuel Antonio. *The Chilean Political Process.* Boston: Unwin Hyman, 1989.

Garrido, José, ed. *Historia de la reforma agraria en Chile.* Santiago: Editorial Universitaria, 1988.

Gil, Federico. *The Political System of Chile.* Boston: Houghton Mifflin, 1966.

González Camus, Ignacio. *El día en que murió Allende.* 2d ed. Santiago: CESOC, 1990.

González Errazuriz, Javier. *El Partido Demócrata Cristiano.* Valparaiso: Instituto de Estudios Generales, 1989.

Grayson, George. *El Partido Demócrata Cristiano Chileno.* Santiago: Editorial Aguirre, 1968.

Hauser, Thomas. *Missing: The Execution of Charles Horman.* New York: Simon and Schuster Touchstone Books, 1983.

Hersh, Seymour. *The Price of Power: Kissinger in the Nixon White House.* New York: Simon and Schuster Summit Books, 1983.

Hirschman, Albert O. *Journeys toward Progress.* New York: Twentieth Century Fund, 1963.

Horowitz, Irving Louis, ed. *The Rise and Fall of Project Camelot.* rev. ed. Cambridge: MIT Press, 1974.

Humphreys, R. A. *Latin America and the Second World War.* 2 vols. London: Athlone Press, 1982.

Ingram, George. *Expropriation of U.S. Property in South America.* New York: Praeger, 1974.

Israel, Ricardo. *Politics and Ideology in Allende's Chile.* Tempe: University of Arizona Press, 1989.

Jensen, Poul. *The Garotte: U.S. Policy towards Chile.* 2 vols. Aarhus, Denmark: Aarhus University Press, 1988.

Johnson, Loch K. *A Season of Inquiry: The Senate Intelligence Investigation.* Lexington: University Press of Kentucky, 1985.

Kaufman, Edy. *Crisis in Allende's Chile.* Westport, Conn.: Praeger, 1988.

Kaufman, Robert. *The Politics of Land Reform in Chile, 1950–1970.* Cambridge: Harvard University Press, 1972.

Kinsbruner, Jay. *Chile: A Historical Interpretation.* New York: Harper and Row, 1973.

Kissinger, Henry. *The White House Years.* Boston: Little, Brown, 1979.

Kissinger, Henry. *Years of Upheaval.* Boston: Little, Brown. 1984.

Labarca Godard, Eduardo. *Chile invadido.* Santiago: Editorial Austral, 1968.

Levinson, Jerome, and Juan de Onis. *The Alliance That Lost Its Way.* New York: Quadrangle Books, 1970.

Loveman, Brian. *Chile: The Legacy of Hispanic Capitalism.* 2d ed. New York: Oxford University Press, 1988.

Lowenthal, Abraham, ed. *Exporting Democracy.* Baltimore: Johns Hopkins University Press, 1991.

McClintock, Michael. *Instruments of Statecraft: Counterinsurgency and Counterterrorism.* New York: Pantheon, 1992.

Mamalakis, Markos. *The Growth and Structure of the Chilean Economy: From Independence to Allende.* New Haven: Yale University Press, 1976.

Marin Madrid, Alberto. *El arbitraje del Beagle y la actitud argentina.* Santiago: Editorial Universitaria, 1978.

Monckeberg, Maria Olivia, et al. *Crimen bajo estado de sitio.* Santiago: Editorial Emisión, 1986.

Moran, Theodore. *Multinational Corporations and the Politics of Dependence: Copper in Chile.* Princeton: Princeton University Press, 1974.

Moss, Robert. *Chile's Marxist Experiment.* London: Newton Abbott, 1974.

Muñoz, Heraldo, and Carlos Portales. *Elusive Friendship: A Survey of U.S.-Chilean Relations.* Boulder, Colo.: Lynne Rienner, 1991.

Muravchik, Joshua. *The Uncertain Crusade: Jimmy Carter and the Dilemmas of Human Rights Policy.* Washington, D.C.: American Enterprise Institute for Public Policy Research, 1986.

Mutchler, David. *The Church as a Political Factor in Latin America.* New York: Praeger, 1971.

Nixon, Richard. *RN: The Memoirs of Richard Nixon.* New York: Grosset and Dunlap, 1978.

Novoa Monreal, Eduardo. *La batalla por el cobre.* Santiago: Quimantu, 1972.

Nunn, Frederick. *The Military in Chilean History.* Albuquerque: University of New Mexico Press, 1976.

Olavarría Bravo, Arturo. *Chile bajo la Democracia Cristiana.* Santiago: Nascimiento, 1965–71.

Orrego, Claudio. *El paro nacional.* Santiago: Editorial del Pacífico, 1972.

Orrego, Claudio, and Florencia Varas. *El caso Letelier.* Santiago: Editorial Aconcagua, 1980.

Packenham, Robert B. *Liberal America and the Third World: Political Development Ideas in Foreign Aid and Social Science.* Princeton: Princeton University Press, 1973.

Payne, Douglas, et al. *Latin America after the Cold War.* New York: Americas Society, 1991.

Perloff, Harvey. *Alliance for Progress: A Social Invention in the Making.* Baltimore: Johns Hopkins University Press, 1969.

Petras, James, and Morris, Morley. *The United States and Chile.* New York: Monthly Review Press, 1975.

Phillips, David Atlee. *The Night Watch.* New York: Atheneum, 1977.

Piñera, José. *La legislación minera.* Santiago: Editorial Juridica, 1982.

Pinochet, Augusto. *The Crucial Day.* Santiago: Editorial Renacimiento, 1982.

Pinochet, Augusto. *Camino recurrido: Memorias de un soldado.* Santiago: Instituto Geográfico Militar, 1991.

Pipes, Daniel, and Adam Garfinkle, eds. *Friendly Tyrants: An American Dilemma.* New York: St. Martin's, 1991.

Politzer, Patricia. *Altamirano.* Santiago: Ediciones Melquiades, 1989.

Politzer, Patricia. *Fear in Chile.* New York: Pantheon, 1989.

Politzer, Patricia, and Elizabeth Subercaseaux. *Ego sum Pinochet*. Santiago: Zig-Zag, 1989.

Powers, Thomas. *The Man Who Kept the Secrets: Richard Helms and the CIA*. New York: Knopf, 1979.

Prats, Carlos. *Memorias: Testimonio de un soldado*. Santiago: Rehuen, 1985.

Reisman, W. Michael, and James E. Baker. *Regulating Covert Action*. New Haven: Yale University Press, 1992.

Remmer, Karen. *Party Competition in Argentina and Chile, 1890–1930*. Lincoln: University of Nebraska Press, 1984.

Rettig Guissen, Raúl, et al. *Informe de la Comisión Nacional de Verdad y Reconciliación*. Santiago: Secretaría de Comunicación y Cultura, 1991.

Rogers, William D. *The Twilight Struggle: The Alliance for Progress and the Politics of Development in Latin America*. New York: Random House, 1967.

Rojas, Isaac Francisco. *La Argentina en el Beagle y el Atlántico Sur*. Buenos Aires: Editorial Diagne, 1978.

Rojas Sandford, Robinson. *The Murder of Allende*. New York: Harper and Row, 1976.

Sampson, Anthony. *The Sovereign State of ITT*. New York: Fawcett Crest Paperback, 1974.

Scheman, L. Ronald, ed. *The Alliance for Progress: A Retrospective*. New York: Praeger, 1988.

Schoultz, Lars. *Human Rights and United States Policy toward Latin America*. Princeton: Princeton University Press, 1981.

Scully, Timothy. *Rethinking the Center: Party Politics in Nineteenth and Twentieth Century Chile*. Stanford: Stanford University Press, 1992.

Sigmund, Paul E. *The Overthrow of Allende and the Politics of Chile, 1964–1976*. Pittsburgh: University of Pittsburgh Press, 1977.

Sigmund, Paul E. *Multinationals in Latin America: The Politics of Nationalization*. Madison: University of Wisconsin Press, 1980.

Smith, Brian H. *The Church and Politics in Chile*. Princeton: Princeton University Press, 1982.

Staar, Richard F., ed. *Yearbook on International Communist Affairs, 1990*. Stanford: Hoover Institution Press, 1990.

Stallings, Barbara. *Class Conflict and Economic Development in Chile, 1958–1973*. Stanford: Stanford University Press, 1978.

Swift, Jeannine. *Agrarian Reform in Chile*. Lexington, Mass.: D. C. Health, 1971.

Touraine, Alain. *Vie et mort du Chili populaire*. Paris: Editions de Seuil, 1974.

Treverton, Gregory F. *Covert Action: The Limits of Intervention in the Postwar World*. New York: Basic Books, 1987.

Uribe, Armando. *The Black Book of American Intervention in Chile*. Boston: Beacon Press, 1975.

U.S. Congress. Senate. Committee on Government Operations. Subcommittee on Foreign Aid Expenditures. *U.S. Foreign Aid in Action: A Case Study*. Prepared by Senator Ernest Gruening. 89th Cong., 2d Sess. Washington, D.C.: Government Printing Office, 1966.

U.S. Congress. House. Committee on Government Operations. Subcommittee on Foreign Operations. Hearings, *U.S. Aid Operations under the Alliance for Progress*

(Feb. 4, 1968). 90th Cong., 2nd Sess. Washington, D.C.: Government Printing Office, 1968.

U.S. Congress. House. Committee on Foreign Affairs. *Foreign Assistance Act of 1969.* pt. 3. 90th Cong., 2d Sess. Washington, D.C.: Government Printing Office, 1968.

U.S. Congress. Senate. Committee on Foreign Relations. Subcommittee on Multinational Corporations. *Multinational Corporations and United States Foreign Policy.* 2 vols. Washington, D.C.: Government Printing Office, 1973.

U.S. Congress. Senate. Judiciary Committee. Subcommittee on Refugees. *Refugee and Humanitarian Problems in Chile* (Sept. 28, 1973). 93d Cong., 1st Sess. Washington, D.C.: Government Printing Office, 1973.

U.S. Congress. House. Committee on Foreign Affairs. Subcommittees on Interamerican Affairs and on International Organizations and Movements. *Human Rights in Chile.* 91st Cong., 2d Sess. Washington, D.C.: Government Printing Office. 1974.

U.S. Congress. House. Committee on Foreign Affairs. Subcommittee on International Organizations and Movements. *International Protection of Human Rights.* 91st Cong., 2d Sess. Washington, D.C.: Government Printing Office, 1974.

U.S. Congress. House. Armed Services Committee. Special Subcommittee on Intelligence. *Inquiry into Matters regarding Classified Testimony* (Sept. 25, 1974). 91st Cong., 2d Sess. Washington, D.C.: Government Printing Office, 1975.

U.S. Congress. House. Committee on Foreign Affairs. Subcommittee on Interamerican Affairs. *United States and Chile during the Allende Years, 1970–1973.* 92d Cong., 1st Sess., Washington, D.C.: Government Printing Office, 1975.

U.S. Congress. Senate. Committee on Foreign Relations. *CIA Foreign and Domestic Activities, Hearings, January 22, 1975.* 92d Cong., 1st Sess. Washington, D.C.: Government Printing Office, 1975.

U.S. Congress. Senate. Select Committee on Intelligence Activities. *Alleged Assassination Plots involving Foreign Leaders. Interim Report* (Nov. 20, 1975). 92d Cong., 1st Sess. Washington, D.C.: Government Printing Office, 1975.

U.S. Congress. Senate. *Staff Report of the Select Committee on Intelligence Activities: Covert Action in Chile, 1963–1973.* 92d Cong., 1st Sess. Washington, D.C.: Government Printing Office, 1975.

U.S. Congress. Senate Select Committee on Intelligence Activities. *Hearings, December 4–5, 1975.* 92d Cong., 1st Sess. Washington, D.C.: Government Printing Office, 1976.

U.S. Congress. Senate. Select Committee on Intelligence Activities. *Intelligence Activities.* Vol. 7, *Covert Action.* 92d Cong., 1st Sess. Washington, D.C.: Government Printing Office, 1976.

U.S. Congress. Senate. Select Committee on Intelligence Activities. *Supplementary Detailed Staff Reports on Foreign and Military Intelligence,* bk. 4 (Apr. 23, 1976). 92d Cong., 2d Sess. Washington, D.C.: Government Printing Office, 1976.

U.S. Congressional Research Service report to the Senate Committee on Foreign Relations. *Human Rights and U.S. Foreign Assistance* (November 1979). Washington, D.C.: Government Printing Office, 1979.

U.S. Congress. Senate. Subcommittee on Interamerican Affairs. Committee on

Foreign Relations. *Human Rights and Foreign Aid in Chile.* 94th Cong., 2d Sess. Washington, D.C.: Government Printing Office, 1980.

U.S. Congress. House. Committee on Foreign Affairs. Subcommittees on International Economic Policy and Trade and on Interamerican Affairs. *U.S. Economic Sanctions against Chile* (Mar. 10, 1981). 95th Cong., 1st Sess. Washington, D.C.: Government Printing Office, 1981.

U.S. Congress. House. Committee on Banking, Finance, and Urban Affairs, Subcommittee on International Development Institutions and Finance. *Human Rights and U.S. Policy in the Multilateral Development Banks* (July 21 and 23, 1981). 95th Cong., 1st Sess. Washington, D.C.: Government Printing Office, 1981.

U.S. Congress. House. Committee on Foreign Affairs. Subcommittees on Human Rights and International Organizations and on Western Hemisphere Affairs. *Human Rights in Argentina, Chile, Paraguay, and Uruguay* (Oct. 4 and 21, 1983). 96th Cong., 1st Sess. Washington, D.C.: Government Printing Office, 1984.

U.S. Congress. House. Committee on Foreign Affairs. Subcommittees on Human Rights and on Western Hemisphere Affairs. *Human Rights in Chile.* (Mar 20–21, 1985). 97 Cong., 1st Sess. Washington, D.C.: Government Printing Office, 1986.

U.S. Congress. House. Banking Committee. Subcommittees on International Development Institutions and Finance. *Human Rights Abuses in Chile* (July 30, 1986). 97th Cong., 2nd Sess., Washington, D.C.: Government Printing Office, 1986.

Valdés, Juan Gabriel, *La escuela de Chicago: Operación Chile.* Buenos Aires: Editorial Zeta, 1989.

Valenzuela, Arturo. *The Breakdown of Democratic Regimes: Chile.* Baltimore: Johns Hopkins University Press, 1978.

Valenzuela, Arturo, and J. Samuel Valenzuela, eds. *Chile under Military Rule.* Baltimore: Johns Hopkins University Press, 1986.

Vekemans, Roger. *CIA-DC-DESAL.* Bogotá: CEDIAL, 1982.

Varas, Augusto. *Los militares en el poder: Régimen y gobierno militar en Chile, 1973–1986.* Santiago: Pehuen, 1987.

Varas, Augusto, ed. *El Partido Comunista en Chile.* Santiago: CESOC-FLACSO, 1988.

Verdugo, Patricia. *Los zarpazos del puma.* Santiago: Ediciones Chile-America, CESOC, 1989.

Verdugo, Patricia, and Carmen Hertz. *Operación Siglo XX.* Santiago: Ediciones Ornitorrinco, 1990.

Vergara, Pilar. *Políticas hacia la extrema pobreza en Chile, 1973–1988.* Santiago: FLACSO, 1990.

Villalobos, Sergio. *El Beagle, la historia de una controversia.* Santiago: Editorial Andrés Bello, 1979.

Walker, Ignacio. *El Partido Socialista de Chile, 1933–1973.* Santiago: CIEPLAN, 1986.

Walker, Ignacio. *Socialismo y democracia: Chile y Europa en perspectiva comparada.* Santiago: CIEPLAN-Hachette, 1990.

Wayland-Smith, Giles. *The Christian Democratic Party in Chile.* Cuernavaca, Mexico: CIDOC Sondeos, no. 39, 1969.

Whelan, James R. *Out of the Ashes: The Life, Death, and Transfiguration of Democracy in Chile, 1833–1988.* Washington, D.C.: Regnery/Gateway, 1989.

Winn, Peter. *Weavers of Revolution: The Yarur Workers and Chile's Road to Socialism.* New York: Oxford University Press, 1986.

Wolpin, Miles. *Cuba and Chilean Foreign Policy.* Lexington, Mass.: Lexington Books, 1968.

Woodward, Bob. *Veil: The Secret Wars of the CIA.* New York: Simon and Schuster, 1987.

Yocelevsky, Ricardo. *La Democracia Cristiana Chilena y el gobierno de Eduardo Frei (1964–1970).* Mexico City: Universidad Autonoma Metropolitana, 1987.

Zeitlin, Maurice, and Richard Ratcliff. *Landlords and Capitalists: The Dominant Class of Chile.* Princeton: Princeton University Press, 1988.

Index

Book Design by Hillside Studios

Composed by World Comp
in Galliard text and display

Printed on 50 lb. Glatfelter Eggshell Cream
and bound in Arrestox
by Princeton University Press